Highland Postbag

The Correspondence
of Four MacDougall Chiefs
1715-1865

JEAN MacDOUGALL

SHEPHEARD-WALWYN

First published in 1984 by
Shepheard-Walwyn (Publishers) Limited
26 Charing Cross Road (Suite 34)
London WC2H 0DH

British Library Cataloguing in Publication Data

Macdougall, Jean
  Highland postbag.
  1. Highlands (Scotland) — Social conditions
  I. Title
  941.1'507   HN 398.H5

  ISBN 0-85683-071-2

Typeset by Alacrity Phototypesetters,
Banwell Castle, Weston-super-Mare.
Printed in Great Britain by
St Edmundsbury Press, Bury St Edmunds, Suffolk

Contents

List of Illustrations and Map

Preface

Every book has a beginning somewhere. The idea for this one came out of a box, smelling faintly of cedar wood and West Highland damp, in which bundles of old letters lay.

Those chosen for this book cover a hundred and fifty years — 1715 to 1865 — and concern four generations of MacDougall chiefs: the Jacobite Iain Ciar, his son Alexander, grandson Patrick and great-grandson John, the Admiral.

What emerges from their correspondence is a remarkable patchwork of family life: love and romance; social occasions and quiet domesticity; illness and bygone medicine; disasters, battles, quarrels; journeys across the oceans and Highland affairs at home. The pattern of birth, marriage and death is constantly repeated; history is seen from a personal angle and flashes of humour brighten the whole.

Together these letters make up a picture, however modest, of a past when life was so different and yet in many ways so much the same as today. There is fascination in both the familiar and the strange, and it is perhaps the mixture of the two which gives the correspondence a piquancy and stirs the imagination.

The struggle with illegible handwriting, faded ink and heavily criss-crossed pages has been undertaken by three sisters of the MacDougall family — spurred on, no doubt, by the clan motto *Buaidh No Bas* (conquer or die), though they were not prepared to go to quite such extremes. It is impossible to say which sister gathered the most material: it was a team effort. But the credit for most of the work on the naval and military letters must go to my sister Coline, the present chief, who served in the Navy herself and has a special interest.

My other sister, Hope, has a particular interest in the concerns of the people working on the estate — in the fields, on the ferries, in the mills and on the peat. It is a subject hardly touched on in this book as she has already included much of the material in her book on Kerrera, part of the Dunollie lands.° This has not, however, prevented her from giving energetic and cheerful assistance with this book.

° *Island of Kerrera, Mirror of History*, by H. MacDougall of MacDougall, published by the author, Ganavan House, Oban, Argyll, 1979

I have also had the valued support of my husband Stephen, himself half a MacDougall, who has dispensed both criticism and encouragement with equal charm.

Thanks are due to Michael Starforth for his kind help with some historical details, to the late Dr I. F. Grant, M.B.E., for encouraging the start of the project, and to Anthony Werner of Shepheard-Walwyn for seeing it through with patience, wisdom and a sense of humour.

Punctuation and spelling have been altered in the letters only where the original would have made tedious reading.

View across Oban bay to Dunollie Castle. 19th-century mezzotint

1

Background to the Letters

During the first three decades with which the letters deal the MacDougall home was Dunollie Castle. Iain Ciar lived here all his life, except for the years when he was a fugitive after the 1715 Rising; his son Alexander was born here; and here Alexander's wife gave birth to the first six of their fifteen children.

The Castle consisted of a tower-house of four storeys with one room on each floor, and a curtain wall which enclosed a courtyard and outbuildings. Its ruins still stand solid on the top of an ancient sea cliff, overlooking the northern entrance to Oban Bay. The site has a long history of occupation: Dunollie was mentioned in the Annals of Ulster as early as the 7th century.

In 1745 Alexander, who was by then the head of the family, built a new house below and included in it stones and beams taken from the Castle. The hoard of letters then existing moved with the family and was to be added to by each generation. Their contents give as wide a view of human experience, failings and virtues as the sweeping view from the Castle gives of hills, sea and islands.

Even though the site below was more sheltered, it is difficult to understand how Alexander could have brought himself to leave the Castle rock. Blow the gales from all quarters and leak the roof as it might (the reasons given for the move), surely that panoramic view could compensate for anything. Blending with its beauty is a haunting strangeness; a wisp of sadness woven into the pattern of sparkling water and sleeping hills; a touch of that indefinable something which runs through the Celtic tales and legends. One can visualise how through the generations members of the family who sailed to far corners of the world might sometimes have been haunted by the memories of the satisfying shapes of hill and island, the kaleidoscope of ever-changing colours and the happy mingling of stillness and movement.

On some days, however, the view is blotted out by horizontal rain sweeping across an angry sea and driven by gale-force winds.

The house that Alexander built below the Castle was low, whitewashed and slate-roofed. It was added to a small house already there, known as the Laich Biggin, the two together making the shape of an L. Though modest in size the new house was well-built, with three-foot thick walls (though these would have seemed unsubstantial to the family after the six-foot ones at the Castle).

It was in this house, and later also in the three-storeyed Georgian addition which filled up the L, that Iain Ciar's descendants were to live.

Alexander's main rooms were in the newly-built house, but the kitchen was part of the Laich Biggin, a house mentioned in records of 1617. The kitchen floor was covered with massive slates embedded with pyrites (fool's gold), and the great fireplace was arched in stone.

About seventy years after the building of the new house, the wife of Alexander's son Patrick was complaining in her letters of its mean appearance and referring to it as 'our poor cottage'. But her husband was perfectly content with it and criticised his friends in the district for ruining themselves by replacing their modest houses with grander ones. It was left to his son John in the 1830s to follow the current fashion and build — under fantastic circumstances to be related later — an ambitious addition.

In contrast to the original house, John's addition had high ceilings, large windows, and a wide, elegant, curving staircase with wrought-iron balustrades. The two main rooms were the dining-room on the ground floor and the drawing-room above.

The dining-room probably always had its distinctly masculine character: harsh textured tartan curtains hanging from the high windows against severe brown shutters; male family portraits covering the walls. Even the wind in the chimney had a masculine roar.

Upstairs, the drawing-room was completely feminine, with the petit-point fire-screen by the fireplace worked by the Admiral's daughter Louisa; the seventy-two china plates above the picture rail (all to be taken down and washed at spring-cleaning time); the gilded harp in the window; bowls of sweet-smelling potpourri and pictures of the ladies and children of the family upon the walls.

Unlike many Highland houses, Dunollie has no family ghosts, but there are two mysterious noises for which no explanation has been found and which have been heard by at least five generations of the MacDougalls.

The first is heard only in the old part of the house. It is very loud, sounds rather as if something heavy is being dragged over corrugated iron, and is accompanied by a hollow bellowing. A traditional, but most unlikely, explanation is that Alexander built an underground passage from the house to the shore for smuggling purposes, and that when the right direction and force of the wind combine with a rough sea, then the

19th-century photograph of the Dog Stone (foreground) and the ruins of Dunollie Castle in the background

noise of shingle being drawn up and down, and the roar of the water, echo through the passage to the house. Most of the family, however, throughout the generations, have believed that the noise has super-natural origins.

The second sound sometimes heard is a carriage driving up to the front door, swishing the gravel as it comes. But on looking out there is nothing there. Curiously, since cars have replaced carriages it is the sound of a car that is heard — but still accompanied as before by the swish of gravel.

Although the Castle has fallen into ruins since the beginning of the period of the letters, and the old house had been added to by the end, the outdoor surroundings must have looked very much as they did in the days of Iain Ciar and his predecessors.

Dunollie is surrounded by a pattern of sea, fields and hillsides — and woods which come and go through the generations. Standing back from the present sea shore is a broken line of ancient cliffs whose caves once sheltered prehistoric man. In a field beside the road to Dunollie stands a forty-foot high sea-stack of conglomerate rock, the Dog Stone, to which the giant Fingal is said to have tied his dog Bran.

From the top of Cnoc Carnach, the hill behind the house, there is a wide view of the letter-writers' surroundings. To the West stands the Castle, high on its cliff and silhouetted against the sea, with the mountains of Mull beyond. Sometimes the silhouette is dark and grim, sometimes bright with sunlight; and sometimes in winter, if its covering of ivy has caught the snow, it gleams white. Below it, nestle the house and stable-yard, sheltered, but not hidden, by trees.

Towards the South rises the wooded hill which hides Dunollie from Oban. Trees planted there by two of the letter-writers, Patrick and John, still flourish.

Further off across the water, but within easy distance by rowing-boat from Dunollie, lie the Island of Kerrera and the small uninhabited Stirk Island (Shepherd's Hat), Lamb Island, Maiden Island and Heather Island, all with their share of the magic of the West. They too have a link with history, being the remnants of considerable island possessions held by the early MacDougall chiefs in the twelfth and thirteenth centuries, possessions which included Mull, Tiree, Coll, Lismore, Jura and Scarba. (See Appendix)

How the letters reached what was a remote part of the country is an interesting story. For much of the period covered by this book, the men who brought the postbags came on foot. They walked from Dumbarton to Inveraray and then on to Oban.

The postmen, or post-runners as they were then called, must have been hardy and vigorous, for on some routes they were expected to walk over thirty miles a day. The roads in this part of the country were in earlier times not much more than rough tracks over rock and bogland, whose surfaces suffered continually from the wet climate of the West Highlands, and at times from the plodding of herds of black cattle, driven over them on their way to the southern markets. Along these tracks the mail was carried in all weathers. The task of the post-runners was sometimes made more exhausting by blizzards of snow, deluges of rain or gale-force winds in winter, and in summer by the heat of hemmed-in glens and the torment of swarms of midges.

The route to Inveraray varied throughout the period, sometimes crossing Loch Awe by ferry from Kilchrenan to Port Sonachan, sometimes going round the Loch and on via Dalmally.

In the nineteenth century, when the mail became too heavy for the men to carry, they travelled on horseback and their pay was increased to allow for maintaining a pony. Later on, with the roads improved, the post-bags went by mail gig. And so the transport of letters progressed from foot to hoof and then to hoof and wheel during the 150 years to which this book relates.

Until almost the end of this period, letters arriving at the Post Office had to be collected by their owners, and tradition has it that the Dunollie bag for this purpose was made of leather. Until the introduction of stamps in 1840 the postage was normally paid by the recipient. One correspondent, whose husband had an unusually frugal mind, wrote in 1816: 'You know how welcome letters are although there is sometimes a *row* about postage.' It has been said that the reason postage was paid on receipt was that this made the Post Office more careful of the letters. Anyhow the practice made a nice excuse for not writing, an excuse often used: 'I would have written to you ere now but the truth is I had nothing particular to say and grudged putting you to unnecessary postage.' Or: 'You would no doubt be surprised at my having been so long in writing but I thought it unnecessary troubling you with postage in these hard times.'

That a letter once posted would arrive at its destination seems, from the correspondence, not at all certain, especially those letters sent abroad. Iain Ciar wrote to his wife from France in 1718: 'though few may come to your hand take no bad thought for letters are subject to many accidents.' His wife Mary in her turn wrote: 'this is the 25th letter I sent my Dearest but I am not so fortounate as that any of them is com to my Dearest.'

For members of the family who went abroad, often for long periods, letters were especially valuable. One son wrote: 'I hope you will write to me very often and the most trifling occurance in Scotland will be exceedingly interesting to me.' But so often letters to and from Dunollie never arrived. In 1779, for instance, a member of the family wrote: 'I cannot help being displeased at 6 ships having sailed from England 3 months after us and not hearing from my friends by them ... But I cannot attribute this to neglect so I must suppose accident or something else must be the cause.' In May 1812, a mother wrote to her son in the Navy: 'I am afraid your letters may have been on board some of those vessels from Malta that have been taken by the French. We have not heard from you since November last which is a long time.' The same son is disappointed at Halifax, Nova Scotia in May 1815 and wrote home: 'I am a good deal surprised and not a little mortified at not finding any letters here from you. I have not heard from Dunollie since August.' His mother writes back that altogether six letters from the family have been posted to him.

Sometimes letters failed to arrive because they and their ship were at the bottom of the sea. A son of the family wrote from India in 1853:

I have not heard from you for some time and am afraid I must have lost one or two letters as the vessel that was bringing the mail on 24th June from Aden to Bombay was totally lost. The steamer of the Indian Navy which ought to have brought the mail broke down and the mails were forwarded from Aden by a Pilgrim Ship from Mecca. This class of ship is not accustomed to be exposed to the S.W. Monsoon and her loss was expected before the news arrived ... This loss will cause the inefficiency of the Indian Navy to be exposed as the mails are continually delayed by the breaking down of some one or other of the steamers, and it is to be hoped that the carrying of the mail will be given to some private company. It is so great a disappointment to be deprived of ones home letters, not to mention the loss it must have occasioned to some people, and above all the lives of the unfortunate pilgrims.

As late as Victorian times the reliability of the post within Britain was sometimes questioned in the letters: in 1720 'he had no desyre to trust his letter by the post'; in 1782 'I chance this letter by the post'; or into the next century in 1827: 'I have no way of remitting the cash but by the Post which is not a very safe conveyance.'

Many letters, especially in the eighteenth century, did not go by post at all but were delivered by friends, servants or the servants of friends. Although this was often a quicker way of sending letters than by post, it was sometimes slower! A correspondent in 1718 wrote: 'I am heartily sorry my last was so long in comeing to your hands, it was none of my fault for he that gott it undertook to delyver it a month sooner.' Then from Edinburgh in 1745: 'Yours I received 4 days ago but Barcaldine's servant by whom you sent the letter was gone out of town eight days before it was delivered to me, otherwise had written to you by him.' In 1753: 'I am just now favoured with yours which is ane old date but your man says he contracted a fever in Glenorchy where he lay six or seven days.'

Often the messenger seems to have been in a great hurry. In 1720 an agitated correspondent wrote: 'I might particularlie inform you but the bearer's exceeding great haist will not allow me the time. I'd give you all the inteligance I can but your servant's haist makes me a little uneasie so that I can not do what I would.' Then, in another letter: 'if your servant can be prevailed upon to stay till tomorrow I will speak to Mr Campbell and send you his answer.'

Besides by friends and servants there was another, though illegal, method of sending letters — by a carrier who was nothing to do with the Post Office. He was known as an Express. In 1756 a correspondent wrote to Dunollie from Edinburgh: 'I have sent this by Express in order to save time.' In 1780 another said: 'I'll send you ane express with all the money I can forward.' In 1782 one of the family writing from Dunollie seemed in two minds as to whether to use the Express or the post. He wrote to Edinburgh: 'Notwithstanding there is an express going to Town for Betty Macdowal's musicale Instrument yet have ordered him to drop this letter in the post office at Inveraray which insured it goes safely and regularly ... On second thought I have sent this letter by the Express ... P.S. The bearer has no time to spare at Edinr. as I have given him but 10 shils to go and return.'

As to the letters themselves, until after the introduction of stamps in 1840, when the use of envelopes became general, they consisted usually of a single page folded and sealed (two pages were charged double). It is interesting that the single sheet folded and sealed, which became obsolete in the Victorian era, has now returned in the form of the air letter or aerogramme.

Whatever changes in the post the passage of time has brought, a riddle posed by one of the Victorian correspondents remains true today: 'What is it that does not speak but makes itself understood, and walking not it arrives?'

IAIN CIAR
? — 1737

JOHN MacDougall, 22nd Chief (1695-1737)
(known as Iain Ciar)

JOHN, ? - 1737 *m* MARY MacDONALD of Sleat, 1712

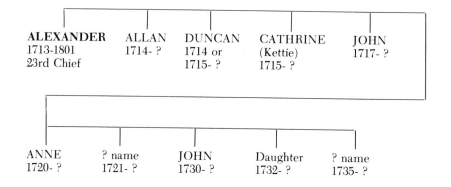

ALEXANDER	ALLAN	DUNCAN	CATHRINE	JOHN
1713-1801	1714- ?	1714 or	(Kettie)	1717- ?
23rd Chief		1715- ?	1715- ?	

ANNE	? name	JOHN	Daughter	? name
1720- ?	1721- ?	1730- ?	1732- ?	1735- ?

The family of John

His father: Allan, 21st chief, married Mary MacLachlan, died 1695.

His mother: Mary, daughter and heiress of Ian MacLachlan of Kilbride.

His wife: Mary, born 1696, daughter of William MacDonald (third son of Donald MacDonald of Sleat, 3rd Bt). She married Iain Ciar in 1712 and died in 1776.

The children

Alexander: succeeded as 23rd Chief in 1737, married Mary, third daughter of Patrick Campbell of Barcaldine.

Allan: became a doctor and went to St Christopher's (now St Kitts) in the West Indies.

Duncan: was out in the 1745 Jacobite Rising.

Cathrine (Kettie): married Maclaine of Lochbuie.

John: died young.

Anne: nothing known of her life.

Another child: name unrecorded.

John: nothing known of his life.

A daughter: name unrecorded.

Another child: name unrecorded.

2

Iain Ciar

Prologue to Battle

Of the four MacDougall chiefs with whom these letters are concerned, Iain Ciar[1] and his great-grandson John were the two who carried on the warlike tradition of their forebears. They both led courageous and adventurous lives, and both travelled far from their native land, though for very different reasons.

Even now, Iain Ciar is a legendary figure in the district: an intrepid warrior, passionately devoted to the Jacobite cause. His letters, while supporting this image, also reveal more gentle characteristics. Those written to his wife, Mary, show a tenderness and sensitivity which makes an interesting contrast to the rough age in which he lived. They also spotlight his vivid religious belief, which enabled him to remain optimistic in the most unlikely situations.

'You are never to despair of enjoying my company,' he wrote to his wife from exile in France, two years after the failure of the 1715 Jacobite rising. 'I trust in god to live and dye within them old rouinish stones of my predecessors.'

How his trust was fulfilled can be read in the bundles of his letters, their paper now yellow with age and their ink faded.

The story begins in the year 1715 when according to tradition Iain Ciar was about twenty-five years old. At the beginning of this year he was living quietly in Dunollie Castle with his wife Mary, a MacDonald of Sleat. It is said that three years earlier, fourteen galleys, manned by MacDougall clansmen, had been sent to Duntulm Castle on Skye to escort the bride to Dunollie. Since then Mary had given birth to three sons, and now there was another child on the way.

The first letter in the bundle for this year includes a peaceful and domestic subject: a bill for garden seeds ordered from Glasgow —

---

1   Most Gaelic scholars translate Iain Ciar as John swarthy or dark. Traditionally he has always been known in the family and in folklore by his Gaelic name, and so it will be used in this narrative.

marigolds, parsley, watercress, thyme, carrots, cabbage, parsnips, beets, radishes, and white peas. But by the time the seeds had grown to maturity rumblings of trouble were in the air and the Jacobite plans to put James Stewart on the throne were well advanced.

Much has been written about the 1715 rising: its political aspects, its mismanagement and its leaders. Iain Ciar writes of it as personal experience.

On August 27th the Duke of Argyll wrote from London to the Gentlemen of Argyll, including Iain Ciar, warning them of the danger of 'the intended rebellious attempts to destroy our Religion and liberties'. He spoke of James Stewart as 'the Pretender to the Crown of these Kingdoms and the usurper of his Majestie's royal titles', and ended the letter (which is quoted in full on page 50), 'I shall immediately, as your heritable Lord Lieutenant, appoint Deputy Lieutenants and other Officers to command our fencible men and shall neglect nothing which may tend to your safety and prosperity. I am Gentlemen, your most obedient and most humble servant, Argyll.'

About a month later, Campbell of Dunstaffnage, a friend and neighbour whose land marched with Dunollie, wrote to Iain Ciar — somewhat breathlessly:

Dunstaffnage
23rd September, 1715

Sir, His Grace as heritable Lord Leut. of this shyre has been pleased to nominate and appoint me as one of the deputy Leuts. of this shyre, and it being necessary that such men as I formerly nominated to join the militia of this shyre be in readiness to march with me to Inveraray against monday next, and sooner if further orders come from the Duke to order us to be there sooner than the said day. I hereby order and desire that you and your men do meet me at Kilmore against 8 of the clock forenoon monday next being the 26th instant, and that each of your men take along a fortnights provision and be sure that all your men take along all their defensible arms, as you'll be answerable to the Duke of Argyll as our Lord Leut. and his deputs, from Kilmore to march on munday, and sooner if ordered by our Lord Leut., and if sooner I'll inform you for tomorrow being the 24th instant my orders were to march tomorrow which being impracticable I onlie receiving orders the night.

from, Sir, your humble servant, Hugh Campbell,

I require you see that the people of Kerrera and any there you are concerned in be not deficient, and consider what I told you formerly, a word to the wise is enough I hope you pardon my freedom. yours sincerely.

Iain Ciar, who was actually on the other side, now wrote with surprising optimism to Inveraray asking that arms should be sent for his men. He received the following reply:

Inverary
25th September, 1715

It is not practicable to give out any arms till once the men come in and they must take care to bring all they have with them since they are so to depend upon it.

I wrote to you last day by Baylie Dugald signifying how much it was to your interest at this occasion to behave yourself so as to oblige the Duke of Argyll who certainly will have a particular regard to such as desire well of him, as he cannot but take notice of those that do otherways. I need not tell you how much its to your interest to behave dutifully to my Grace. This will remove all suspicion that those who are not your good friends were readie to rise, but I am glad that I can with assurance tell you that my Grace will believe no ill thing of a man till he see it.

Its necessary the men be here upon monday or tuesday and that they bring with them forteen days provision. Pray fault not in this which at present is all from Sir your most affect. humble servant A. Campbell.

While the Duke's supporters were uncertain which side Iain Ciar meant to support, he himself at this time was receiving instructions from his Jacobite friends. On 21st August Stewart of Appin wrote:

I have yours by your servant and you are more afraid of ill news than perhaps you need. I had a letter yester-night from Glengarry and another from Lochiel. We are to keep a right understanding and all mistrust is out of the way and they beg that we may all be more wary than ever, they bid us take special care of ourselves, for there are orders out to seize us all ... I wish Sir Donald and Clanranald were both at home, for so long as we keep together we need not fear any events. If Glengary or Lochiel get anything that's worth it he'll acquaint me and I you.

On 27th September Colin Campbell of Glendaruel, (not all Campbells were on the side of the Duke of Argyll), wrote to Iain Ciar.

Dear Sir, I left a Double [copy] of my instructions from the Earl of Breadalbin with Duncan who will send it to you. I will write to you from Glenorchy. I have sent the bearer Syms to Sir John McLean and I beg you may see him safely ferried. [Sir John McLean was Maclean of Duart so the messenger had to be ferried to the Island of Mull] it is to haste Sir John and to incourage him and telling him how all goes and what we have resolved here.

I am your faithful servant Colin Campbell

There is a tradition that during this autumn Iain Ciar had kidnapped a blacksmith named Campbell from Taynuilt, and had set him to work putting all the swords and other arms that could be mustered in good order. He worked in a cave in a rock just below the Castle cliff, a place known to this day as the Blacksmith's Rock. When the man was released he was made to swear not to reveal where he had been or what he had been doing.

That same autumn, Iain Ciar and his men set off to join the Jacobite Army. Tradition has it that they didn't get away unseen: as they crossed Loch Etive, guns from Dunstaffnage Castle were fired at them continually — but the shots fell short and did them no harm.

Although they landed safely on the other side of the Loch, an incident then occurred which made a bad start to their journey. As the party prepared to march, a sudden storm arose and a whirlwind blew the bonnet off Iain Ciar's head. There was consternation when the MacDougall seer, from Ard A Choric on Kerrera, stepped forward and warned his chief to turn back, for if he did not he would be a wanderer for seven years. To this Iain Ciar is said to have replied; 'No! I will go on and see the end of it even though I am to be a wanderer for seven years.'

At nineteen years old, Iain Ciar's wife was left to defend Dunollie Castle. Her youngest child Cathrine (Kettie) had only recently been born and was still at the breast. Mary had not long to wait for trouble, for on 9th October an order was issued from Inveraray to garrison Dunollie in his Majesty King George's name 'and to that end to require John MacDougall of Dunoleich and any other persons residing there to surrender the said hous under all highest pain'.

When Iain Ciar, by this time in Perth, heard that the Castle had been attacked, he wrote to Mary 'the base cowards why did they not attempt to meet myself.' The letter continues:

> Praise be god the Conduct you had in keeping them out of the house. I hope in a few days you will hear better tidings than ever ... Keep the house and cause, line the door with turfe in the inside. Once Sir Donald comes up you shall be supplied so dearest keep good heartt and the Lord that creatted all things give you both strength and courage and preserve you and yours from the power and malice of their enymies.

The next month, on 6th November, he wrote to her from Perth again:

> Dearest and only Comfortt,
> This day I was in Company with Earle of Marr who is very well pleased with your conductt. I'm hopeful you have not surrendered the house. You are desyrd to keep it as long as you can and so I

hope in God in a few days you will have a good account of this Army. I'm to joyne Sir Donald who came here three days ago. You may depend to hear from me with mony as shoon as possible.

[He then asked that more men be sent but added] Keep noe less in the house than twelve and for Gods sake keep courage for all things goes very well.

Let my horse be sent and my cloak and all my clothes if you can see anny savety for them if nott it cannot be helped. Lett me have all the account of the Country, of who is kindest to you.

Lett me know of the children. I dare nott be very free, once more I crave your stoutness in keeping the house and for the love of God keep good heartt and be noe ways concerned aboutt me for I am in noe danger nor doe I see anny danger in our undertaking, belive nothing you hear aboutt us except what you hear to our advantage. You shall hear from me very shoone. Haste back Donald and cause him travell night and day till he come up. Your father [Mary's father was William MacDonald, the third son of Donald MacDonald of Sleat] and brother and all other freends minds their service to you and soe doth him who shall live and dye.

Yours while I am J. McDougall

The Battle of Sheriffmuir and afterwards

Iain Ciar wrote to his wife describing the Battle of Sheriffmuir:

Perth
19th November, 1715

Comfort and only dearest,

I doubt not but you have got a doleful account of me and the whole of the King's party. But, blessed be god, our behaviour, at least a part, is honoured by this time in most of Brittain.

The matter of fact was this: on Sunday, being the thirteenth instant, we engaged the enemy; we had my Lord Argyle's left wing. We were placed on our own right wing with Glengarry, Clanranald, Sir Donald Maclean's and a small battalion of my Lord Breadalbane's four troops of horse commanded by the Earl Marischal.

The enemy being unanimously attacked by us whom I named was utterly defate, for of five regiments of foot and the Black horse there never entered Stirling of the five hunder men but the whole were killed or taken. For I can assure you such of them as engaged, I mean Sir Donald's men, there was never a score that left the field of them.

Our left wing was indeed put in a confusion and was a good way gessed [dispersed] by the enemy; and then our horse made extraordinary good resistance, keeped their ground and artillery

Stones marking the site of the battle of Sheriffmuir,
13th November, 1715

and camped that night where they had fought it and so we keeped the field of battle. My Lord Argyle was obliged to betake himself to Stirling that night with the loss of eight or nine hunder killed and two hunder at least taken prisoners, Blessed be god our loss needs not be recorded, for Sir Donald there was not twenty of his whole men killed and not one gentleman in the whole of his nor twenty wounded — and I have the honour my dearest to be amongst the wounded, for I received a slight one through the right thigh and, praise be to god, it may be so called for my danger is already over. So my dearest for the love of god be nayes concerned for me for upon my honour I inform nothing but the truth, and we have all the encouraging news desireable that our army in England consists of about 15,000 and meets with no opposition as yet.

I will not be fashing you with all the news we have, but all are good, but begs you may not give ear to the country clashes [gossips] for I know the country will quean news to dishearten you, but god is still in heaven on whom I have still my dependence, god give you grace to do the same.

The few that came with me are very well, without losing a drop of blood except a slight wound Hugh Krekanich's son got in the arm. There are four of them away home with a full handful but please god I get home some of them shall not escape the widdle [whip] as they deserved. I admire [wonder] what keeped little Donald.

I durst not ventue to send you money or any other thing for fear to lose the haill by reason that there is robbers on the way Haste back the bearer and let little Donald come along with him by all means, see likewise to send Neil the millers son in their company that he may return to yourself with things that I'll not name at present.

I am hopeful you'll keep the house and do it till get better or worse. Hastening back the boys will be a means to relieve part of your straits. I intreat you, as you incline to oblige me, keep good heart for the fear I lay under about you keeps my mind still in grief. Manage everything, live to the best advantage you can. The bearers will report the rest of my mind to you. Let me know how the children are or if they are in life. Your father and brother has their service to you and all others of your friends.

Sir Donald was a little tender but is on the recovering hand and was not at the engagement at all but remained at Perth and I supplied his place, pray to god with honer to him and myself.

The best here are daily in letting me mind my service to such as are your friends. I conclude with a kiss to yourself, heart and all I have.

Yours in all sincerity while I am J. MacDougall

The only loss we regrett is the Captaine of Clanranald who was killed on the spot and my Lord Strathmore but our enemies lost many of their principal officers and 2 or 3 Lords, the same of Isla is wounded in the thigh and body.

Written on the outside of the letter

Upon leaving there is sent with the bearer 3 pairs of gloves, 1 pound figgs, 1 pound raisins 1 unce cinamon, 4 unces white candy and 8 unces liqorice.

The bearer of the Sheriffmuir letter, together with the little Donald mentioned in it, disappeared while on their way back to Perth. This meant that Iain Ciar was for a time without news of his wife. 'The frequent letters I have sent you without return,' he wrote, 'perswuades me to my sad grief things are nott right' with you but if you be in life and well all othere things can not in the least trouble me ... Lett me hear from you for I can have noe rest night or day till once I know your state and conditione.'

The mystery of the men's disappearance was solved after a time when it was discovered that they had been captured, and imprisoned in Dunstaffnage Castle. Luckily for them the neighbourly feelings of Campbell of Dunstaffnage over-rode his duty to the government and he soon let them free. 'I was informed,' wrote Iain Ciar, 'that my neighbour Dounstafnadge had set Donald and Allan at liberty.' In another letter he writes to Mary: 'Mind my kind respects to Dounstafnadge and his Lady for I'm informed they are very kind to you in my absence ... I will write to Dounstafnadge.'

Iain Ciar himself, it seems, was not averse to doing a good turn to a neighbour who happened to be on the opposite side. He wrote to Mary about MacDougall of Gallanach's brother-in-law. 'You may tell Gallanach's wife that her brother Sanders was taken up here for a spy and lay in the dungeone some time before I was informed. I went to the Earle of Mar and procured his liberty. He is in a most miserable condition, he has nothing unless I give him, soe if they think it worth their while to write to a rebell, as I am, I shall give him here whatever they advance to you. He is not in his right wits.'

Meanwhile Iain Ciar was nursing his wound. 'I bless god,' he wrote, 'my wound is nearly closed but I am not as yett very strong by reason of the strict dyett that I am obliged to keep to prevent a fever. Thanks be to god I am free of all distempers save my wound which in a few days will be fully cured. I will have nae halt so, my dearest of all living, but be not in the least concerned about me.'

And then a few days later: 'I am fully recovered only my wound is nott altogether closed for the ball was very big but I can with all ease

walk in my chamber.' In another letter to Mary he said he would come
home to recruit more men but 'I durst nott venture to travel or ride so
shoone after my wound ... I trust in god that it has been to my weelfaire
both for soul and body that I was wounded.' In his efforts to reassure
Mary he even went to far as to prophesy: 'Let me undergoe what
dangers there will be no more of my blood spilt and though there would
be it will be slight and in a good cause.'

All through the letters written at this time the need for more men to be
recruited to the Jacobite army is stressed. There had been many
deserters after Sheriffmuir and Iain Ciar wrote on 1st December: 'There
is gentlemen sent to their respective countrys to bring back all the
possible men they have.'

As Iain Ciar couldn't go home himself, because of his wound, he sent
his brother Duncan and wrote to Mary of his coming. 'I wish he may
bring many for the bringing of men would be much to our advantage
and honour. 'But,' he warned Mary, 'lett none of the men you have in the
house come with Duncan.'

From letters written later in the month it seems that Duncan's
recruiting wasn't going too well and Iain Ciar asked for Mary's help. 'I
doubt not,' he wrote, 'but my last letter will prevail with my friends in
sending other men with my Brother. I know it is uneasy for them to have
passage but willing people will still fall on means ... and it is the Lord's
will to place our undoubted sovereign on his ancestor's throne.'

He begged Mary to see as many as she conveniently could and to tell
them to come as soon as possible. 'If they disobey,' he wrote, 'for my
pairt I fully discharge my interest in them.' Those who will not appear
for him in time of need, he told her, were no friends of his.

In Mary's worrying position, waiting daily for the Castle to be
attacked again, unless messengers failed, she was never long without her
husband's advice, encouragement and praise. 'Pray keep a stout heart,'
he wrote, 'and depend wholly on your creator. I entreat you take care
not to expose yourself to any danger for save the concerns of my soul
you are the only thing that concerns my mind ... Your name is well-
known here and they admire your courage ... God is with us and we
have a just cause.'

Sometimes the encouragement took a more material form: when Iain
Ciar could trust the bearer he sent Mary presents. Following the gloves,
figs, raisins, cinnamon, white candy and liquorice sent almost from the
field of Sheriffmuir, he sent her two silk napkins and a piece of lace
measuring 5 ells and a quarter. At the same time he sent her 'Rob Gibs
contract', [a toast of friendship] which: 'you are to wear about your
neck and not to pairt with while you live. That is a handsome piece of

gold which I bought here and paid two guineas for it and that is worth three or four. It is to tie about your neck with a ribbon.' In his next letter he repeated that she was to wear it every day and to keep it while she lived, adding: 'I pray god if that it be his pleasour I may never hear or see the day of your death.' Would she like, he asked, an ell or two of Holland and as much mussoling?

In another letter, he wrote: 'I have sent calico for a frock for my daughter but nothing to my dearest, for things round here are very dear except provisions but blessed be God they are cheap.' Later on, however, he evidently felt a little more affluent: 'I have caused your Cosine Mistress Mary shop a dress to you which I have sent home. I have sent a pair of gloves to Flory, I have sent one ell of linen to your dy [dye or colour], and ane apron to your nurse.'

On Dec 29th a jubilant letter left Perth for Dunollie. The long-expected had happened: the King had arrived — and Iain Ciar wrote to Mary that he had seen his face and kissed his hand.

> Blessed be to god, I have the best news to give you that was since ever you were borne. This morning the King arrived with a throng traine ... I bless god we are very hearty and I hope this will encourage you to give all your company the King's health and success to his arms. I hope you will not neglect mine for I do boost myself by drinking of yours. I trust in god your couching [sleeping] neighbours will think shame on themselves ... I conclude with his health, success to his friends and all them that is his reall friends.'

In the following month the outlook still sounded cheerful. 'We had news just as I was writing, that two ships landed belonging to the King with fourteen stand of arms ... I hope we will want for nothing neither need my Dearest be concerned for depend on gods grace you will have comfort for I have honor and reputations for the blood I lost.'

But Iain Ciar's high hopes came to nothing.

> 17th February, 1716
> Comfort and only Dearest, The misfortunatt relations of our undertaking is grevious to be reported for we were most unhumanly betrayed by the Earle of Marr, Marquis of Huntly and the Earle of Seaforth by whose doings we were obleiged to fly and disperce, many of our Nobility have left the Kingdome so that I durst nott venture to go to my dearest. My design is to go with your father for a time. I doubt nott butt your life and living will be very uneasy to you as it has been long since, as for your house if they please you are to give it up. I am hopefull they will use you more kind than to extend their severity.'

My humble opinion is you should go to Inverary and apply to Stonefield [Campbell of Stonefield] for your peace. You are nott to make known what way I am gone. Iff they allow your peaceable possession of your own I would advise you to continue where you are this side of May. God Almighty may be pleased to send releif before that time. We have applied for our peace, what effect itt may have is hard to know ...

If so be they will not use you kind and will putt you out of the possession of your own then you are to make your best way to your father's. As to the children, if you be obliged to leave your own you are to dispose of the lads as they are and for your daughter you can doe nothing with her till once she be done at the breast. I hop in god things will nott come to this degree of hardship.

Pray take nothing in ill pairt for god who provided hitherto for us will nott forsake us, though it were our fate both to go to Spain we will not want bread. The rest of my mind the bearer will communycatt to you. My only joy take good courage and never dispair for blessed be god I am yet in life. I will add no more till meeting I wish how shoon it is, all pleasure, comfort and only dearest from my dear your affectionate and loving husband, J. MacDougall.

The letters now stop abruptly. Iain Ciar had become a hunted man, and Mary was likely to be turned out of the Castle by the government forces. There were no more letters until the following November.

What happened during these nine months can be only speculation. The facts known are that the Castle had to be given up and that Mary became pregnant again. There is, however, a strong family tradition which contributes something towards filling in the gap: namely that Iain Ciar lived for a time in a cave some way up a cliff on the mainland opposite the island of Kerrera. Mary, who was by now living on the island, brought him food by night.

Exile

In November 1716 Iain Ciar went into exile. He wrote to Mary from Lochmaddy of the ship in which he was about to sail for France.

My dear Life and only Comfort.

The day I pairted with you we arrived at the ship where we were very kindly received by the master and crew. The ship is a comely good one and by appearance stoutt att sea my jewell. They wait impatiently for a fair wind which I pray God they may have. Since I pairted with my Comfort and only Company I pray the Almighty may be pleased to make our meeting more joyful than our pairting

... Dear Honey keep up your heart and trust in God night and day and he will in his deew time relieve your difficulty and give us the enjoyment of one another which is all under heaven I wish for.

In spite of the stoutness of the ship the voyage turned out hazardous. Iain Ciar described it in a letter to Mary from Brest: 'My dearest Life, Since pairting we met with many hardships at sea butt blessed be god and his name be praised we all are arrived at Brest safe.'

They left Lochmaddy on 18th November and reached Ireland six days later — but were then driven by a contrary wind back northwards again to the west of Uist. When the wind became favourable they sailed back to Ireland and then made straight for France.

On 3rd December, sixteen days after they had started, the ship made land but Iain Ciar wrote 'our sea men did not know the place so that we came too close on the shore and with great difficulty we gott againe to sea.' Next morning at five o'clock they made again for the land.

It blew most horribly, so that we all thought to have perished but the hand of God preserved us, blessed be his name. I never, my jewel, so spaired of my life as we ran straight to the coast. The inhabitants ran to the shore in order to share of our spoils, but god almighty prevented their design for we found a small creek where we dropped anchor, but such was never seen for a harbour for the rocks of Aird or any place in Treshnish was nothing to it, however god was pleased to make it safe for us. The next day ... we got a pylott who brought us safe to this town ...

'So blessed be god,' he added in another letter, 'and hope no more to do with the sea. I bless god my only dearest did nott know the many dangers we were in at sea and indeed I never knew what fear was till then.'

'Had I all France to myself,' he wrote, 'I had rather have bread and water with my dearest ... I do not value Children, friend or relation in comparison to my Pleasure day and night who is my only pleasure on all occasions and the Lord, that never failed us, send me the opportunity either that I may come where you are or you to me ... I conclude with a thousand kisses to my dearest enclosed in this line and assure yourself on all occasions I will not be failing writing to the mother of my little ones though perhaps few may come to your hand take no bad thought for letters are subject to many accidents.

Iain Ciar was also worried about money for his wife's subsistence as the small allowance which later came from the forfeited estate had not yet been granted.

For God's sake do not want. If once ye settell bring your pott and caldrone from Mull and rather than they would be idle hire them to a brewer or sell them for your support. They are your own and dispose of anything rather than want, and woes me how little my satisfaction has for her support ... To God the Father, son and Holie Ghost I would commend the care of your soul and body, the same Lord will give us a merrie meeting.

Unfortunately Mary's letters failed to reach France and Iain Ciar became more and more impatient for news of her and of the arrival of their expected baby. In December he had written: 'I suppose ere this come to my dearest you will have run the hazard of your life, may the Lord support you in your labour and grant you a safe delivery. The only thing I now long for is to hear from my only comfort which makes me very impatient till I hear from you.'

January and February of 1717 passed and by March there was still no news. Full of anxiety, he wrote: 'the greatest comfortt I have in this country is my constant writtings to you tho' I never yett had the good fortoun to hear from you or anny others since I left that Nation ... I entreat to know about the children or if your last is in life ... There never was a man living under soe many uneassyness as I am for want to ane account from you whereby I might know your conditions.'

On 22nd April he wrote again:

It is butt needless to rehearse the extassie I lye under this six months for want of hearing from you which still gives me grounds to suspect my dearest is nott in life, or that none of my letters are come to your hand, but a line I had from your Cousine Mary from Blair dated the 21st March persuades me that some of my letters arrived safe. She informs me of you being safe delivered, what grounds she may have for itt I know nott for I can give no credit to any accounts I hear about you till I see itt from yourself and almost I lost hopes of that satisfaction.

Meanwhile he wrote to Cousin Mary at Blair and said that he was afraid that she was concealing from him the fact that his wife was dead.

At last, in October, almost a year after Iain Ciar had left Scotland, two letters arrived from Mary. The only good news in them was of the existence of their latest child. 'I keep Johnny with myself; he will sometimes make me greet and other times make me laugh. He's as good a child as ever went on woman's knee.'

The first letter begins: 'This is the 25th letter I sent my dearest that you might know of your poor miserable wife's conditions which is but miserable.'

'I have never received a letter with greater pleasure,' Iain Ciar replied, 'nor never read any with mor melancholy understanding your caise to be most miserable ...'

Mary's two letters *are* full of misery: at the age of twenty-two, her thoughts were much on death. She told her husband that there was a lump gathering in her breast which would be like to make an end of her, and that the gown from France which he had promised to send her would come too late. 'You tell me that I may expect my gown shortly and that you hope to be the bearer of it, but its past to be for a summer gown and I'm afraid it will be over cold for a winter gown, and you never tell me which of the two you desire it for, but I fear it shall fall me about my gown as befalls the sheep when they wait for the new grass.'

She went on to tell him of another worry:

I am eaten up with lies and malicious stories raised on me ... if there is a hell on earth I am in it with your friends doings, if they see a man stay one night in the bothy that I am in they will raise bad reports of me. If my precious jewel were as doubtful of me as your friends are it were better for me to be dead than alive, and as it is, if it were the Lord's will, it were better for me to be dead than the torment that I am in.

Iain Ciar wrote back much distressed and gave her advice as to how to deal with this gossip:

I advise my life nott to be concerned aneant the malicious storys raised by the wicked crew that are about you, for the more you slight them the less they'l be at pains to invent ... I am hopeful you have mor reason [sense] than to take to hart anny thing they are capable to invent ... can the wretches think there is any scandall or lys they are able to invent can obleidge me to prove unkind to my dear Mary.

Then in another letter:

20th October, 1717

As to the aspersions of knaves and villains be they male or female or both aginst my dearest — I can not believe you are so much changed by what I have known my only pleasour to have been as that their malicious and wicked reports should in the least dauntten you ... God almightie strengthen you and give you heartt and courage to undervallue all their pernitious aspersions.

As to Mary's health Iain Ciar wrote:

You inform me to my great greef that ther is a lump gathering in your brest which if nott timeously prevented will certainly make

an end of you; my only dearest advise in time a man of skill anent
your distemper befor it com to a length surpassing all cure and
then my coming will be too late ... Pray be advised and do not dy
in greef and despaire, low as we are, and god in his due time will
raise us ... I know all your distemper proceeds from greef so my
dear as ever you have been tractable in taking my advice use all
means for your health and god in his due time will bless you with
all your reasonable demands.

The bothy where Mary was living was at Gylen on the island of Kerrera.
The Duke of Argyll, Mary told her husband, had confiscated the estate
and she wrote on 4th October that 'the bousie rider of the white horse'
[Campbell of Glenmacrie] 'is factor of it, he's living where we lived. I
bless god I do not want bread though I get nothing of my own allowed
me as yet.'

She continues: 'As to the children they are in health which is all I can
say of them at the time. I have settled Kettie in the mill with Barnabuck's
sister. I was forced to bring Allan to myself by reason he was not well
keept where he was so that I have Johnny and Allan with myself. The
Miller's wife is dead, they dare not but keep the child right as long as I
am here, my pleading it seems is needless for allowing to myself our
children.'

In spite of her miserable state of depression, Mary had the courage to
plan the perilous journey to France to join her husband. Iain Ciar was
against this. In 1717 he wrote to a Mr Gregory who travelled between
France and Argyllshire and who had seen and was about to see Mary.

You may believe its noe small greef to me shee had noe house or
entertainment sewtable to the kindness you are pleased to show
for us both. I flatter myself to think she did not want the
inclenatione to do itt. May the Lord hasten how shoon it may be
my hapyness to give and take a boll with you. [On the subject of
Mary coming to France, he continued] I can nott be so crewall as
to desyre her to come to Bordeaux, it being so long a voyage for a
persone of her constitution and very uncertain of my own time tho
still I persuade myself itt can nott be long where I am, but I am
sensible one day of my absence is more than a year with her, where
it proper I could say the same. We must all submitt to provdence
still hoping for the best and not doubting to attain our wishes att
length.
    All I can say is that if I thought my abode would be six months
where I am I would with all my heart consent to her coming, the
voyage being soe dangerous and her present state soe bad that itt is
impossible for me to advise her save to intreat she keep courage
for I'm seur all her distemper proceeds from greef which is meer

folly still being seur I'm well and in life, and still there is hope for a living man. This I hope you will communicate to her ...

'You say', wrote Mary, 'that I am your only concern you have which I do not doubt butt I am very sure if you were as fond of my company as I would be of yours you would not be so long without me.'

During 1718 Iain Ciar was evidently trying to make some money by doing trade in wine with an Edinburgh friend who wrote to him in March:

The Skipper is not yet come to Leith, how soom he arrives I shall enquire after those goods you have on board of him for me and dispose of them to the best advantage. The pryces of all sorts of victualls is rising for our merchants have bought considerable quantities to send abroad... Write me when you expect to saile with the wine and wether your owners design for Glasgoe or Leith. I wish you a good mercat. [The letter is unsigned.]

Then in May Mary received a letter from her husband: 'I hope nott long that my cargo is like to be reddy, god grant it a safe landing and a good reception. Things were never on soe good a footing what success it may have is nott known to man, a little patience and time will show it.'

In November Iain Ciar's friend in Edinburgh wrote again: 'I am glad of the good vintage this year. But if I may advise you doe not offer to risque your cargo without passes from Spain and Sweden, which I hear may be gott for little money, however I expect you'l advise me in your next if I may bespeak hands for your wine this year. I heard last night that 3 of our wine ships wer seized on the English coast by Swedish privatters.'

Meanwhile, in June, Mary had some good news in a letter from Patrick McDowall W.S. (Writer to the Signet) who was a cousin and the family lawyer in Edinburgh.

I had wryten to you sooner but still waited till there should be a meeting of the Duke of Argyle's managers which was only last week. I made a petition for you and gave each of them a copy of it, and gave in your contract of marriage to them upon which they came to this resolution: to order the factor to pay you three hunder merks yearly untill further orders and that they have seen and considered the land — but they will not allow you to meddle with the tennents but on the contrair some of them proposed that you should be obliged to retire to Sky and live with your own friends upon that 300 merks. All of them seemed to favour you because the factor had written up here that you behave your self very prudently both in words and actions, which some of your sisters in affliction has not done.

A month later Mary received an unsigned letter of warning which illustrates the divided loyalties involved in any civil war. Considering the last sentence of the letter it is surprising that it can be read centuries later!

Dear Madam, Altho this is sent you upon a melanchollie occasion yet the great love and respect which I ever had and shall have for you makes me give you this advertisement and tho' I know you are safe at last yet to prevent present trouble I could not miss such an opportunity.

It is to tell you that Glenkindy is to be in your country within ten or twelve days and is to take an account of McDougall estates. I know it holds of the Duke of Argyle yet Glenkindy will survey it. But what I am to Guard you against is that whatever Cattle or other valuable furniture you have in or about the house ye putt it in some secure place till Glenkindy leave the Country for he will be very exact to take Inventary of Cows, horses and plenishing.

Madam you need not be anyways concerned about this for the time will soon come perhaps when you can doe me service upon which I would depend. I will goo along with Glenkindy and hope to see your ladyship at your own house.

I am not sorry upon any account that I wish very well to King George's interest unless it is that I think it contrary to your inclination for which I have extremest respect. I therefore wish you all happyness and what you wish, providing ye do not wish myself hanged. You'l please believe whether this warning be of any use to your ladyship or not, yet it proceeds from the good will and affection of your ladyship's most devoted servant. I believe you will know the hand having seen it formerly from Inverness before now.

Madam burn this when you read it. Bona 14th July 1718.

Towards the end of this year the letters from the Jacobite exiles seem to have a certain optimism running through them.

Keep good Courage,' Iain Ciar wrote to Mary, 'god in his due time will putt ane end to your calamity and that shooner than you imagine ... as I begun so hop to end towards my King and my dear. I trust in god I shall have no reason to [word torn] for when a man loses his honer its the same whether dead or alive. I have all the reson in the world to beliv my absence will nott be very long.

As I told you in my last our king is married to a daughter of Sobieski, late king of Polland, hir name is Clementina she is butt yours of age, she is one of the greatest beautys in Europe and very rich and hop a great party. I doubt nott but his maryage will be a means to convertt his very enymies in a shortt time. I trust in god will produce of the fruits of it.

George Mackenzie, an exile in Rome, wrote to Iain Ciar:

5th May 1718

'I hope in God the world will turn as you and I wish it and give us yet an opportunity of being agreeably and innocently merry as we have been ... Please know that the K ... s affaires are in as good a situation as his friends can wish and that I hope in God to drink a dram of Usqi with my friend soon, at the foot of a Rock which, if not so weal furnisht with wine as what you usually see in Languedoc, supplys that want by plenty of water and one of the blessings of the promis'd land Milk.

I'll be very weal satisfied to know how your kind and virtuous Heroine does when you heard last from her, and how the fatherless are. God allmighty be their protector until its his pleasure that this storm should blow over.'

The Earl Marischal wrote to Iain Ciar: 'I long for the time when I shall see your claymores and bagpipes again that honest and brave men may be rewarded and then I'm sure you will have a good share, you may be assured that if it depended on me you would have no reason to complain.'

In January 1719 Iain Ciar wrote to Mary: 'Chances and accidents fall out soe oft that I dare say no thing as to news butt I am very hopefull that a short time will produce things to comfortt you. God almighty grant you a good and successful new year and depend upon it, please God, wee once more will have a merry meeting ere six months of it pass.'

This seems to have been a hint that the Jacobites were about to make another attempt to put James Stewart on the throne.

Return to Scotland

In March 1719 Iain Ciar, together with other Jacobite exiles, landed at Stornoway and joined the Earl Marischal and his Spanish troops. The rising seems to have been unlucky from the start. There was disagreement between Tullibardine, eldest son of the Duke of Athol, and the Earl Marischal, as to who was to be in command. At the end of April the news that the Duke of Ormond's fleet, coming in support of James, had been destroyed by storm made Tullibardine counsel retreat. However, he was persuaded to go forward and the Battle of Glenshiel took place in June.

This battle marked the end of the Rising. There is no description of it among the letters, but there is a record elsewhere of Iain Ciar being present. When it ended, the Spanish troops surrendered and were taken prisoner. As to the rest, in the words of the Earl Marischal, each 'took the road he liked best'.

Iain Ciar evidently stayed in the country. Being still a hunted man, he was of course unable to return to his wife and could only meet her secretly. The following letters to him give a little idea of the uncertain atmosphere of the times. Alexander McDonald, a cousin, wrote:

> I take this occasion of saluting you with all sincerity and beggs you'll endeavour to excuse me to our friends you know, and assure them they may depend on my fidelity, which with God's assistance I shall not violate while I breath; would to God they did not believe false reports of me. Could I once get out of ye confinment I am now in I doubt not I would convince them there is unjustice done me. I shall not insiste further on this subject expectin to have the good fortune to see them shortly if possible. God allmighty in his due time will comfort us all and relieve us from our sufferings, let us take heart and hope still for the best, for my part all the stories I can hear shall not make me despair — far less unfaithful to our Master.

In August another cousin (unsigned) wrote:

> I received yours which was noe smale comfort to me and I bless my createur who has brought you safe out of all periles both by sea and land. I trust in his grace that he will conduct and protect you till he restore you to greater contentment.
>
> As to your Lady she is whiles tender which was her ordinar which was occasioned by your dooings. I trust in god ther is noe fear of her which is noe small comfort to you and to me as a well wisher ...

In the same month there was a letter from Colin Campbell (Glendaruel?):

> I am surprised how that idle storie cam of my lord's desine of going suddenly away. I can assure you there is no truth in it nor will he think of it befor he receives his majestie's further commands and we would all gladly hope that ere long afairs may take so good a turn as might prevent our taking banishment a second time, but if our hard fate should bring things to that extremytie you may be sure my Lord will acquaint you which is all need be said to you on that subject at present ... My Lord Tullibardine gives you his service and desires you may make his compliments to Sir Donald ...

In October Mary wrote a very worried letter to her husband:

> I received yours with the tou quadrupels. I desine god willing to

make off within the second or third day and shall folow my dearest's directions. As for your coming to see me for God's sake doe not propos itt for my life itt is certen your enemies is very numerous and your friends very few, butt my comfort I am afread ye desine to leiv the kingdom and to com to take the last farewell of me, if soe god healp your poor children for assure yourself they may be called both fatherless and motherless. I shall not inlearg on this subject, all this time whatever ye doe I shall continou your obedientt loving spouce till death.

The year 1719 was kinder to Mary than the four previous years. Not only was her husband again in this country but in November she was granted a tack (lease) of Dunollie, to take effect from the following Whitsun. She was at this time pregnant again.

The tack was granted by the Duke of Argyll's Commissioners to:

Mary McDonald spouse to John MacDougall, late of Dounnolich and her heirs and assigneys All and Haill the five merk land of Dunolichmore and Dunolichbeg, the toun and lands of Slatrich [on Kerrera] and Miln of Oban with houses, biggins, yards orchard, parts pendules and pertinent thereof whatsoever lying in the parish of Kilbryde, Lordship of Lorn, Sherrifdome of Argyle ... and begin at the term of whitsunday next to come in the year of God one thousand seven hundred and twenty and from henceforth to be peaceably possest and enjoyed by her and her foresaids during the said space with free [word torn] and entry thereto freely, quietly, well, and in peace ... and the said Mary MacDonald obliges her and her foresaids to keep and uphold the houses and biggins of the said lands windtight and water tight during the said space and to leave the same in as good condition at her removeall therefrom as she receives the same at her entry thereto ...

In the spring of 1720, Mary's baby was born, a girl who was named Anne.

About this time it seems as if Iain Ciar was thinking of going abroad again, for there is a letter from Tullibardine discussing the subject, a letter which gives a good idea of the state of uncertainty and inefficiency that was dogging Jacobite affairs. Tullibardine wrote:

29th February, 1720

Sir, Receive inclos'd the letter you desir'd; and am at a loss what to wryte you since it cannot be affirmed we have gott any certain accounts or true lights from the first beginning of the late rare undertaking, which has put all here quite out of patience. So that not to lye longer deluded or erre in loyttering in these parts to no purpose we were forced to come to a resolution with ourselves that if satisfieing accounts came not against a reasonable day, we would be oblidged on all considerations of right reason to flitt our quarters. Accordingly we designe to sett out soon and are the mor confirmed in that by letters just come from Edr. which are so far from clearing matters that all seems still more confused. Therefore ClanRanald, Lochiell, Glenderuell and I are to make the best of our way to the other side.

Without being able to give certain advyce to people that are left, as weell as my Brother, only in my private oppinon it seems best for you and others to continue, at least if possible, in the Country till directions can be gott from the King how to dispose yourselves most for the service at this ticklish juncture, which you may be assured will not be long of coming to you. If once it should happen to be any way in my road to know his Majesty's intention on this head, and the first opportunity that happens I'll not be wanting to our Master more than to myself in thoroughly acquainting him with the particullars of your firmeness, and the honourable pairt you, as well as others, acted for his service even under the bad aspect of our late fracas.

So depend no service will be wanting that lyes under my power to doe you which is all can be said at present from him who truely is, Sir, your most humble servant and cusin, Tullibardine.

Enclosed in the above letter is the following note:

29th February, 1720

To Mr Wm. Dundas, Merchant in Rotterdame, Mr William Gordon Banquier at Paris and Mr Robert Gordon Merchant in Bordeaux.

Gentlemen, The bearer hirr of Lieutennent Collonell McDougall may have occasion to be subsisted before new orders can be had from the King and it is being for his Majesty's Service that he be taken care of in the mean time. Therefore this is earnestly desireing that wherever he may be obliged to land you'll have such a regaird for the service as to subsist him at the same rate as formerly and as other Lieutenent Collonells who are on the Establishment till the King's mind can be known on that head. In the meantime be so kind as to place it to my account which will be a favour done to Gentlemen your most humble and reall servant Tullibardine.

Iain Ciar was in Mull the following month and from there wrote to 'Mr Brown, Merchant, att the present att Scalpa' signing himself John Houston, the name he adopted during the troubles.

Dear Sir, I am surprised you have forgott to acquaint me which makes me very uneasy being here exposed to severall dangers which I would willingly shun, and being informed you are to contynou on that coast to wait the sommer fishing I would gladly wish to know itt whereby I might join my small stock with yours. You may readily know the state of my affaires and may intrust what you please with the bearer.

There is a rich ship com in to Craiknish, the crew have deserted hir. The ship is seased and the most of the crew, who was richly provided with, got off all coins. The ship's loadening was beef, pork, flour and bisketts, som silk stuffs and other things of value. She had 12 or 14 field peeces in the hole, she is butt small. Ther are different accounts of hir, the generall opinyon is that she is a pyratt.

Pray fail nott to lett me hear from you, pray remember me kindly to all with you,

I am in all sincerity your aft. humble servant, John Houston

The ship at Craignish is mentioned in a letter from Archibald McQueen, 'to the Much Honoured Mr John Houston, to be forwarded to by him to the Lady MacDougall'.

Much Honoured, I had much pleasure by receiving and peruseing your letter and the more that it contained the agreeable tydings of your own and your Lady's well being, to both whom I wish your young daughter may be the forerunner of many comfortable yeares.

You have such account of your friends and how they have desposed themselves as makes judge it only superfluous in me to repeat since I cannot add to what you have received.

The ship taken at Cregenish makes news here as to its riches in cash and apparell and if it be true, as its said to be, that it belonged to the Pretender it is a further indication of his misfortune. I pray the Lord may direct and preserve you and comfort you under all your pressures.

During the summer Iain Ciar left Mull and went to Lochearn. While there he received the following declaration from his king.

The King's most gracious declaration to all his loving subjects of what rank and degree soever

James R.

The cryes of our people having reached our ears at this distance we deem it incumbent upon us to declare in this public manner our paternall concerne for your sufferings. We are well satisfied that God has long since touched their hearts and that your affections are with us, we now hope the same almighty power has opened

your eyes to show them a sure and safe way to be your own
delyvers by uniting in our Restoration.

Whilst our country remained in any tolerable conditione of
prospect wee were the less sensible of our own misfortunes. But
now that so great a calamity is brought upon it by the varice of a
few miscreants our tenderness for its reestablisment in plenty and
peace increases our impatience to return to our dominions not so
much out of a desire to find justice ourself as to doe to others, and
to have an opportunity to show ourself the father of our people.

We'd wish for no other method for our mutuall deliverance but
by repentance and unanimity of our subjects that all past errors
may be effaced by their further behavior that such a 'storatione
may be effected as was that off King Charles the second our Royall
uncle, without the Least bloodshed, domestick Disturbance, or
obligatione to foreign assistance.

That the King and his people may be embraced with hearts
overflowing with affectione, that trade may againe florish, Creditt
and publick faith be restored, and honest industry be encouraged
wee call god to witness, who inspires and directs the heart of
Kings, that our ambitione is not so much to wear the crown of our
ancesstors as to show that wee deserved it.

But whatever fate may attend our own persone the preganncy
off your Queen att this very tyme gives us a near prospect by the
blessing of God off a joyfull increase of the Royall family in the
Right Line, how farr such blessings may multiply hereafter
Remains in the breast of providence but this is certain that as long
as theres ane heir to the crown English born remaining Dispos-
sessed its impossible should dye or Brittain be happy.

Wee are unwilling to enter into any personall Reflectiones upon
any sovereigne prince, we disdain to sett so ill ane example, but
experience may have convinced you that no people can be happie
under the yoke of a foreigner lett his possessions be what they will,
let his intentions be what they will, yet innate love to his country
will always persist and be prevalent and indeed ought to be so for
what vertue either so natural in a prince or so commendable in him
as affectione to his own people.

As our Birth was English soe is our heart Intirely English and
altho driven from our Cradle to wander and exile in forreign
countryes our Educatione has also been truly English.

Wee have made the constitutione off our country our first study
and in that search have been delighted to find that our ancient
Laws have provided every thing that a just reasonable King can
desyre either for his felicity or Grander, and it is that ancient
constitutione wee wish to see restored with our persone and being
restored resolve to maintain.

We Conjure you therefore not to lett slipp the present opportunity of employing your thoughts, and off joyning hearts and hands to attain soo desyrable ane End, and wee promise on the word off a King that upon my first accesione to the throne we will soo far referr the State of the natione under all its heads of grevance to a free parliament that you shall have nobody to blaime but yourselves if the least article should be wanting to your future security and happiness.

    J.R.

Given att Rome this 10th octr. 1720 and in the 19th year off our reign.

What effect this declaration from his king had upon Iain Ciar is not known but, read centuries later, it doesn't seem calculated to set the heather alight. Was it tactful of the King to refer to his heart being entirely English?

Mary was at this time pregnant again and in January ordered a maternity gown from Edinburgh. It was sent with a letter in which references to materials, a tablecloth and christening clothes were mixed up with a momentous piece of news for any Jacobite.

                            21st January, 1721

The gown was made by Lady Southesques measurements being the nearest I judged to your size. It is made after the newest fashion and has outletting if needful.

    I was obliged to take a whole piece of the mussleburgh stuff not knowing what fashion of a bed you designed, if there be too much of it the rest will sell or be of use to you.

    If there be too much of the dornik sent for napkins return 4 ells of it which the merchant will take back but I bought the tablecloth large which can be made use of double or single as there is occasion for it ...

    I am obliged to pay ready money for the Christening clothes which are made as near as the directions as possible.

    None has a greater concern for your late and daylie sufferings ... though I am not without hopes of better times, and for your comfort the Lady is safely delivered of a brave boy the 20th of last month, Charles ... [Prince Charles Edward] —

    I would gladly know if all the things sent does fit ... With the utmost sincerity and affection, dear Madam, Your Lady's most humble servant, A.Wm.

There is some pieces of the gown in one of the pockets thereof.

By May the baby had evidently arrived, for Pat McDowall, W.S. in Edinburgh, complained that Mary hadn't told him whether it was a son or a daughter. He was at the time corresponding about a legacy which a Colonel MacDougall in Holland was said to have left to Iain Ciar. Her

father wrote of it: 'You have reason to be thankful to him who has
provided in your great necessity, wishing you much joy in this and
success in all your other undertakings.'

Pat McDowall wrote to Mary enclosing a letter from a John Oliphant
in Rotterdam which reads:

> 13th May 1721
>
> Yours of the 30th March is sent me in my wifes letter and being by a
> friend itt came only to hand yesternight. I do observe itts contents
> which refreshes my memorie of a Legacy left by Collonell
> Mcdouall to Laird of Mcdouall.
>
> [He goes on to say that a Mr Campbell who was going to
> Scotland] fairlie undertook to informe the Laird of Mcdouall of
> the same, in his returning he'd the misfortoune of being drouned
> ... The accounts I had was thatt there was of houses and Lands in
> the Bush [?] to the value of fourty or fifty thousand florens left to
> the Laird of Mcdougall by the Collonell and the tennants would
> not pay their rents till the heir appeared.

Mr Oliphant said that he had written for a copy of the will and would
write again shortly; he added that a floren was equal to a pound Scots or
rather better (a pound Scots was the twelfth of a pound sterling).

Of the legacy Pat McDowall wrote to Mary:

> 21st July, 1721
>
> I do think there is something in that affaire worth looking after,
> and its most proper for your friend to Look after it himself for any
> body else will make but a prey of what they gett. His expense will
> be but small and he will gett acqaintences at Rotterdam that will
> direct him how to manage itt, and I think he should goe as soon as
> possible before the days turn short.
>
> But if he does not take along with him the depositions of some
> witness's of character, taken before Majestrats of Invereray signed
> by them and the town's seal appended by the Clark, as to what
> your friend's relation is to the Col, and that none nearer are in life,
> his going will be to noe purpose.

Iain Ciar was still an outlaw, so there were certain difficulties about him
going to Inveraray and appearing before the Magistrates! Mary
therefore wrote for advice from Campbell of Stonefield who, though
on the Government side, seems to have been a good friend to the family.

Stonefield replied to Mary with a possible solution:

> 5th August, 1721
>
> I was favoured with your letter of the second instant last night and
> would be ready to go all the length that was possible for me to
> serve that gentleman you speak of, but there can be no assistance

got under the touns seall unless the magistrats who have the keeping of the seall should sign it and you know you doe not allow me in your letter to communicate this secret to anybody ... there are also some other difficulties about attesting the place of residence which arises from the speciality of the present circumstances.

If the legacy seems to be ane affair of Consequence that deserves his own presence, and that he is resolved to go there about it, I humbly think he might instantly go to Holland and I'm sure it would be very easie for him to get ane attestation under the seall of the city where he stayed formerly in, or some other city, that he is that Child that was brought over by the Collonells order which might be done by taking the oathes and affidavits, in presence of the Burgomasters there, of such as knew him there, whereof I think some must be still alive; least he should be disappointed in this he might carry one or two men with him who could make oath upon it, and likewise of him being representative of the family ... nor do I think he would have the least difficulty to find some Scotch people there of his acquaintance ... who could make oath before the Burgomasters ...

I doe not think it advisable to trouble the D. of A. for any attestation considering present circumstances.

This seemed a good plan and hopes must have been high. But they were suddenly dashed. About a fortnight later Pat McDowall wrote to Mary: 'I did not know that the Collonell had a half brother or sister or any nearer relations as your friend soe that the case is verrie much altered, for if there be not a special wryting, either by testament or elseways made in his favour his going abroad will be useless. I had a letter from my friend in Rotterdam that he had caused make inquiries for a testament but could find none.'

After this disappointment there is a gap in the letters until 1725. Nothing is known of Iain Ciar's movements during this period, but tradition says that he spent part of his time in Ireland where he had some good friends. A story has been passed down in the family from generation to generation about his encounter there with the Red Robber. Iain Ciar and his henchman Livingstone, having landed in the north of Ireland, were making their way to visit the Earl of Antrim, when they were told by a woman in a cottage that the path they were about to take was very dangerous. Lurking in the forest, she told them, was the Red Robber, on whose head the Earl had put a price of £1000. She had been asked to warn travellers not to go that way.

Iain Ciar and Livingstone continued undaunted on their way. Half way through the forest they met the Robber and immediately seized his whistle so that he could not summon his gang. Iain Ciar then challenged him to single combat. The fight was long and desperate but eventually the Robber lay dead on the floor of the forest. Livingstone cut off his head and his silver buttons and then they made their way to the Earl of Antrim's castle, where they were received with much delight, feasting and rejoicing.

Returning from tradition to the letters: there is one to Iain Ciar, dated 12th September 1725 from Sir Duncan Campbell of Lochnell, which was of the utmost importance to the family. It brought a strong hope that Iain Ciar might be able to obtain a pardon by applying to General Wade.

> I received yours and you may assure yourself that with pleasure I embrace any opportunity by which I can be of any service to you. Now the most favourable opportunity offers that any in your situation had had and which all in your circumstances in the Highlands I find doe embrace, and that is by applying to Generall Wade to procure your remissions to you from the King upon your professing your mistakes for bygone and promising to be dutifull subjects in the future. As for oathes theres no such thing required and I'll engage myself for your good behaviour in tyme to come, unless you discharge me, nor need you come from home yourself but only wryte to the Generall under cover to me. Lett the letter that comes to me be from your lady, to show if neccessary because I myself can not legally correspond with you but can always deliver to the General any letter directed to him enclosed in a ladys letter.
>
> And for your further ease, and to make your business safe, I have sent ane double of the letter I would have you wryte to the Generall. You may think the letter verrie strong but that it cannot be so for I have seen much stronger from some in your circumstances to him alreadie since his coming to this countrie, and upon your writing this letter your business is certainly done in which I hope you'll not neglect your owne interest. As to your scruples anent the Duke of Argyll what is done by Generall Wade is done by him for they are in the same interest and partie.

Iain Ciar followed his advice, and Sir Duncan wrote to Mary: 'Yours last night I received with ane letter enclosed to General Wade [unfortunately this letter has not survived] which I shall be sure to deliver safe into his hands. You may rest assured that nothing will be wanting on my part to procure McDougalls remission which I may venture to tell you will be done with others upon the King's return or before the end of next session of Parliament. In the meantime he shall meet with no disturbance from anybody . . .'

Once again, high hopes came to nothing. Iain Ciar's faith was still further to be tested, and when his pardon eventually came, two years later, it snatched him from disaster at the very last moment. According to contemporary records, Iain Ciar, together with others including Stewart of Appin and Rob Roy, had been taken from Newgate to Gravesend to be put on board a ship for transportation to Barbados. The pardons arrived only just in time. 'His Majesty with his usual clemency', wrote the *Weekly Journal* of 24th January, 1727, 'had pardoned the following Jacobites who had been convicted capitally of High Treason in the first year of his reign.'

So ended a fugitive period in his life. The conviction he had expressed in his letter to Mary ten years before had been fulfilled: 'I trust in god to live and dye within them old rouinish stones of my predecessors.' And so he did.

During the ten remaining years of his life Iain Ciar and Mary increased their family by at least three, thus forming a second little family much younger than their older children. The first was born in 1730, a son named John who arrived in much happier circumstances than the John he replaced, who had been born during the bleak period of Iain Ciar's exile in France.

The three eldest sons were sent during the early 30s to Edinburgh for their further education: Alexander and Duncan to Chambers of Law and Allan to train as a doctor. Kettie, the eldest daughter, was also sent to Edinburgh. Iain Ciar had hoped that she would stay with his wife's cousin, Mrs Mary McDonald, but he received from her the following letter explaining why this was not possible. It gives a good idea of how cramped were the houses in the Royal Mile, where many of the aristocracy lived:

> Cannongate
> 31st July, 1731
>
> I received your letter and I am sorrie that it was not in my power to grant that which you proposed of your Daughter staying with me ... For all the accomodation is but a Dineing-room and two little Bedchambers, a little Kitchine and Pantry. My cousin Mrs Peggy and me lys in one of the Bed Chambers and the two Janets, Sir Alexander's sister and Castletoun's sister, lys together in the other Bed Chamber and they are so little that none of them will hold two Beds, so that you may easily see now how impossible it is for me, for as is already we are already very much straited for want of room.

The letter goes on to give news of Kettie:

> I had the pleasure to see your Daughter who is with me just now,

and though she is not to Lodge with me you may be sure I will endeavour to have her as offten with me as I can, and that her time will allow of, and she shall get always the best advice I am capable to give her. She is to go this night Home to her new Quarters to one Mrs Melvile with whom her Brother has agreed for her Board and teaching her the white seam. I hear her called a very descreet woman and uses her Boarders they say very well but a great Presbyterian there fore my cousens, Sir Alex.'s sister, and me will take your Daughter to our meeting-house to sitt with us.

Kettie Macdougall is in my opinion a very sweet tempered agreeible Girle and carried herself alreadie better as some that has been years in this place so that her Mother needs not be ashamed who sees her, either for carriage or anything else and you may tell my cousen her daughter has so much descration and good sense that she will not willingly go by the directions she has given her about the taking of her cloaths. All she has taken is a silk Plaid which she would not grant to take but of the slight sort because her Mother allowed her to give but a Guinea for one she said. But them they pay but a Guinea for are so slight that she would not have a month's wearing of it when it would be like a Clout, for the air spoils such slight silks. So that with much ado I made her take a better Plaid which is ten shillings more price, and as to everiething else she has gotten of my cousens, Sir Alexrs. sister and me choised them for her and oblidged her to take some things better than her Mama allowed her, or she herself inclined to do ... Just now your Father-in-law is as he uses to be, but his wife is fallen worse again and few but himself regrates it.

Meanwhile Iain Ciar was doing all he could to get the family lands restored. There is a letter from Pat McDowall W.S. on the subject:

Edinburgh
3rd July, 1730

I had your letter and have several times been with my Lord Advocate since he came home. He says that the Duke has not granted a Charter to any of his Vassalls as yet and desired yours may be delayed for some time because upon his Granting of yours he would be importuned by other People to do the like and since you might depend upon yours there was no loss in the delay, however I shall continue to importune the Advocate that the thing be done.

Importuning, as it turned out, had no effect, and there was much loss in the delay, for the land was not returned until fifteen years later, eight years after Iain Ciar's death.

In order to try and make a fortune and so relieve the family problems

Iain Ciar's second son Allan went to the West Indies. There remain a few letters which tell of his life between the ages of eighteen and twenty-five. He began his medical education in Edinburgh in 1732. Medical training in Scotland had for long been of low quality but now, thanks to the recent appointment of efficient professors, the Medical School of Edinburgh was beginning to gain a good reputation.

As was then the custom, Allan was apprenticed for three years to a Chirurgeon Apothecary, the G.P. of those days, and a McDowall cousin wrote to Iain Ciar: 'I had the honor of yours by your son who is a lusty young plant. He enters this day to Mr Kennedy with whom I am perswuaded he will be very well, the young gentleman himself seems resolved to mind his business carefully.'

The next letter gives more details of Mr Kennedy: 'A Cherugeon Apothcare in this City a gentleman verie weill imployed. He was a Chief Surgeon in a Man-of-War and long in hospital in Paris. I sent his indentures to Garthland to signe, I expect them back soon with his Prentice fee.'

The Garthland referred to was Colonel Dowell of Garthland in Wigtonshire, who was helping his Chief with the education of his sons. Garthland, who had made a considerable fortune from his sugar plantation in the West Indies, wrote to Iain Ciar: 'I do assure you, dear Cusin, I will never ommit any opportunity I can to serve you and your family.'

If Iain Ciar had fears that his son would run wild in the City a friend reassured him: 'You need not doubt his being close keept for he cannot be absent one hour without his Maister's leave. His Maister is to acquaint me of any complaints he may have and I shall give my advice to your son as occasion offers.'

It does not seem, reading the indentures of the time, that the life of a medical student permitted much freedom. He had to bind himself 'to serve his master by day and by night, holy-day and week-day'.

Allan apparently made a good apprentice, judging from the letters to his father from friends in Edinburgh: 'I received yours from your son who I expect will answer all our expectations. He attends his affairs punctually and I have made an interest with some of the doctors that attends in infirmary to allow him to come and see the operations which will do him the best service ...'

And then later: 'Your son Allan had the recomendation of everybody he converses and especially his master commends him highly. He never misses him out of the shop [surgery] nor finds him idle but always improving himself one way or other.

By 1735 Allan's training was finished, and he celebrated his new skills by sending home some medicine for the child that his mother was expecting: '. . . an ounce of oil of sweet almonds and as much syrup of violets for the young child, if it is God's will to bless you with one, and give a teaspoon now and then. If you don't up it to your child it shal be usefull to any of the Rest that shall be troubled with the cough.'

The following year a friend wrote to Iain Ciar from Edinburgh: 'Your son Allan is gone for St Christophers [now St. Kitts in the West Indies], I pray he may be as the Colonel at his return, the Colonel went as poor and in the same employment to that place. It is a luckie cast for him and I hope it shall throw up well to him.'

As far as can be gathered from the letters, things didn't 'throw up' particularly well. In answer to a suggestion from his brother Alexander that he should contribute towards his sister Kettie's dowry on her marriage to Maclaine of Lochbuey, Allan wrote from St Christopher's:

22 September, 1737

I do assure you that tho' you are pleased to banter me annent being helpful to the paying of her portion that there is not a brother she has, or ever will have, whose love was, is and shall be more sincere towards her than mine. I would to God it was in my powers not only to do her Service but to all the rest of the poor family I have the honour to owe my birth to, but in my present situation its the most I can doe to support myself, but I am hopefull God Almighty will be pleased through time to redeem us all from this laberinth of trouble.

[Allan went on to thank his mother for a plaid and his father for six pairs of garters.]

I am sorry I cannot make them no better acknolegement than to thank for the same but I shall endeavour by the next opportunity to send a barrell of sugar to my mother which will serve her for some time for Common use.

[He then asked for a strange assortment of things to be sent:] I wish you could see to pick up a sword, pistoll and dirk as likewise a shoulder belt and one of your brass mouthed purses, and send me them as soon as possible you Conveniently can. I wish you would let my Mother know that I would be obliged to her if she would send me by the first ship half a dozen dried ling and two or three reested [smoked] salmon . . . if you know any person you could put trust in at Greenock or Port Glasgow that she would send by one of the Skye birlins [half-decked galley or rowing boat] thats bound for either of the aforesaid places a Barrell of her best march or septr. Ale together with a small Cask of aquavita. The Ale must be very well brewn and hoped otherwise it won't keep.

Later he wrote: 'Expecting by every ship that you would send me the

*MacDougall coat of arms on archway leading to
family burial ground at Kilbride*

Armes. I wish you would send me a Sett of handsome Armes for the highland dress ... likewise send some highland Garters. I wish you would endeavour to send them by the first Oppertunity that they may be here before the 30th Nov. [St Andrew's Day].

In this letter, dated 16th June, 1739, he acknowledged two letters from his brother Alexander, one dated the previous October and the other in January, both of which arrived in April.

> I have kept health very well since I last wrote except a touch I had of a pestelentiall fever that raged here during the months of Oct. and Nov. last, which had like to have done my business. I was the only white person left alive on the Estate, in short the plague at Athens did not kill more people in proportion to the inhabitants than that Damned fever did here.
>
> Upon the death of the Colonell's nephew, who was manager of his Estates here, the Gentlemen who are the Atturneys were pleased to give me the Management, and the Colonell, from whom I had a letter since, approves of it. I have about Eighty Pound Sterling yearly Salery with which I can make a Shift to live, and I do assure you I have toyl and fatigue enough to go through, but while I keep health I don't value it for I see idleness produces nothing but want.
>
> I wish you would send me all your news for we have a report here that you're like to have a Civill war at home.

Death of Iain Ciar

Iain Ciar died on 8th December, 1737. Although his wish to die within the stones of his ancestors was fulfilled, he was not buried among them. The family burial ground was on Loch Etive, at Ardchattan Priory, founded in the thirteenth century by Duncan, a former MacDougall Chief. Tradition has it that on the day of Iain Ciar's funeral the Loch was so rough that the cortege could not get across. The storm continued to rage for three days, so the funeral party decided to give up the attempt to cross and wound its way to Kilbride, a graveyard among quiet hills, where Iain Ciar's mother had been buried. This was now to become the family burying place.

Allan, who is not heard of again after this, wrote home from the West Indies to his brother Alexander of his poor mother: 'I beg you would comfort her to the utmost of your powers.' Mary survived her husband thirty-nine years.

A gaelic bard, Donald MacIntyre, wrote a lament for MacDougall of Dunollie, which the Rev. John MacLeod of Oban has kindly translated. These are a few verses from it.

Great is the loss of Lorne this year,
Lamenting is my tale which will not change,
Iain Ciar, his head laid low,
The country is aware of MacDougall's loss.

The weather changed when you died,
The clouds were constantly raining,
The harvest of the woods was lost,
Its produce, its flower, its fruit.

You were pitying the poor,
You were generous, wise,
Wisdom of nature with the best advice
You had in abundance as a gift.

You were brave, of splendid appearance,
As Oscar was in Fingalia,
A kind man, without bending, without flaw,
I cannot see anyone like you.

You were good at awarding merit,
You were hard going into the fight,
Loving, merciful in wrath and victory,
Your reputation remaining in many lands.

But let us submit to the high Lord,
Who has not left the place without heir,
It is good that Alastair is present,
Though Sorrowful is our loss.
Let us be virtuous and content,
That your sons are kind and worthy,
Farewell to the chief that went away from us,
It is from God that Glory comes.

Ane Account of the Funeral Charges of John (Iain Ciar)
MacDougall of Dunollie, December 14th 1737

	£	sh	d.
Imprimise for Necessars from Inverery	6	14	1½
Itt. one boll meal from the Miller att Clye		10	
Itt. 3 stone Butter as per accounts	1	4	
Itt 10 Gallons Aquavita as Do.	6	13	4
Itt 3 pints double Distilled Rum as per Do		6	
Itt one bottle Brandie as per Do.................		1	
Itt 4 Dozen Clarett as p Do		16	
Itt ane half stone candles as p Do	3	3	4
Itt 8 Bottles Madaira Wine as p do		9	4

Itt 6 Wedders as p Do.	1	
Itt to Cash for expresses & morte-cloath.........	18	6
Itt four Dozen Poultrie	3	
ten Ducks	2	6
six gees..................................	6	
three Turkis	4	
To the Cook................................	6	
To Mrs Livingstone Cook Maid................	5	6
To charges for returning the Morte Cloath.......	1	
To Murning for the Widdow 5		
To Alexander Campbell — Surgeon 8		
Itt to the Coffine.............................	15	
To charge Alexr Steward Nottar publick 1	1	
To ten stone Cheese at 3sh per stone 1	10	

'*Inventory of Household plenishings and limber*'

There is among the letters 'An Inventory of Household plenishings and limber left by MacDougall [Iain Ciar] att his Decease Decr. 8th 1737.' The total value comes to £50. 11s 11d for all his belongings. (It is interesting to note that the bill for his funeral comes to not very much less, as it adds up to nearly £40.) Some of the items in the inventory are valued separately, but others are lumped together, in some cases rather incongruously: 'an old bed covering and an old saddle and bridle'; 'two old Curtains and a Walking stick'; 'an earthen porrenger and a pair of Garters'; and 'a pick Axe and 3 doz silver buttons'.

The furniture listed in the inventory gives a picture of how the Castle was furnished at the time: 2 large tables, 3 small ones, 3 old frames of tables and an old dresser, 2 doz chairs, 2 old armed chairs, 3 large chists and 5 small ones, 3 presses [cupboards], and 6 old doors not in use.'

As to the beds and bedding: 'to the timber of four beds' runs the list; '5 other old bed posts and sides', a Box bed and small press. The bedding consisted of '8 pr. bed linnin', '4 cod (pillow) covers and 22 pairs blankets', '3 feather beds with pillows and bolsters', and the nicely described 'near the making of a bed of feathers'. To complete the scene were 'two old peuther [pewter] Chamber Potts' and two earthen ones.

To cover the table there were '9 table cloathes', and in reserve 21 yards of coarse Dornick, (a kind of table linen from Tournai with a geometric design). There were also thirty napkins.

Pewter predominated on the dinner table: pewter dishes, basins, a salt and mustard dish, '15 broth peuther pleats' and 42 plain ones. Of china there was a china punch bowl, 8 Delph plates and 5 dishes, a small posset dish of Delph and 2 Delph bowls.

The cutlery listed is half a dozen knives and forks, a dozen silver spoons, half a dozen tea spoons,silver tea tongs and a dealing spoon which is listed with 2 silver salts.

There were 2 flagons, a glass decanter and a dozen drinking glasses.

One entry in the kitchen list reflects a method of cookery of the time: 'a Rack and 3 spitts and a small caldron'. There were '3 Big Potts' and 2 small ones, 2 small Copper skillets, 2 brass pans, a frying pan, an old girdle, a brander, 3 pairs of tongs, a ladle, a strainer and a grater.

Looking at some of the items in the inventory it is evident that besides cooking, the women of the household busied themselves with many other useful activities — such as brewing ale, churning butter, making cheese and spinning and weaving.

When Allan, Iain Ciar's son, wrote home in 1737 from the West Indies begging his mother to send him a cask of her home-brewed ale, perhaps it would have been made in the 'working and masking vat for ale' that is mentioned, along with 10 ale casks and a dozen bottles, in the inventory.

Two churns and numerous milk vessels and pails tell of the butter-making and 'a cheese setter and presser' of the cheese.

There were 2 large and 2 small spinning wheels, 2 pairs of cairds (wool carders), 4 stone of wool and 2 of lint (flax), and also various tools used in the weaving of wool and linen. Spun woven yard is mentioned, 5 yards of tartan at 6d. a yard and 'a webb undressed black Cloath 24 yards' valued at 10/- for the whole piece.

Reflecting the family's outdoor life are two fishing nets, herring casks, fowler's pieces (guns), saddles and bridles, horse comb and brush, 'Plowing and Harrowing Grath', other agricultural tools, 'A Bees Scape', peat spades, slyps and creels.

The list of Iain Ciar's clothes is short: a coat, a plaid, two pairs of tartan trews, 8 linen shifts, a pair of garters, a pair of gloves, a pair of boots, two small leather belts and 'two Handcur Chiefs.'

Personal possessions seem also very sparse: a Bible and 8 small books, a broad sword, shoulder belt, pistol, 2 razors and a whone [hone], small brass inkpiece, snuff box, pen knife, purse, 'cash in his purse 17/6', 3 doz.small silver buttons and a pair of silver buckles, and two silver pocket pieces. A pocket piece was a coin, not usually in current use, which was kept in the pocket.

The valuation of the various items is interesting. To give some examples — large tables are valued at 7/6 each, chairs at 1/4 each, 3 feather beds with pillows and bolsters £1, pewter dinner plates 8d., a china punch bowl 4/-, silver spoons 8/- each, a dozen drinking glasses 2/- the lot.

In the kitchen Big Potts were 4/-, while small copper skillets were 1/6 each and brass pans 1/3. The vat for making ale was valued at 5/6.

The four spinning wheels were valued at 10/- altogether, while the fishing nets were 10/- each, the fowler's pieces 2/6 each, the 'plowing and harrowing grath' 10/- and the 'Bees Scape' 10/- also.

The ratine (rough woollen cloth) coat and three linen shifts came to 10/-, while 2 tartan trews and a cane were valued at 1/-, and a pair of boots and a plaid were 4/-.

The Bible and 8 small books were valued at 8/-, the pistol at 10/- and a pair of small silver buckles at 3/6. The most expensive single item in the inventory is 'a Dung Cart with its harness' at £2, and the least expensive an old hamper at 2d.

It is probable that many of the family possessions were lost during the time that Dunollie Castle was forfeit after the failure of the 1715 Rising.

Family Post

Usually, unconnected bits and pieces, some trivial and some important, make up a family post and the Family Post sections of this book follow the same pattern. The selected letters, or parts of letters, do, however, all give a strong flavour of the times.

Angus

In March 1715, one Robert Colhoun, who had undertaken to do some smuggling business for Iain Ciar, wrote to him relating the contrariness of a character named Angus. He had accompanied Colhoun to Glasgow as a guide, and had hatched a plot that could have wrecked the whole undertaking.

'Angus and I,' writes Colhoun, 'fell almost by the ears at Loch Lomondhead and Angus would be for returning home which was not a little uneasie to me, then with much ado I gott him persuaded to go further on his journey.' Colhoun blamed Angus for 'the rise of the discord' and explained: 'I was only desiring such and such things to be done which indeed he took very ill, and he put the other two men in such bad humor that we could get nothing done with them but with playing with them as they had been children.'

The party eventually arrived in Glasgow, but here more trouble with Angus arose. 'When we were unloaded and got all lodged in safe houses, I sent your servant Donald for Angus to take up his quarter with me which he refused but had gott a lodging for himself and the other two men where they made shift to eat and drink seven pound Scots — which was another clamour, the man coming to me next morning with their account.'

It had been arranged that Angus would be paid five pounds for his services, but now he turned awkward about this. 'He thought five pound sterling was too little and we could not get him pleased at all, but at length with five pounds and twenty pence he seemed pleased but grumbled within as I thought — which was not ill-founded. He went off without any good night.'

However, this was not the end of Angus's awkwardness. Two days after he and the men had departed, the town officer, one Allan McDougall, came to Colhoun with a fine story about them.

'They had plotted amongst themselves,' wrote Colhoun, 'to inform against us for importing prohibited goods — for which they thought they would get some money. Allan McDougall told me with much persuasian he gott them driven off that lay, for the lad had a kindness for me and waited on them till he seed them away incase they had done damage. And I blame nae but Angus for all.'

The other business Iain Ciar had entrusted to Colhoun was the buying of seeds for the garden, which Angus was to bring back to Dunollie. But Angus, when asked to pay for them, absolutely refused, saying 'is not MacDougall's word nae better than my money?' Colhoun had to pay and he enclosed the account in his letter — at the same time asking Iain Ciar to buy him a horse. 'if you can get one as broad as long almost and cheap you may send him, and I shall send the money by the bearer or pay to any you desire here.'

An account of Seeds, Spade and Shevel sent to Mcdugall
28th March 1715

One unce meray gold [marigold]	at 26	....	0 - 2 - 2
″ do of time [thyme]	at 16	....	0 - 1 - 4
4 do of Cabitch	at 3	....	0 - 1 - 1
2 do of Carrats	at 3	....	0 - 0 - 6
2 do of Pasnips	at 3	....	0 - 0 - 6
2 do of turnipes	at 2½	....	0 - 0 - 5
2 do of beets	at 1½	....	0 - 0 - 3
1 do of persal [parsley]	at 2	....	0 - 0 - 2
2 do of Carses [watercress]	at 1½	....	0 - 0 - 3
2 do of Refords [radish]	at 2½	....	0 - 0 - 5
2 do of white pees	at 9	....	0 - 0 - 9
shovell and spade cost		....	0 - 3 - 6
			0 - 11 - 3
	Money I got from you	....	0 - 2 - 0
	Balance due to Rob. Coloun	....	0 - 9 - 3

Sir, the above seeds are as cheape as I could purchase them. If you send the horse lett him be verry broad and something handsome not Exceeding four pounds sterg. which is the needful of your humble servant at command Robt. Colhoun.

Letter to the Gentlemen of Argyll

To the Gentlemen of the Shire of Argyll from the Duke of Argyll London.

27th August, 1715

Gentlemen, I think my self obliged to return you my thanks for the zeal you have showed in your late meeting for the peace of the Country, and for the defence of his Majesties Government. I shall not fail to do you the justice to acquaint the King of the alacrity and duty you have expressed upon this occasion against the intended rebellious attempts to destroy our Religion and liberties. I don't doubt but it will appear at this time how false those suggestions have been which have been made of late Years that the Pretender to the Crown of these Kingdoms and the usurper of his Majesties royal titles had increased in his interest in the shire of Argyll, so famed in the worst of time for the supporting the Protestant Religion and the resisting of Tyranny. My family, and consequently you, have formerly suffered for this cause, I glory in it and I hope you do so too, but I can with great satisfaction acquaint you the King has taken much precautions and is so much resolved to protect his faithful subjects that we cannot run any hazzard but from too great security.

Our old and our new Enemies will soon see their errors and those who have always been ready in the worst of times to assist the right cause will now with the greater pleasure follow and support their principles in the best.

I shall immediately as your heritable Lieutenant appoint Deputy Lieutenants and other officers to command our fencible men, and shall neglect nothing which may tend to your safety and prosperity,

I am Gentlemen,

Your most obedient and most humble servant,

Argyll

Rob Roy's work?

Unsigned letter sent from Leuchars to Iain Ciar in exile, 21st Aug. 1718. Believe me I long much to see you and drink all our friends health and shall be glad to know when I may expect to enjoy that happiness.

There wer severall baraks [barracks] a building this summer in the north and west highlands. Its reported that in one night they were thrown down and the workmen stript naked and made to swear they would never return on such ane errand again, its said Rob Roy has had a hand in it, be that as it will, its certain, as I am now informed, that its mater fact that the workmen came back to Edinburgh.

The Family Doctor

Ken Ocomhour to Iain Ciar.

Gerline
5th September, 1719

Much Honnored Sir, I had the good fortune and honnor of receiving a line from you wherein you are pleased to thank me for kindness done to your lady and children whereof I was very uncapable and anything I could doe was far less than my duty and your honor may believe that I am stile mindfull of former favours and shall study to recompence them soe far as in me lays and I wish I may not have occasion to serve you Lady and children often as I am willing to obey and the more because its your desyre and your Lady is deserving of any kindness that can be done to her for she is ready to serve any whom she knew you had a kindness for, she makes freends to herself and looses none. I doubt not but you heard some asperations that went abroad of me the year yr honor went abroad but I shall not study to exculpate myself at such a distance I shal only say that it would be very ungrate in me to be guilty of the like, being soe much indebted to your kindness and I conclude wishing your honeur health and happyness and I presume to subscribe much Hon., Your Hon. most obedient sert. Ken. ocomhour.

Sad News

John McDougall to Iain Ciar.

July 1731

My wife died the 5th July to great loss, as every man makes who loves a good one. A better wife I believe never lived, from that you may easily enter into my grief. The Lord giveth, the lord taketh, blessed be the name of the Lord.

Wood for the Miller

Campbell of Dallfuir to Iain Ciar

November, 1731

I know no timber in my wood fit for a wheel Kimm but birch and alder. I judge your miller may be served of that kynd and you may send him when you think fitt, and he may call at my miller when he comes who will direct him where he may be best served, which I shall order him to doe whether I be at home or not. I am heartily sory your Lady is so very tender. I wish her better health with all my heart.

Poor Innocent Man?

This story, though tantalisingly incomplete, is included because it gives a flavour of the times when a man could imprison someone who annoyed him without bringing him to justice; and because it gives an insight into Iain Ciar's character.

Campbell of Dallfuir, to Iain Ciar

13th July, 1732

Sir, I receaved yours the other day wherein you begin with being surprysed that I doe not Liberate Mcallvory or bring him to a tryall in the shyre.

I own to you I am in no hurrie about either and tho I were inclyned to sett him at Liberty, as I cannot say I am, I doo not think it would be acting civilly by Sir Duncan Campbell in me to doo anything with that villan but by his approbation, since his releasement in the manor you propose it, must at least depend upon him and his aunt as much as upon me.

You give it next as your opinion that there is neither pleasur nor profit in extorting a confession from a poor innocent man to which I agree, nor doo I know that he has mett with any treatment which looks like extorting a confession, tho I know nobody that has a poorer claim to honesty or innocence than he, whereof you would be soon convinced if you took the half of pains to find out his villanies that you do to make him appear ane innocent person.

You mention lykeways that iff his releasement is not agreed to you hope not to be blaimed iff you look to his liberation after another manor. It is certain I cannot hinder you to follow any legale method you have a mynd to ... I make a supposition should you gett that villain so farr protected from justice as to prevent him being hanged or transported (wherein its very possible you may be disappointed), Mcallvories character must be better established before you can reap any other honour by it than supporting the cause of a known rascall ...

I am heartily sorry that anything should have happened that obliged me to differ with you, which I doo not out of choise but necessity and I appeall to all the world whether I am more to blame exposing a known villan than you are by setting up for his protector.

News from the newspapers is often quoted in the correspondence.

Trouble in Holland

Jo. McDowall to Iain Ciar
Edinburgh,

24th October, 1732

The dutch are like to be distroyed by a sort of worm which eats through all their dikes, earth and timber, and makes them like honeycomb ... they have made an universal fast for it to deprecate the vengeance of heaven.

National News

John McDowall to Iain Ciar

Edinburgh, 1734

Our assembly sitting is as hott as fire, never considering the merits or reasons of things butt gives a clean vote. I hear they are to be dissolved to prevent mischief. It is suspected that they may occasion more. All is in a flame both at home and abroad, Whigs as well as Tories are discontented and all out of houmour.

Burden to his Family

John MacDougall to Iain Ciar

Pendennis Castle December 1736

His son Coll is a hopefull Lad, the misfortune is that he has no friend which can incourage him, therefore the best thing he can do is to look out for some frugall person in order to be married, providing she has some small fortune in order to set him up that he may not be burdensom to his father or the rest of the family.

ALEXANDER
1713-1801

ALEXANDER MacDOUGALL, 23rd Chief (1737-1801)

ALEXANDER, 23rd Chief *m* MARY Campbell

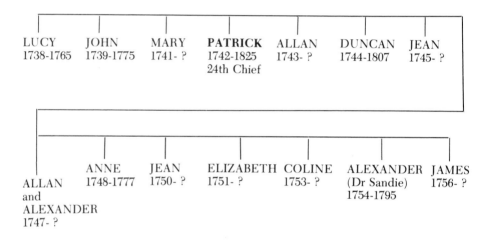

LUCY	JOHN	MARY	**PATRICK**	ALLAN	DUNCAN	JEAN
1738-1765	1739-1775	1741- ?	1742-1825	1743- ?	1744-1807	1745- ?
			24th Chief			

ALLAN and ALEXANDER 1747- ?	ANNE 1748-1777	JEAN 1750- ?	ELIZABETH 1751- ?	COLINE 1753- ?	ALEXANDER (Dr Sandie) 1754-1795	JAMES 1756- ?

The Family of Alexander
(also known as Alastair Dubh or Sandie)
23rd chief, born 1713, died 1801

His father: John (Iain Ciar), 23nd chief, died 1737.

His mother: Mary, born 1696. She was a daughter of William Mac-Donald, third son of Donald MacDonald of Sleat, 3rd Bt, and married Iain Ciar in 1712. She died in 1776.

His wife: Mary, third daughter of Patrick Campbell of Barcaldine. She married Alexander in 1737 and died in 1782.

The children

Lucy: born 1738. She married James Macdowal of Edinburgh and had at least two children who survived — James and Betty. Lucy died in 1765.

John: born 1739. Married Isabell, second daughter of the 3rd Lord Ruthven. John was in the army and then in the armed forces of the East India Company. Both he and his wife died in Bombay in 1775.

Mary: born 1741. She married Alexander MacNeill of Oronsay, and had children.

Patrick: born 1742. He became 24th chief. He married Louisa Maxwell, daughter of John Campbell of Achallader. They had twelve children. Patrick died in 1825.

Allan: born 1743, died in infancy.

Duncan: born 1744. He married Jean Campbell, daughter of Captain Neil Campbell of Duntroon. They had thirteen children. Duncan died in 1807.

Jean: born 1745, died in infancy.

Alexander and Allan: twins born 1747. Alexander died in infancy and Allan is not heard of again, so probably also died young.

Anne: born 1748. She died unmarried in 1777.

Jean: born 1750, died young.

Elizabeth: born 1751, died young.

Coline: born 1753, died young.

Alexander (Dr Sandie): born 1754. He became a surgeon, and married first Anne, daughter of John Hay of Edinburgh; secondly Jean Fisher. By his first wife he had one daughter, Mary, who married Charles John Viscount Mountjoy. Alexander died in Russia in 1795.

James: born 1756, died young.

3

Alexander

In contrast to his father, as Chief Alexander lived a quiet domestic life. But for the difficult decision he took in 1745, his life could have been a repetition of Iain Ciar's: banishment and many years spent as a hunted man, or he might well have met death in his support of Prince Charles Edward. Despite the Jacobite blood inherited from both parents, however, he seemed to have lacked the fire of his forefathers, and for good reasons, which his father would probably have rejected, he did not join the '45 Rising.

Alexander's dedication was to his family, his property, and those who lived there. His aim was to improve the Dunollie lands returned to him after their forfeiture and, in company with many others of the time, he took advantage of the new ideas then reaching the Highlands for improving the land, cattle and crops.

The Uneasy Years

Writing from France in 1717, Iain Ciar called his children his poor orphans. And so they were until he was able to come home to Dunollie ten years later, having by then been pardoned for his part in the 1715 Jacobite Rebellion.

Alexander was his eldest child. When he was about five years old, he was sent to a clansman at Dumbarton who, on hearing of the misfortunes of the family, had offered to be responsible for the care and education of his future chief.

'I am glad to understand,' Iain Ciar wrote to his wife Mary, 'that poor John in Dumbarton has called for my son Sandy ... I entreat you may not faile to send him.'

The friend in Dumbarton wrote of Alexander at the age of nine:

> Your son here gives full hopes of his being a good scholar and a towardie boy, so that evrie bodie loves him as your ladyship may be verie sure of. I do and shall take as much care of him as if he were my own.

The schoolmaster, one Mr Love, also approved of the boy, and in 1721 gave him a good school report.

> I gladly embrace this opportunity of Acquainting Your Ladyship anent your son and his proficiency att this school ... Your son Madam was entered to the Latin Hallowday last and I must really say tho' he be very Young yet he was amongst the best schoolars of his Class, is a Most Excellent scholar and makes as good proficiency and advances att his Book as those who are double his Age ... I take a very narrow Inspection of him and I look carefully to his writing, in which he also makes very great progress ... I am with the greatest Affection and Respect Madam your Ladyship's much obliged and most humble Servt.

Alexander was then eight years old. Mr Love added: 'I am persuaded he will be an ornament to the ancient family which he is descended off.'

The next mention of Alexander in the letters is when he was nineteen and about to enter a lawyer's office in Edinburgh. A friend wrote to his father:

> 30th July, 1731
> I had the honour of yours by your son whom I have conversed with several times and have found him a young man of very good parts. I hope you and all concerned in him will have the pleasure of seeing him spring up a fine gentleman and a fit representative of your family.
>
> It is thought proper that he study the mathematicks and french till November when the session sitts down and Crichen and I shall have our thoughts by that time about a writing chamber to settle him there. To have him in one before that would be to lose his time when no business is going.

Alexander went to Edinburgh with his sister Kettie (Cathrine), who later married Maclaine of Lochbuie. She went to finish her education and lodged with a very 'descreet' woman who was to teach her 'the white seam'. There is a letter from a Macdonald of Sleat cousin complaining that Alexander was preventing his sister from spending necessary money on clothes!

> But for that, Kettie has not gotten so many things for her Brother has keeped a night goun off her which she was allowed. Her Mama desired she would get a Hambrugh nightgoun and a fustine night goun but her Brother would give her but the Hambrugh Goun and she very modestly yeilds to what ever he pleases. She has got one suite of Edgings at 2 shillings the yard, but she has gotten but that one suite of Edgings so that you may write to your Son and desire him to give his sister what more little necessarys she wants.

Hide-covered trunk brought to Dunollie by Alexander's bride,
Mary Campbell, in 1737

Alexander married in 1737, when he was twenty-four. His bride was Mary, third daughter of Patrick Campbell of Barcaldine. She left one castle home to live in another, and brought with her a wooden trunk covered with deer hide, studded with brass nails and inscribed with a date 1731.

Alexander has written the exact date of his wedding, 15th September, 1737, in a large Bible given to him when he was fifteen by Dugald MacDougall of Ardmore, on the island of Kerrera. In this Bible he was also to write the date of birth of all his fifteen children, and in it his successors have recorded all the family births, right down to the present day.

This edition of the Bible is dated 1707 and proclaims on the title page: 'Newly translated out of the original Tongues and with the former translations diligently compared and revised by his Majesty's Special Command. With most profitable Annotations upon all the hard places, and other things of great importance. Which notes have never before been set forth with this new translation. But are now placed in due order with great care and industrie.'

Iain Ciar died about three months after Alexander's wedding. Sir Alexander Macdonald of Sleat, a cousin, wrote from Skye:

> 26th January, 1738
> I am extreamly sorry for the loss your Family has sustained by the Death of your Father, but regretting it will be of no use to you or any that were concerned in Him and there fore the only means of repairing so great a loss is to look forward so that your care and concern ought to devolve on what is left behind.
>
> It is impossible for me to give you any particular Advice at this distance as not knowing very exactly the Circumstances of your Affairs, however this I know — that nothing will mend them but your own prudent Conduct and diligence. I cannot but rejoice that you have hit on a partner of Life who (by all I can hear) will be helpfull to you in everything that will forward the Interest of the Family.

The 'care and concern' mentioned by his cousin seem to have dogged Alexander for many years to come. A letter from McDonald of Largie written in the same year gives a gloomy view of the situation in Argyllshire; he suggested that they could do worse than emigrate — to be free of oppression.

> 21st February, 1738
> There is nothing in life I think we should so much prize as liberty and I appeal to McDougall if we can much want of that in this part of the world. No, it is even a crime to breathe — I mean for any of

Sorles [Somerled's] race ... What are we but speckle birds the butt of their malice, they will never be at ease till they extirpat us root and branch, it is long since they have begun with me but I am determined to fight my way through them as best I can. I pray God you and yours may be rid of their yoke as soon as I would wish — and God knows that should be tomorrow.

Mary and Alexander's first child, a girl they named Lucy, was born at Christmas time, 1738. Alexander's brother Allan wrote home from St Christophers in the West Indies: 'I wish you much joy of your daughter, and desire you put in for a son next if you have not done it already. I am sure my sister [in-law] and you are come of a good brood so that I need not be afraid of barreness.'

The next baby was a boy, John, born just about a year after Lucy.

Since the death of Iain Ciar, Alexander and his wife had been sharing the castle with Mary, Iain Ciar's widow, and probably also with her younger children. Now the decision was made for the two families to live separately. There is among the letters a document dated 19th October, 1739, setting out what the widow was to have when she left the Castle.

It was agreed that in the case for the said Allexr McDougall my son should incline to separate our liveing together in one family that in that event I was to restrict my liferent provision and joynture to the sum of four hundred merks scots money of annuity yearly to be paid to me att Martimas and Whitesunday by equall portions out of the first and readiest of the rents of the lands [of] Slaterich and Geyline ...

It was also agreed by the said Allexr McDougall in the event of our separating families, upon his own expence to stock the fourth part of Geyline in Kerera with labouring horses, cows and sheep and seed corn ... and give me the possession of the said fourth part during my lifetime in satisfaction always of soe much of the said annuity of four hundred merks as the rents thereof will amount to on the same terms and conditions that the other tennants thereof possess it.

And it was further agreed betwixt us that in case of our said separation I was to have the third part of the Household plenishing and furniture ...

And now seeing I have thought it more my interest to live separate than to remain in one family with the said Allexr MacDougall my son ...

Mary settled in Kerrera, but in 1741 was living in Inverness with her younger children, apparently for the education of her son John who was then twelve years old and attending school there.

As Iain Ciar's ambition had been to change the dynasty of kings, Alexander had been left with the task of getting back and improving the family estates which had been lost in the Jacobite cause. Up to the time of his succession all efforts to get the forfeited land returned had been unsuccessful and the situation summed up in a memorandum of 1734 from Alexander to the Duke of Argyll was still the same when Iain Ciar died in 1737.

'And not dessigning to take any benefit by the misfortune of the familly His Grace [the Duke of Argyll] frequently promised to grant a chartour in favers of the said Allexr MacDougall, the memorialist, of the lands which belonged to his father but which was delayed from time to time by some Interruptione or by comeing in the way.'

Much continued to come in the way. In 1741 Mary wrote from Inverness: 'Sir Alex. left this morning ... I did not neglect to spake to him concerning your charter. My Lord President said to him that when the Duke of Argyle wid come to Scotland that all of you was to have your charters.'

But by 1745 Alexander still did not have his charter. Duke John had died by this time, and had been succeeded by his brother Archibald. Donald Cameron, Lochiel, wrote to him from Edinburgh:

14th April, 1745

As to our affairs: by what I am told, it is probable they will come to a conclusion soon. The justice clerk is gone to London and has carried my charter with him as it is said to be signed. I have often spoke to Archie Campbell concerning yours and Appin's but could learn nothing in particular only in general that your business would be soon done and I am indeed of opinion that all of us will gett our Charters about the same time, but it is probable not till the Duke comes down.

I propose to leave this, with my family, about the middle of next month whether my charter comes or not for I am heartily tyred of this place. Our country is in a miserable condition and I am affrayed of the consequence ...

Your affectionat cousine and most humble servant Donald Cameron.

In August Alexander at last received the news that his charter had been signed and that his forfeited estate was now his own. In the letter from Andrew Fletcher (Lord Milton) it is delicately suggested that there were means by which not only Alexander but his wife as well could show their gratitude.

Roseneeth
5th August, 1745

Sir, Upon the Dukes coming to Scotland your charter was signed

at Brunstane in the way you wished. So you may come to Inverary
or this place as soon as you please to receive it. If you can get some
men to send Col John's Company, the Duke's cozen and apparent
heir, it will be doing a right thing and will plese the Duke and
confirm him in the good opinion I have endeavoured to give his
grace of you and your family.

My wife desires her compliments and begs the favour you'll
bring her some recepts from your Lady about Dyeing scarlet and
other colours.

On 19th August, the Jacobite Prince Charles unfurled his Royal
Standard at Glenfinnan. The '45 Rebellion had begun.

Family tradition has it that at this juncture Alexander's wife, Mary
Campbell, poured a kettle of boiling water over his foot as he prepared
to join the Prince.

In any Jacobite family whose chief did not fight for the cause in 1745,
there must be much speculation throughout the generations as to the
reason. The picturesque story of the boiling water, whether taken
figuratively or not, conveniently puts the blame on Alexander's wife.
But it is pertinent to remember that though Mary's father was a
Campbell her mother was a Cameron of Lochiel, a Jacobite family
famous for their support of Prince Charles Edward. If Alexander had
allowed his wife to influence him, her pleading might not necessarily
have been for him to stay at home.

According to tradition Alexander had much difficulty in deciding
whether or not to join the Prince and his final decision, not to do so, was
made only at the last moment. If this is true he must have still had in him
something of the Jacobite spirit of his father, in spite of experiencing in
boyhood the suffering of his family for the cause. On the other hand it is
probable that he lacked Iain Ciar's idealistic nature. When the
restoration of the Dunollie lands, for which Alexander had been
working most of his adult life, was made, almost at the same moment as
the raising of the Prince's Royal Standard, the more practical side of
Alexander's character prevailed. As he was not one of those who had
already promised the Prince support this was no dishonourable
decision.

Another tradition has it that when Alexander went to Inveraray to
collect his charter he had a conversation with Lord Milton (with whom
he was friendly) that convinced him of the folly of joining a venture
which many Highlanders, Jacobites included, felt was doomed to
failure.

Anyhow, for whatever reasons, Alexander stayed at home, and
moved into the new house he had built below the Castle. There is no

evidence that he gave any assistance to the Government side, nor does it seem that he particularly restrained his men. He left it to his brother Duncan to lead the Jacobite MacDougalls in the '45.

A letter written in the following year by Andrew Macdowall, a cousin in Edinburgh, points to another aspect of Alexander's dilemma: had he joined the Rising, he would have let down those of his friends who had sworn he was a loyal subject in order to get him his charter.

> 13th May, 1746
>
> Yours gave me Great joy. I was informed for Certain of your good behaviour both as to your self and Restraining your men Concurring in the late ffoolish Wicked project ... My wife Rejoyced much to hear of you remaining peaceable that you might bruik [possess] the Charter you had so much pains and Expence in producing and on that occasion I past my word of honour for you to the Justice Clerke, as I doubt not but you did to his Grace at getting it, both of which you have sav'd and acted the part of an honest man as well as a good subject and a ffriend to our Country.

The fact that Alexander and others in the same position did not join the Rebellion did not mean that they were unaffected by it. On 24th October, 1745, John Campbell wrote to Alexander: 'Dr Sir, It has been judged for the Service of the government to Disable all boats as they saw Occasion. Your best way therefore to prevent any hurt to such boats as you are concerned in is to send them to Dunstafnage where I reckon the ships will not meddle with them but I doubt they will give any Receipt for them.'

The last remark sounds a little ominous.

The following letter was written a little over a month before the Battle of Culloden:

> Inverery
> 3rd March, 1746
>
> Gentlemen:
>
> As we have certain Intelligence that the King's army will be very soon att Inverery in pursuit of the Rebels who continue to retire before them, it is obvious that they will find themselves so hard pressed they must retire to Lochaber. There they cannot continue for two reasons: the approach of our Army and the want of provisions. Men reduced to absolute dispair will attempt any thing to prolong their Lives. They have no way to shun the Danger they are at present exposed to, but by coming into this shire or forcing their way to the Low Country by our frontiers, in either case it is highly necessary for us to look to our own saftie; a visit from our Declared Enemies must be attended with fattall consequence if they catch us unprepared.

General Campbell is Determined to make a stand for his country, we hope every body will think it their Dutty to give him all the assistance in their power and we have considered it as ours to Lett the Gentlemen of the shire know our present situation and judge it highly necessary that every Gentleman able to carry arms do repair to this place with all possible dispatch and bring with him all the Volunteers he can.

We are Gentlemen etc.

Archd Campbell Sheriff, Neill McNeill Ugudale, Archd Campbell Jnverliver, Alexr McMillan Dunmore.

It is proper that such Gentlemen as brings servants take care that they be fitt for service.

John Campbell, Appin, wrote to Alexander:

11th May, 1746

Sir, I have received yours of the 9th inst. You know advertisements have been sent forth requiring that in such Countrys as are therein mentioned the Arms should be instantly delivered up and proper places appointed, to all which I refer. It is your duty to take care and see the Order complyd with where you are concerned ...

As to protection I can grant none, I shall doe what I can to prevent the innscent from suffering with the guilty.

In October the Chief of the Lamonts wrote to Alexander:

Aird Lamont
19th October, 1746

My dear Sir, I had the favour of yours and you may believe there are few men living would goe a greater length to serve you and yours than I would doe. I rejoyce that the Duke of Argyll has given you your estate. I make no doubt but you will by your prudent management purge all the wadsetts [pay off all the mortgages] and I hope in God you will (before you die) have as good an Estate as any of your Predecessors had.

The Duke of Cumberlands Glorious Victory att Culloden gives me and all loyal subjects the greatest joy, however as we had some friends and well wishers that were ingadged in that Rebellion I cannot but regrate their misfortune and from my heart wish they had never embarked in such a bad cause ...

Two years later, it seems that Lamont, like many other Government supporters, was shocked by the aftermath of the Rebellion, and was willing to help those who were suffering from it. He wrote to Alexander:

Last night I had the Pleasure of yours of the 17th Instant by these poor people who are disposed of the lands they and their

Predecessors enjoyed long before the present tyrants were ever heard of. These poor Creatures are very sensible of your Friendship to them and all of their Name ... I have pitched on a little place for them where I hope they may doe very well.

In a letter written in 1752 Alexander referred to his financial state as 'tottering', but in spite of this he managed to send his eldest son John to finish his education. John, by now thirteen, was sent to a school in Crieff where the schoolmaster was a MacDougall. Certain problems arose and Alexander's half-brother-in-law John Campbell, who was living in Crieff, wrote:

May 1753

When the two Boys [John and a cousin] came here I settled them in a house where I was sure they would be taken good care of in Every Respect. But as the people never had a Boarder they were unwilling to take them and would not at Any Rate name a Boarding fee until they had made tryal. I Inquired these few days and they told me they could not Afford to keep them under three pounds sterling for Quarter Each which indeed I think is Dear as in most other Houses here they are for less than the Half.

Itts true there is a great odds in the living for they have a room to themselves with a fire and Candle, Eat as often and as well as they please, and are kept as clean as any Boys in the Kingdom with the addition of Mrs Drummond's tender care of them when Any thing Ails them. Yett I still think the Boarding dear in such a place as this which made me Inquire at Perth where there is a very good school and in the schoolmaster's house the Board is three pound [presumably for the two?] I could get it cheaper but I was not pleased with the houses ...

In some time the school at Perth will be fitter for Johnny as there are Many Gentlemen's sons there and the Master I believe is justly in great reputation. I have no complaints of your namesake here; he is a Very Discreet man and knows his Business very well. Now I will tell you fairly the case: here they are Lyable to Little Expence but the Boarding; at Perth you will be brought into ane Expence that you Cannot find fault with tho' your purse will feel it. I know this from Experience and you may Judge for your self.

Whether or not John went to Perth is not known, but the following year Alexander was asking John Campbell's aid in borrowing money. He received the following answer:

Crieff
8th February, 1753

As to what you mention of my Joining Credit with you to the Royal

Spinning wheel belonging to Mary, the last girl to be born in Dunollie Castle, before the family moved down to the new house

Bank I am sorie I cannot Agree to do it not that I have any scruples as to your Part, But I am so involved in Ingagements to the Bank Just now that I will not meddle with them More or Less in Money matters untile I get my self somewhat Disingaged. I never Borrowed a shilling from them in My life time for my own use and yett I am Ingaged for a Considerable soume and Particularly for Twelve Hundred pound sterling Borrowed to prosecute Glenure's Murderers. I am ingaged for two other soums for Glenure with the Bank, so that you May see I have reason not to try the strength of My Credit with them least I should meet with a Denyal which would not sitt very Easie upon me.

Glenure was John Campbell's half-brother. The murder referred to was the Appin Murder made famous by Stevenson in *Kidnapped*. Colin Campbell of Glenure had been acting as factor to the forfeited estates in Appin: in May 1752 he was murdered by unknown persons. Local tradition has always maintained that an innocent man, James Stewart of the Glen, was hung for the crime.

Family Affairs

By this time Alexander and Mary had had thirteen children, and there were two more to come. During Mary's child-bearing years life must have been an alternating pattern of birth and death. Three children died for certain in infancy, and subsequent children were given their names. Of the fifteen births entered in the family Bible only seven names are heard of again in all the correspondence. In 1756 Mary bore her last child, James, who died young, and in the same year her eldest daughter, Lucy, was married.

The Courtship and Marriage of Lucy

Among the letters there is a bundle relating to Lucy's courtship and marriage to James MacDowall, an Edinburgh merchant. She had been sent to Edinburgh in 1756, at the age of eighteen, to finish her education under the patronage of Alexander's friend and namesake, Alexander MacDougall of the Exchequer and his wife. Lucy wrote home that she was living in elegant society and was 'the fine lady'. She wrote of assemblies and plays, begging the loan of her mother's flowered silk dress and permission to buy an embroidered riding jacket. Her friends had given her a handsome cardinal (cloak) costing 50 shillings. In a letter in March that year she made no hint that she was involved in a love affair.

She chatted lightly of this and that, mostly of clothes, and adds: 'You was wanting some news. On Friday last my Cousine David was married to one Miss Campbell ane heiress of a thousand pounds and this day the Cross of Edinburgh is brought down to the Ground which is a peace of antiquity. There is no other news only everybody talks of having War.'

Early next month, however, the secret was evidently out and Alexander wrote to Alexander MacDougall to know his opinion of the young man. His friend replied: 'As to what you mention with respect to Miss Lucy I can give you no particular information with respect to the Young Gentleman, only in General that he is well spoke of and commended for Affability, Descretion and good nature, and reckoned in a very good way in the World. However I shall make particular enquiry with respect to what you recommend and write to you by the next post.

The next letter was from the young man himself:

4th May, 1756

The confidence your Daughter has put in me in showing me your Affectionate letter to her lays me under the strongest obligations ... and, as I have reason to think that my proposals are not at all disagreeable to her, should by this have wrote to you, particularly as to what settlements and made you acquainted with what provision I intended for her in the event of my Decease, so as to Accelerate my happiness. But I thought it a more proper Subject of a verbal conversation than of letters.

Would Gladly hope when things are in this situation you and your Lady will concur to have the affair brought to a conclusion as Speedily as possible, as many both of her and my friends have been entrusted with my intention so that it cannot remain long secret — and it would be extremely disagreeable to Miss Mcdougal to have the matter talked of before it was concluded. You being here would make all easy and soon put an end to the Affair. I am certain nothing would be more Acceptable to your Daughter than your presence with her in this important Step and I need not tell you how much I should esteem the favour.

Not doubting that you'll take such measures as may Accomplish my hopes without any thing that be disagreeable to Miss Lucy or may delay the happiness of Dear Sir your Lady's and Your most obed. huml. servant James MacDowall Junr

Alexander of the Exchequer then wrote that he had waited upon another friend, 'my Lord Bankton' for his opinion. It was somewhat unromantic: 'He seems to be of the opinion that the bargain is feasable and wants the matter to be brought to a conclusion soon.' The letter ends: 'heartily wishing Heaven may direct you and Lucy aright in an affair of such great moment.'

A week or two later, Alexander of the Exchequer wrote again, this time at length. He had been discussing the marriage settlement with James and his father and it had seemed very reasonable. But all wasn't as smooth as it seemed: since then there 'had been a Grand Consultation of his friends where the proposals have been Entirely altered and new ones substituted in their place.'

Obviously rather put out by this, the writer went on to describe with disapproval the wooing of Lucy, who by this time was staying with him and his wife.

> 20th May, 1756
>
> I think it my Duty to Inform you with respect to the method taken by the Lover to carry on this Courtship with your daughter.
>
> Miss Lucy after her arrival in Town it seems had soon been made acquaint with Mrs Betty McDowall who I am informed keeps a house in Town for the Sale of Camricks, Lawns and several other things of that sort and is a great dependant on James McDowal's family, and by the nature of her business occasions a constant resort of young men and women to her house which brought on the Intimacy betwixt Miss Lucy, James McDowall, his sisters, their family and connections, on which proposals for a marriage ensued. And from what I have Learned — have reason to believe — matters were Entirely made up betwixt the young folks before you had any information of it, and Since letters began to pass and repass betwixt you and them that Mrs Betty McDowll's has been the Constant Rendevous.
>
> Since the time your daughter left Mrs Froggos till now she has not dined five times at my house but has continued to Dine, drink Tea and often sup, at the Young man's house, his father's and that of Mrs Betty McDowall or some other of their particular friends and acquaintances. So that it may be justly said that from the beginning of the Courtship till now she has been Entirely under the influence of him and his friends, without any advice or directions from any of her kindred and relations, excepting the Letters from you to her on that subject.
>
> But what gave me still more Uneasyness upon this occasion was her staying several nights in this Mrs Betty's without any good or solid reason for her so doing, considering the distance from the Town to my house is so very small. And I also observe that from their constant behaviour, which I have had frequent occasion of Seeing Since she came to stay at my house, I think matters are come to such a length that there can be no thought of looking back, besides the people of the Town (some whereof are her friends) having taken the same observation with me it would not be prudent even of thinking of a return.

I have taxed Miss Lucy much upon her behaviour and frequently admonished her to be more cautious, but youth and thoughtlessness often bears too great a Part with persons of her age and sex. However she has promised to me this day to be more cautious and to put off the matter till your Consent shall arrive.

From what I have said you can easily perceive upon what footing your daughter is and by what influence she has been brought this length, which I hope will Induce you to come to Town with all Convenient Speed, or at least come the length of Glasgow and send for your Daughter, by which means you will have it in your power to make better Terms for her than may otherwise be expected — and if you can think of coming I shall meet you at any place you shall think proper to appoint, where I would have an opportunity to talk over with you what I do not Chuse to Communicate by writing. However I hope what I have here suggested will be Entirely kept in your own breast and such use made thereof as prudence and good sense shall direct.

Alexander had by this time heard again from young James, who also urged him to come to Edinburgh:

By this time I should have given you the most ample Account of our Affairs was it not that I have reason to believe that in the present juncture most letters especially those directed to the coasts are inspected at the post office. All I shall therefore say is that it is not yet five years since my father gave me £500 as a beginning in Business. It is now more than doubled. My trade is in a flourishing way. But I count this but small when compared with what I expect from him.

With the greatest Cheerfullness I should have waited on you at Dunollie that in person I might have satisfied you of every circumstance but only this is the throng Season with persons dealing in the Woolen and Linnen Manufacture particularly wholesale (which is my way).

James went on to say that his father was the heritable proprietor of the Cannon Mills; that he had recently obtained a decree from the Lords fixing his Thirlage (the obligation to grind at a certain mill), and that a great many Brewers and others were subject to it. They were coming in and settling with his father, but as he was so ill at present James must necessarily attend and act for him.

Alexander now wrote to young James and kept a copy of the letter.

Upon receipt of your Letter Inclosing your father's I wrote to my Daughter to satisfie my Self as to her sentiments of your proposals which I have now received under cover from you, and as her

answer to me has so far paived the way there now only remains one
step to putt your wished for end to this affair.

Your Father's account and yours of the state of your affairs are in
such general terms that it leaves me pretty much in the Dark, as I
know he has a family to provide for and yett at the same time the
regard he expresses for my Daughter convinces me he'll concurr in
making such provision for her and family (in case such should be)
as will enable her to live comfortably in the event of her surviving
you. You are by no means to inferr from this that my intention is to
embarass either your Circumstance or theirs by making extravagant claims for her or Children if any bees.

You'l likewise consider what would be a very competant living
for my Daughter if she was to be settled in this part of the world for
life would be too small att Edinburgh on account of the difference
of living, apparels, house, rent etc. I am so far from being averse to
this affair being brought to a sudden conclusion that one moment
shall not be lost on my side to put a period to it.

[A letter also went from Dunollie to James' father on the same
theme, and Alexander ended:] If agreeable shall appoint a place
for our meeting, as it is not in my power at this season of the year,
on account of the management and Markett of my Cattle, to go
your length, where we can have ane oppertunity of extending
writtes to our mutual satisfaction.

On 20th May James wrote that he would be able to settle £60 sterling per
annum on Lucy in the event of his death, together with a house or £15 a
year for the rent of one. He remarked that all his friends were of the
opinion 'that nothing can be of more dangerous Consequences than
provisions that will render Children in some Measure independant of a
parent or give them a Compulsatory upon him ...'

As affairs are now so far advanced I doubt not you'l forgive my
ardent desire of having things brought to a Conclusion with all
possible despatch ... I should have put off the most important
Business and waited on you at Dunolie but such is my father's
Condition and the oppinion of Phisicians concerning him that we
fear every day shall be his last ... I have sent this by Express in
order to save time and hope by his return every obsticall to my
happiness will be removed.

Such seems to have been the hurry that by 8th June the wedding had
taken place, without the settlement yet being signed. The Bridegroom
wrote to his father-in-law:

Cannon Milns, Edinburgh
8th June, 1857
Your kind letter of yesterday I received this forenoon enclosing

one to your Daughter in both of which so much is showen of the patternal Love and Affection that in the strongest manner it endears you to both of us, and you may in reality and Sincerity upon all occasions address me as your affectionate son.

We had a most agreeable jaunt in here, where we arrived yesterday betwixt 2 and 3 o'clock afternoon from Hamilton where we were Kirked and was received by all your new conections with the strongest Expressions of joy and Affection ... Allow me with the greatest warmth of fillial affection to offer my most Sincere Comps, to that Gentle-woman whom I have now the Honour to Call Mother and to you in the endearing name of Dear Father, Your affectionate Son etc etc James Mcdouwall.

P.S. Direct my wife's letters to her husband's care. We'll if possible see what can be done to order matters so as to be with you in August.'

By June the following year Lucy had had three miscarriages and the marriage settlement had still not been signed. Her husband wrote to Alexander at the time of the third:

25th June, 1758

From all appearance an abortion is now certain and that in the third month. She had last night at Bed time great pain in the small of her Back etc and this morning threw off the forerunner of a total abortion. I just now had a private conversation with Thomas, young Midwife Doctor, who tells me it is improbable she can retain it, if so this is now the third time and as these practices is very dangerous it has just now entered into my head to send her out to you & her mother's care for some months before she has occasion to be again in what I call a good way, but when she'll be fitt for travelling or if this Scheme takes place it is not certain and must be the subject of another letter.

In August Lucy wrote that they had moved to Canonmills again and that she was much the better for leaving the town. Canonmills is now of course very much part of Edinburgh. She continued:

I have waited this long time writing you upon a subject that gives me great Concern and that is my Contract of marriage, to see if you and Mr Mcdowall would agree about it. My Dear father I am very sensible you intended it for my good but there is nothing on earth can be harder on me than you and my husband is not agreeing about everything and particularly a thing so interesting as that, and more than that you insiste upon provision for the oldest son which is more than we could afford to give whether he was foolish or wise. I beg you will allow that Contract to be wrote in such a way as to be agreeable to Mr Mcdowall and what he can afford ...

I do not know but it may be a just judgement on us to have no Children when we are making so many provisions for them. I know a Lady that bought a Cradle when she was married but never had anny use for it — so that may be the case with us ...

But in November James wrote in jubilation to Alexander: 'I can with some degree of certainty informe you that Lucy is once more in what I call a good way, she too is turned very fatt and in intire health except a little Sqimishness in the morning peculier to women in her way.'

A son, James, was born the following year. A daughter, Betty, came later.

The Saga of MacInnish's Cattle

The fact that Alexander refused to go to Edinburgh to sort out Lucy's settlement ('it is not in my power at this season of the year to go your length on account of the management and Markett of my cattle), supports the tradition that he was a keen farmer and an improver of the land. There is among his correspondence of 1757 the saga of MacInnish's cattle, a story which illustrates some of the hazards of cattle-dealing and the amount of time and physical energy that could go into the recovery of a debt of £21.

Alexander's lawyer wrote a memorial giving the facts:

Upon the 25th of Oct. 1757 Duncan MacInnish, Drover in Mull Granted bill to the Memorialist [Alexander] for £21 sterl. for value payable fourteen days after date. The value received for this bill was black cattle which the accepter [MacInnish] immediately drove to the Low country to the Marcates.

After the Marcates were over a Rumour was spread in the Country that MacInnish had absconded and had a design of Defrauding his Creditors by leaving the Country with the Money he received at the Marcates for the price of the Cattle he Sold there, which rumour proved to be true for he left this Country and Carried with him a Considerable sum of money.

Alexander had already written to his lawyer asking if it was in order to go to Mull and seize cattle to the value of MacInnish's debt. The lawyer, one John Marshall at Inveraray, replied:

As the fellow has left the Country your only safe and legale method is directly to apply by Petition to any of the Justices of Peace setting furth that he owes you such a sum and that he has either fled the Country, in meditatione fugo, and there fore crave a summary warrant to apprehend, apprise and secure his effects wherever they can be found for payment of your debt which is the method used every day in the like cases ... Upon getting this warrant you may secure the cattle etc until the days on the charge on your precept [order to pay money] be expired and then poind them in common form.

'Poinding' the cattle meant taking them to Inveraray to the Marcat Cross, a journey of something like fifty miles there and back. Alexander evidently wrote asking if this was really necessary. John Marshall replied:

You ought to cause one officer and two apprisers [valuers] and such cattle as are in your custody of MacInnish's and apprise them and bring the cattle gently with a copy of that comprisement to the Marcat Cross here in order to get the poind legally finished for without the cattle are brought here and apprised at the Cross there is no possibility of legally finishing the poind even if the cattle should suffer.

Alexander applied to Dunstaffnage, who was a Justice of the Peace, and the warrant was granted.

Upon receiving this warrant the Memorialist [Alexander] sett out for Mull and got hold of some cattle of MacInnish the value whereof thought might amount to the Contents of his bill ... He drove away the Cattle he had Seized from MacInnish's farm and carried them over from the Island of Mull to the Continent where they might be kept in Safety till the Expieration of the days of Charge of payment that the same might be regularly poinded, and accordingly after the Lapse of these days the Cattle were regularly and lawfully poinded ... and were valued by the first apprisers at £19.12.8. and by the apprisers at the Marcate Cross at £25 sterl money.

The poinding was Completed upon the 14th day of Dec 1757. As every part of this procedure was gone about in the most regular and orderly method that Could be devised the Memorialist had good reason to think that he would hear no more of the matter and was therefore greatly surprised to have a Summond of Spulzie [plundering] Executed against him at MacInnishes Instance upon the 19th day of Jan 1761, betwixt three and four years after the date of the poinding.

The legal advice given to Alexander on the subject of the Summond of Spulzie was as follows:

... that no Spulzie [plundering] could be made appear against him

[Alexander] as he acted in Every particular in Conformity to the rexive warrant he obtained for securing his Debt, and the only thing of which he hears they are to take hold of is the Memorialist [Alexander] not poinding the cattle in Mull Immediately upon their being Seized instead of Carrying them away to the Continent and there poinding them. The answer to this is at least two fold, first that MacInnish can qualify no damage by this and secondly that had not the memorialist taken away the Cattle Immediately they would have been forced from him by MacInnish's friends and Connections.

Further legal advice from a Mr Montgomery in Edinburgh is found in a letter written just before the case was due to be heard, to the effect that MacInnish had no chance of proving 'spulzie'. But as the 'poinding' was not quite regularly gone about Mr Montgomery thought MacInnish might still be allowed a trial of the value of the cattle. The letter continued:

If they persist upon it, which they will be fools in so doing as the expence of such proof must greatly exceed the difference between their own alledged prices and the sum the cattle were apprised at. But as they may be so foolish Mr Montgomery seems desirous to know in what way the cattle turned out to you after the poinding, what price you got for them when sold, deducting the grassmeal and also taking the value of any of them that casually died.

This you will do as soon as convenient. I daresay they will be offering ane accomedation. But we must not too early agree to it least their expectations may increase.

There was a list of questions to be asked of the men who assisted Alexander over the taking of the cattle. The men were Duncan MacInnish, the sheriff's officer and Constable; Donald MacFarlane and Archibald MacGoyle the assessors; Duncan MacDougall in Soroba, 'my trustee among my cattle'; and Hew MacLucas at the Miln of Oban.

What they were to be asked was whether the cattle brought from Mull were exactly the same as those taken to Inveraray, and there seems to have been great interest in a flecked red cow.

Duncan MacDougall in Soroba. To be interrogate if he saw the next day MacInnishe's cattle after they were ferried to Dunollie from Kerrera and if he saw them the day they were sent to Inverary and if it was the very identical cattle he saw at both times and if it was the same cattle he saw again in Dunollie from Inverery without changing, altering or other substitute in their place, to be interrogate what he knows of the fate of flecked reid cow ...

Hew MacLucas at the Miln of Oban. To be interrogate if it was the same identical cattle that he saw at Dunollie that he and John MacInish the officer and Patrick MacDougall [Alexander's son] brought to the Cross at Inverery and back again to Dunollie or if he could understand that any of them were changed or altered and others substitute in their place ... and what does he know what come of the flecked reid cow, how long they took travelling backwards and forwards betwixt Inverery and Dunollie and what distance and if they were feeding the cattle upon the road with corn and hay and if the cattle were in good order.

There was also the fate of the belted black cow to be investigated: 'Colin MacDougall in Dunollie and Donald Brown there. To be interrogate whither or not in March last they found a belted black cow of MacInishe's cattle dead at the side of the Dunghill in Dunollie after being drawn there and whether they assisted in taking the hide off her.'

The ferry across which the cattle were taken from Mull was owned by Alexander. It went from Auchnacraig (Grass Point) on Mull to the west coast of Kerrera. From there the beasts were either taken across the island to Port Kerrera and from there ferried to the mainland, or else they were driven to the north end of Kerrera and made to swim the channel between there and the shore below Dunollie.

About this time Alexander had been corresponding with the Commissioners of Supply for the Shire of Argyle about a new and safer landing place. He wrote:

The Ferry of Kerrera to Mull having for a long tract of years backward, yea past memory, been used to be keept alternately for three months at Slattrach and three months at Ardmore which lye about two miles distance from one another, the proprietor being sensible how troublesome and uncertain this method proved to the leidges passing that way sought to remedy this inconvenience. Several years ago [he] fixed the ferrying place at Barnabuck, being not only the centre betwixt the two aforesaid old ferrying ports, but also a much shorter and safer run to Mull than either, as is known by the whole people.

The Educating of John

MacInnish's cattle were not Alexander's only worry at this time, for he was much troubled about the education and future of his eldest son, John. John, now eighteen, was keen to join the Army, as the Seven year's War between Great Britain and France (over a dispute about colonies in Canada, America, and India) had recently begun. Alexander, who wished his son to finish his education, was much annoyed with John

Campbell (a half-brother-in-law), who had been using his influence successfully with the Duke of Argyll to obtain an offer of a commission for John in the Fraser Highlanders: they were being recruited for service in America. John Campbell wrote to Alexander:

> 1st February, 1757
> He [John] tells me that he is afraid that you and his Mother will be Averse to his Goeing ... you know my sentiments upon that head ... and as the Duke of Argyle has named him purely in Compliment to you I fancie you will not think it a reasonable step to Appear Averse to what his Grace has done for him ... I think you should write first to the Duke of Argyle thanking him for what he has done for your son and that you think yourself very Happy that His Grace has taken your son under his protectione.

Alexander wrote to the Duke the same day giving his views, using suitably diplomatic phrasing:

> Being informed that your Grace was so good as to Recommend my eldest son to a Commision in Collonel Fraser's Battalion I cannot but with the greatest sincerity make very most Thankful acknowledgements to your Grace's favour, yett att the same time he being very young and not near done with his education I must be concerned to see him disappointed of that which would make him in time useful to himself and Country. I would beg as a favour to gett him altered from this Corps to some Marching Regiment that would have a chance of staying in Britain for a few years where he would have ane oportunity for improving himself ...

To someone else he wrote: 'It is quite inconsistant with my son's Interest to lose his education by going to America ... am convinced his Grace would not desire that my son should leave his education but in a way where he could improve, which is what cannot happen by his going to America at the age he is of.'

John Campbell voiced his disgust: 'I beg you will give over Your Airs and be thankful to god for giving you a son that is thought to deserve a Commision ... once a young Man has it in his power to follow that sort of life that his heart is set upon he will not thrive at any other so that what will not Admitt of a Remedy should be made the Best of ...'

Alexander replied: 'If he lives for a few years I have not the least doubt but he'll very sensibly feel whether his own or my scheam for his appearing in the world were most for his interest. I never doubted your Regard for me and family tho in this particular of your Nephew I am farr from thinking you studied either.'

The following year John was languishing in a lawyer's office in

Edinburgh. From there he wrote to his father: 'I doe intend to make the best use of my time as for the education, as that will be of consequence be my fate what it will. It is to no purpose I have been with Mr Grant as yet ... for not one hour he has bestowed on instructing me as yet ... but he is a good discreet man and I hope he will do better soon.'

Alexander had evidently been making suggestions as to John's future and John replied:

As a stocked farm paying rent is the Best that can be done me in my country it is my opinion if I could only write my name there must be something better made of it than that ... I have no aversion to the Country Business But thinks it next a gallie slave one only stocked farm and a small triffle of credit. And I for my part am resolved to try fifty employments before I once think of it on these terms.

Three years later John is heard of as a Captain in the Army, commanding a Company being formed in Colonel Oswald's Battalion. 'The officers are to have four pounds of levy money for every good recuite that passes at the review with Subsistance from the date of each Attestation.' The Seven Years War was still going on and the Company was 'to be compleated with the greatest Expedition'.

A Recruiting Incident

In the following year Alexander was himself involved in a recruiting drama. It is an interesting story as it shows that in spite of the Act of 1747 which took heritable jurisdiction from the clan chiefs, a clansman, when in trouble, still turned to his chief. It also leaves a suspicion in the mind that the methods of recruiting were sometimes questionable.

The incident took place in Mull, where Maclean of Torloisk was recruiting for a Regiment known as the Maclean Highlanders. He had raised it the previous year to serve during the Seven Years War. It was never to see service as a regiment because it was disbanded at the peace of 1763, but it supplied many recruits to Highland regiments serving abroad.

On 9th January 1762, Alexander received a letter, brought by a messenger from Mull, from Archibald Campbell, Ardnacross. It related how the brother of the messenger, one John Macdougall, had been at the Inn when the Innkeeper had produced a gold coin and asked if anyone could change it. John MacDougall picked it up.

'When it came into his hands,' the letter continued, 'the Innkeeper said, "You have it in the King's name." Whenever the lad heard this he threw it on the Table and said, "I'll have nothing to do with it." The

Innkeeper said, "You are the King's Man," and after so saying he said that the whole Company present had best drink to the King's health . . .'

The following day the lad's employer, Alexander McNivern, went to the Innkeeper to enquire into the affair.

> The Innkeeper told that MacDougall had fairly inlisted with him and Alexander, not knowing how matters was, offered the Innkeeper twenty shillings sterling smart money not to trouble the lad — which he took. But before Alexander left the house he returned the smart money back again and promised that he never would trouble him any more; at this time Alexander believed they would not give the Lad further trouble.
>
> On the next day John MacDougall was arrested without a warrant.
>
> The persuers say that the Defender took Gold for the King's name from the Innkeeper but the witness is well depond [gives evidence] that whenever he had it in his hand and the Innkeeper said he had it in his Majestie's name that moment he threw it on the table. I hope you'll take the poor fellow's part as you have justice on your side and let them know you will not see him wronged.
>
> I think those that went to apprehend him warrentless should be let know that they acted contery to Law. If you was at a greater distance than you are we would have done it, but as you are the person who should do it and is nearer the Law all is referred to you which I hope you will not be slack in doing.

Then by express came a letter from Major Maclean of Torloisk.

> 9th January, 1762
> Dear Sir, This express goes on purpose your length concerning one MacDougall that has always been about my Friends. This John MacDougall listed 9 days ago with one of my people and took a thirty six shilling Piece, but he afterwards repented and his master came to offer the smart money for him about 30 hours after he took the money or more, but the man he offered the smart money to neither could or would take it saying that tho' he could list men he could not Discharge them. Upon this John MacDougall absconded, would not appear, till I was forced to send a party for him but he would not attest.
>
> But this inlistment being clear, and the acknowledgement made in offering the smart money by his master, convinced his brother Lauchlan that good words were best and upon his giving his obligation to me for producing his brother I allowed his brother to go home.
>
> I likewise promised him I would aquaint you with this affair, not that I thought there was any kind of necessity for giving you any

trouble in a case that was so clearly and distinctly proven, but to satisfy the young man's friends, as his brother told me that he had Promised to acquaint you of every thing that would happen to either of them and after my relating you the facts, as I do now, as they really are that if you would not promise to extracate the said John MacDougall he would attest. I told him I would be at the expense of this express but would at the same time assure him that you would never interpose in any man's behalf who was so legally voluntarily inlisted that he sent his master to offer the smart money, tho' too late.

This is the situation of this affair, and to obviate any foolish notions these ignorant People may have of a support of a Chief, right or wrong, would be glad you give your opinion of this matter to satisfy the People...'

Whether Alexander supported his clansman or not is not known, but it is perhaps relevant to note that the previous year he had written to a friend saying that he had advised his tenants and their sons how best to avoid being 'Persuaded' to volunteer!

To return to family affairs: in 1765 Alexander's eldest daughter Lucy died, and was buried in the Dunollie burial ground at Kilbride. It is thought that she died in childbirth, for a bill was sent to Alexander for Sundries at Mrs MacDowall's funeralls' (note the plural), and includes an entry 'to a sett of coffine mountings for Grandchild, 3/6'.

This bill was from the local shopkeeper, one John Campbell, and as Lucy's husband had not paid it after a year it was put on Alexander's account among such items as 'a cow and two stotes [bullocks], tar, tea, corks, paper, horseshoes, a currie comb, bottle of Juice of Leamonds; tarred cordage for fishers, ½ yd linnen, starch, brown sugar and two hanks fine hair'.

To sundries at Mrs MacDowall's funeralls as per separate acct. furnished June 1965 and given a Discharge of the same to MacDougall 23 June 1766 to be sent to his son in law, but still stands good in the Debit.   £15.9.11

To 1 doz. fine screwed wine glasses for family use at said funeralls.
                                                             0.7.0.

Lucy left Alexander two grandchildren, James and Betty. An amusing letter from James, which must have been written about 1770, still remains. James had been sent to a boarding school or college in Warrington — which is puzzling, because he lived in Edinburgh, and his uncle John Warden was well known in Edinburgh educational circles. Soon after arriving, he wrote to his father:

I am just now sitting in my room after supper and taking the
opportunity of that hour, which is the most silent we have altho' at
the same time it cannot be said to be free from noise, for even now
I am entertained with the squalling and yelling of the students, the
thumping of canes and sticks over my roof, loud laughing and
much singing and the noise of German flutes, walking to and fro.
rattling of tables and such other noble amusements. However, so
much for that, let me now proceed to give an account of our
business thro the day.

In the morning we have three different Bells. The first calls us to
rise, the second to put on our cloathes and the third and last to
come to Prayers, after Prayers we get our breakfast, at ten the
French lecture goes in and comes out at eleven, between eleven
and twelve we have no hour at all so that hour may be devoted to
study. At twelve Mr Bright's lecture upon the drawing meets, at
one we get our dinner and after Dinner we go to Dr Aiken's Greek
and Latin Lectures as likewise the Mathematicks. Between tea and
supper we have no Lectures, at ten we must be either in our own
rooms or in the room of our fellows the reason you know yourself.

In his next letter James describes two of his masters:

Talking of Dr Aiken I must own that in my life time I think I never
saw so sensible a man ... every word he utters expresses something
and every subject he explains, concerning what we read, is always
made so perspicious that a Child might understand what he meant.
In short he is a most noble example of venerable old age and
profound learning. Dr Enfield again is much to be admired on
account of his consummate good Nature and altho' he has not had
so much experience as the former yet he is universally belov'd.

James went on to say that he was thinking of writing a letter in Latin to
his uncle, but must have some time to consider it — because when
writing a 'familiar' letter he couldn't write the sort of things that the
Roman authors wrote, but must use different Phrases!

He ended the letter with a P.S. 'I have got a bag of oatmeal into my
room. The Students think it odd. I never mind that.'

John goes to India

About this time Alexander's eldest son John reappears in the letters. He
had by now married Isabel, second daughter of the third Lord Ruthven.
He had also joined the armed forces of the East India Company. For a
time there had been an estrangement between John and his father but
the following letter, written just before sailing to India, in one of the
Company's ships, put an end to this.

12th February, 1770

My dear Sir, Being on the point of biding adieu to this Island for
some years, perhaps for ever, I think it incumbent on me to break
through the silence which has prevailed between us for near two
years, a silence tho' unaccountable, that so far as concerned me did
by no means proceed from a want of duty and respect to you, as I
have never yet had cause to charge myself with a thought but those
of the most tender affection for you.

I have an immensity to say to you in the way of clearing up some
things that have given you uneasiness in regard to me ... The
reports that have been brought to me of your resolves I have
treated in the manner that I thought did most justice to you,
knowing the uprightness of your disposition and conscious I ever
acted in a manner becomeing a Gentleman and an honest man,
principles the most certain to build upon ...

Alexander evidently replied in an affectionate manner for John's next
letter said: 'I was made happy by the receipt of your letter. Did I feel
less I should be better able to express the sense I have of your goodness
and attention. Your repeated assurance of affection is the most pleasing
tale I can hear and as I can with truth aver I rank it amongst the foremost
blessings of my life. I hop you will have little difficulty to believe I shall
use every means to cultivate it and preserve it.'

The voyage went well and Alexander received the following letter.

22nd March, 1770

I have the pleasure to inform you of our having got almost under
the line and being in pretty good health. Our passage has hitherto
been most remarkably fortunate, fine weather with propitious
gales has brought us thus far perhaps sooner than any other ship
outward bound for a great while, this being but the 30th day
inclusive since we sailed from the Downs ...

The heat for some time has been extreme and now 'tis quite
melting and skinning. 'Tis the only thing I feel disagreeable as I am
now pretty free of sea sickness. I assure you I often wish myself the
comfort of being lazed on one of your Banks of Primroses which
by this period I dare say looks beautifull and must appear a
paradise to one used to the heats we have known of late.

From India he wrote home in praise of the East India Company.

18th June, 1771

If I may offer an advice to my Uncle it is that he endeavours to get
into the Company's service in preference to his Majesty's, it is far
more advantageious ...very little money is needed in fitting out.
Six good shirts, six Check ones to wash on board of ship, a coarse

Coat to wear on board, and a good scarlet one, without lace, to land in, a 3 shilling hatt for the passage, a better one to appear in before the Governor, together with a sword, some stockings and shoes and a good liquor case full of brandy is all that is necessary. The Company will give £10.10.0 in advance and good ship's provisions for the passage.

Besides making schemes for his Uncle, John wrote home with one for his widowed Grandmother, who was then seventy-five.

I rejoice to hear my good Grannie is so hearty, it is become very fashionable at home for Ladies who are not marketable in Europe to come to the east for husbands. By your account I declare I am inclined to think the Old Lady would cut no dispicable figure, and she will be sure of the best quarters I am master of till she is provided for. But joking aside tell her I hope she may live 20 years longer because then I shall have a prospect of seeing her again.

Although John and his wife seem to have settled down well in India, little touches of homesickness can be detected in the letters.

'I should be very much obliged,' John wrote to his father in 1771, 'if you would send me a pair of Highland pistols the best that can be made, but larger than common ... Lord that my mother would send me some Cheese, and you some salt salmon. Would that I had a piece of it now, with Oat Cake ...'

The following year he wrote:

Camp near Ellore, India
10th February, 1772

As to Mrs Mac. and myself blessed be he who gave us life, we have never known what it is to be ill. I really believe we are now naturalized, at least I think I am, for you who may perhaps recollect that I was a little subject to a headacke on a hot summer's day at home will wonder to hear that the hotter it is the more I like it, I truly believe a winter in Europe would freeze me to death, however would the time to try it was come. But thank God I feel no anxiety about the matter other than that of returning so as once more in this life to have the happyness of embracing you.

The subject of fortune-making often comes into John's correspondence.

I believe I have already told you that things are wonderfully alter'd in this country, that in former times every blockhead whom chance drove upon the coast must get a fortune whether he would or not, now a man of sense finds much difficulty and it is only time, industry and patience will do it, especially if a person has no money when he comes to India. But on the contrary a person who has capital will even now, without he is a fool, double it every two years of his life and if lucky every year.

The advantages of my profession were never equal to those in the civil line, but were far beyond any thing you can figure, so much so that had I fortunately come here when I first went into the King's service I long ere this must have realized a sum equal to the purchase of most estates in your county.

Charles Campbell made all his fortune the two last years he was in the country, and no less a sum than £40,000 at the last siege where he commanded. In short you will this easily see, that prudence first directs me if possible to go upon sure ground by establishing some kind of capital out of savings. After that is done everything, I trust in God will go on so well as to enable me to return home during your life time in a condition to be of service to my friends ... My expectations are high in the great God who is pleased in the meantime to grant me two of the greatest blessings: health and the best wife poor man ever had. I do assure you all I get may with truth be said to be earned with the sweat of my brow, and I really believe every thing got in that way is most likely to stick by one.

In the same year he wrote again on the same theme:

8th October, 1772

The wonderful rapidity with which fortunes are at times made in the east outshines every other part of the world as will appear from what I am going to tell you. General Smith when I arrived from the coast (two years ago) was reckoned worth no more than £30,000. He goes home this season and is turned master of £130,000. He is the son of a common artillery man to his praise be it told. But be that as it may as to myself I am determined to follow what I look upon as a true and very sensible observation that more fortunes are made out of savings than in any other way whatever, trusting all to the guidence and goodness of that wise providence that rules over us.

In July 1775 Alexander had a letter from his son Patrick in Edinburgh, who had heard that John was very ill. A ship from Bombay, the *Thames*, had arrived in England with a surgeon on board who knew John and his wife. A friend of John's wife who had seen him wrote:

The surgeon on board says the Capt. (John) and his wife lives with the Governour and that Capt. MacDougall was in very bad health ... They were to have taken passage on the ship but were persuaded by the Faculty of Phisicians not to venture, Capt. Mac being so weak it would endanger his life. The surgeon says if he gets a little better or stronger he will come on one of the latest

ships. Mrs MacDougall was very well but had a great deal of
Fatique by Capt. MacDougall being so ill.

Patrick commented to his father: 'This is but a sorrowful account of
poor John yet still he may recover. I wish he had entered in the Thames
as I am satisfied it was his best Chance of Recovery, but still we may
hope for the best. I had some reluctance in transmitting those Accts, but
I never knew the good of concealing the worst Intelligence of one's
connections.'

The family waited in suspense for more news but there was silence.
Six months later, in January 1776, Alexander wrote to Patrick. 'Its most
extraordinary no accts. of your Broyr by the last ship from India, I beg
make all search in your power. I still support yr is some hidden scheam,
do all you can to unreavele it.'

On April 19th Alexander wrote again:

Very extraordinar yr is no reall news of your broyr being either
dead or alive, its most surprising unless yr will be some accot. by
the Northumberland. If yr was a correspondant at London that
would be at the trouble of enquiring of the Capt., or some of the
principal officers aboard, what they know about him its possible
some account might be got of him.

By May 2nd Alexander was convinced of his son's death. He wrote to
Patrick:

Yours of the 27 ultimo I have and now I think yr is no doubt of my
son John's death. I always dreaded it but yours confirms me in it,
its a most severe shock to his family & in particular to his fond
Parents, I doubt not in the least her death as its most certain if she
had been in life she would have write to some of her connections. I
wish you exert yourself to be informd of the particulars as to his
death ...

Then on May 6th he wrote: 'Yours of the 4th received wt the
confirmation of my Dr sons death and his poor wife all wh. put
together must be a severe shock to all concerned and in particular to
me.'

John had died on the 27th April 1775, a whole year before the family
heard of it. In fact when they first heard of his illness he was already
dead. His wife had died about four months later.

The settling of John's affairs caused the family much worry. To
complicate matters he had, like so many young men of the time, left an
illegitimate son. It was rumoured that John had left everything to his
wife and his wife had left all to John's natural son. However, despite all
efforts, no will could be found.

The mother of the child, who was referred to by the family as 'the Bratt', had subsequently married a Mr Swinton in London and the boy lived with them. Some years later Alexander wrote to Patrick:

> 23rd July, 1784
>
> Mr Swinton has Acted very inconsistent from the beginning in this affair. He would not part with the young spark while yr was hope of his having a fortune and now to throw him upon us, who are quite uncertain whether we have a concern in him or not is most impudent, who knows but he is a production of his own, and put in place of the one aledged we had a concern in. But laying aside all that I by no means wishe his being in Scotland and my resolution is that he upon receipt be returned back to england and bound prentise to some handycraft if something betwixt £20 and £30 will defray the expense ... Therefore upon Receipt return him back the expence of ych I'll indemnifie you.

Alexander's youngest son Sandie wrote on the same subject:

> It was ever my opinion from the moment I saw him that he was not akinne to us, be that as it may, we may be mistaken ... and however awkward the circumstances of his birth may be we are in my opinion bound to put him in a situation of bread ... What I think is that the boy should declare the profession he gives a preference to and if his time of life, education or abilities does not absolutely forbid it he should be indulged.

A few months before the family heard of John's death, Alexander's mother, Iain Ciar's widow, died — without knowing if her grandson was dead or alive. Alexander wrote to Patrick:

> 2nd February, 1776
>
> I have sett down to accquaint you of your Valuable worthie Grandmother's death who dyed this day about 12 o'clock. She was in all stages of her life a most Dutyfull Parent, a sincere and Generous friend and a devout Christian. I intend her interment to be Thursday next, you should accquaint her cuss. Sir Hew MacDonald of this event. Duncan [Patrick's brother] is at Fort William with Sandie, I have sent express to him. Put in the newspaper the post script with any amendments you see proper or economiums ...
>
> P.S. Dyed at Dunollie the 2nd of Fevruary aged 80 Mary MacDonald, niece to Sir Donald MacDonald of MacDonald and relict to John MacDougall Esq of MacDougall.

In another letter Alexander described the funeral as 'very expensive and genteel', of his son Duncan he wrote 'I assure you Duncan made good use of the Drams three nights running after the burial.'

Sandie goes to India

Two years later another of Alexander's sons embarked for India, hoping to make his fortune. This was Sandie, who had trained as a doctor at the Edinburgh Medical School. His brother Patrick, who was twelve years older, had advised him against this profession and had written to Alexander on the subject in 1772:

> As to the Surgeon business I entirely dislike it. I declare I would sooner bind him to any thing else for I plainly see he is as much at a loss for Bread the day his prenticeship is over as at present, after being out of pocket near £300 stl. at least, most certainly a house apprentice is the cheapest than boarding which will cost £40 stl. per annum and doubt not but he can be settled without the house for about £30 stl with a Good Master.
>
> If he can put up with such fair as I have to my self during his Apprenticeship he is most welcome for what ever consideration you please which we will not readily differ about, tho' I know the Youth have the Devil for a stomack.

In May 1778 Sandie wrote to his mother on the eve of his departure to India with the recently formed Lord Macleod's Highlanders (the 73rd). Britain was at the time fighting the American War of Independence and France had recently joined the Americans against her. French troops, together with some Indian states, were also making trouble for the British in India.

Sandie, who had lost all his luggage, wrote from Southampton:

> 12th May, 1778
>
> Since I joined the Regt. my situation has been particularly disagreeable. My mate Mr Horseman has not done one days duty owing to sickness and poor McLean has had a fever which was contagious here amongst our men, so that I had everything to do myself and God knows what a Gauntlet I have run. However I keep my health and has the pleasure to think I did my duty to every person's satisfaction.
>
> I have been by my father and Duncan provided in linens etc and by my Aunt in bed linen in so much that I shall be able to do pretty well without my trunks. I bought Blankets and Mattress in this country with every other thing that I thought I should most stand in need of. Considering that my Brother wrote that my trunks were put on board at Leith some time ago its very odd that they did not make their appearance, nor did he mention the name of the ship.
>
> No doubt you would hear that our Regt. is going to India, it is now beyond a doubt that we are destin'd for Bengal. For my own part, as I have embarked in this affair, I am determin'd at all events

to go through with it and I think it a fortunate event for me our going to that country as it is certain that in 3 or 4 years I shall be able to put myself in a situation very comfortable, with my other Industry, for life.

As to the Voyage and climate I shall endeavour to make myself easy, my Constitution tho a little hurt I apprehend to be better fitted for an expedition of this kind than the strongest or most vigorous, and no care shall be wanting on my part to preserve my health.

As it happened Sandie's Regiment did not go to India, but to Guernsey, and the day after they sailed Sandie became very ill. He wrote to Patrick from Guernsey:

16th June, 1778

The day we sailed I found myself much indisposed, not from seasickness. I turned much worse next day so much so that I was obliged to send for McLean from the ship he was in to Blood me. The following day I was delirious, and continued so. We came to Anchor here and that evening I was immediately carried ashore. The 5th day I continued delirious, fortunately on the 6th day a Rash came out all over my whole body as thick as any small pox you ever saw in your life, that day I turned perfectly sensible and in 2 days the fever left me intirely. I was very weak but found my appetite returning in such an amazing degree that I had the utmost difficulty in keeping my self from devouring every thing I saw, lest overeating would bring back the fever, considering the weakly situation I was then in. However in a few days my strength returned in a surprizing degree and it would do your heart good to see the play of knife and fork now.

My fever has not been attended with any bad Consequences, only that every bit of skin is come off my body, this you'll say is an advantage if it should contribute to make it any fairer. I never enjoyed better health than at this moment and indeed it is not surprizing, considering that this is the most delightful Island and the finest climate I was ever in ...

Every man in the Regt has got the Malla de Ecopois, this you see is French — in plain English the Itch, but called here the Scotch disorder. I have not had less than 50 men in Hospital under care at a time and then I must take another set in when those are cured. It expends a great deal of butter and Brimstone. I suppose this disorder will be £20 out of my pocket before the Regt. is clear of it.

We are under constant fear here of an attack from the French. The people of this Island speak all French, we are within 2 or 3 hours sailing of the coast of Normandy and sees it as plainly almost as you see Fife from Edinburgh.

Eight months later the Regiment had returned to England and were once again on the point of sailing for India. Sandie wrote from Spithead, on board the East India Company ship, Atlas:

27th February 1779

We are all of us turning very impatient, for a fair wind is all we wait for. We will be a most formidable fleet and I believe well appointed as ever left this country. There are 12 India men, 20 sail of the line besides Frigates and near 200 sail of transports and merchant ships. 12 Sail of the line return to England after convoying us 300 leagues off the Lands End and the remainder are intended for the India station, except 2 or 3 who remain on the coast of Africa. 400 of the Welch Volanteers go under Lord McLeod's orders who are said, in conjunction with this regt., to be intended for the taking of Gorrie [an island off the African coast]. They remain to Garrison the place and we proceed on our voyage to India. So this is the great armament about to leave this place.

The fleet arrived safely at Funchal, Madeira, 'after a very tedious passage of 32 days', and Sandie wrote from here to his Father.

23rd April, 1779

You'll Naturally expect that I am to give you some account of the Island of Madera, at about 9 miles distance at sea it has a most Gloomy and Barren aspect and little promise of any refreshment whatever, the hills are as high, as steep, and as Craggy as any in Lochaber, but when you approach nearer the scene changes considerably and you can perceive an infinite number of delightful vine yards extending to the very tops almost of those mountains with a great variety of Valleys abounding with every luxury of life.

Yet notwithstanding this the peasants are the most starving wretched sett of animals that ever existed. The only flourishing people are English, Scots and Irish, the Portuguise are a sett of the Damdest Rascals that ever lived, they gape for the arrival of an English fleet as a hungry Dog for a morsel of meat and how soon the fleet arrived the price of everything was so shamefully augmented that the poor inhabitants were starving ... The first night I went on shore I paid a Guinea for a very bad bed in a room where there were six others and every thing else in proportion ...

The inhabitants and our soldiers and sailors have had several squables, one or two of the sailors were stabbed behind their back, our men drew their broadswords and had not the officers interfer'd I believe they would have taken possession of the Island and would not have desired to have gone any further.

The People of this place are the greatest bigots existing. Their churches are small but excessively rich in proportion to their size, fully as much so as any in Flanders.

I have found the weather rather disagreeably warm as I have been obliged to lay aside the clothes I wore in England, we have a disagreeable kind of wind almost every fore noon called a Lavanter which blows from the Coast of Africa, and so far from being refreshing is hot and suffocating. For my part, tho I find it excessively disagreeable, yet I enjoy good health. It is not so with others for within these 5 days my sick return has increas'd 100 Men and Officers.

The ship left Madeira for the west coast of Africa, where Sandie's Regiment and the Welch Volunteers were to do battle with the French for possession of the island of Gorrie. Sandie evidently was not looking forward to this expedition and wrote his feelings in a letter to his father before they embarked:

There is hardly a doubt remaining that we are going to Gorrie before we proceed for India, where if we are landed and obliged to carry on war, however short, tho we should suffer little by the sword the Climate will make up for it. Should we but be embarked for a week I doubt much if I don't lose the one half of our men as we shall be there in the rainie season which is the most unwholesome part of the year in that at the best bad climate. For my own part I do not by any means relish this expedition but a millitary man must like whatever happens. Should I survive this same jaunt of pleasure to the Coast of Guinea you may expect to hear from me an account of our proceedings there.

The taking of Gorrie, which Sandie described in a letter to Patrick, was hardly what had been expected:

> Ship Atlas, off Gorrie
> 9th May, 1779

Yesterday morning we came in sight of this island with 7 ships of the line, 3 Frigates, two [Boml? Page torn] 2 tenders, 12 India men and 7 Transport.

After anchoring before the place an officer was sent on shore with a Flag of Truce ordering the place to surrender. Soon after his landing, to our great astonishment, we saw the British colours flying upon the Fort and soon after understood that the French had evacuated the Fort last February.

A French officer with a few men had remained to convey away their cannons, military stores etc into vessels which lay in the harbour. How soon our fleet made its appearance the french officer and soldiers made the best of their way in boats to the African shore. The vessels fell into the hands of our Admiral.

The Lt. Col. of the 75th Regt. is by Lord McLeod appointed Governor, 550 men of the same regiment is left to Garrison the place with a proper train of artillery, provisions, stores etc. God knows I do not envy them their situation for all of the places I ever saw this is the most damnable. I do not believe there is the thickness of a sheet of grey paper betwixt the island of Gorrie and Hell. The day is immorately hot and suffocating and the nights cold and damp with a great fog. We are to sail the day after tomorrow and well for us it is, so I shall think till then an age.

We have been exceedingly sickly though I can not say we have lost many considering how exceptionly crowded the ships are and the formidable appearance of the fever we had amongst the men and many of the officers were in a most alarming situation.

Three days ago I was seized with my old acquaintance the shitters. As there are several of us in the same situation it would divert you exceedingly to see the constant demand on the Quarter Gallery. The Hon. Capt. Lindsay offered me (having got possession) 5 shillings if I would resign him my seat but being above bribery I rejected his offer with disdain and informed him I would maintain my ground to the last extremity, by which means a pair of new washed linen britches of the Captain was rendered totally unfit for service.

On arrival at Table Town (Cape Town), Cape of Good Hope, Sandie wrote to his father:

15th August, 1779

You may believe after being four months at sea that I longed not a little for vegetables, had I landed at Dunollie have mercy on your garden and my mother's milk house, as to every other thing no man in Argyleshire kept a better table than we did on board ship.

I am affraid that any description I can attempt to give you of the heat of the weather between the tropics and under the line will convey to you but a very faint idea of what it really is. For my part, who in Scotland did not know what it was at any time to perspire, I had to change myself 5 or 6 times every day and notwithstanding my dress only consisted of a shirt, a thin muslin jacket and drawers which every time I changed them were as completely soaked as if they had been over board the half of the day. I had little or nothing of the prickly heat yet my appetite, my spirits and my health was better than I ever remember.

[Then followed a description of the style of life in Table Town]

Since my arrival here I have been constantly on shore and were it not for the infinite superior degree of Elegance in the mode of living, and for the high hills that encompass their Beautiful city I should imagine myself in Holland. Every luxury that the most Epicurean fancy could suggest is here in the utmost profusion. For my own part I live in a style that makes me alreddy begin to think that I am an Eastern Nabob, there is no such thing as Publick houses but you live and lodge in a private family.

My style is as follows: I have an elegant Parlour and bed-chamber and dressing room, and room for Black Allan [his servant] who, by the by, is I am afraid turning a man of too much fashion, tea, Coffee and Chocolate with every kind of fruit you can imagine in the Greatest perfection for breakfast, two Elegant courses and a desert, with as much wine as I chose to drink, for dinner, coffee in the Evening, a good super with wine, rack, punch etc and two good courses. At my service 4 slaves to attend me, Victuals for my servant and with all overwhelm'd with kindness all for a duccatoon a day ...

Since our arrival here we have got our sick on shore, the number from the men of war are 800, those from the Indiamen, including Company's recruits, are 500, and those from the 73rd Reg. about 250; the disorders in general are scurvy and fluxes. We have lost 30 men since we sailed from Europe, the loss of sailors and recruits for the Company's service has been much more considerable ...

We shall all be perfectly recovered of our complaints before we leave this and for my own part I think no more of the remainder of the Voyage than I would of going from Dunollie to Duart [Oban to Mull]. With the Ships and accommadation we have I do not think there is anything formidable in an India voyage.

Make yourself and my mother perfectly happy with respect to me, my income as Surgeon to this Regt. was above £200 a year, the officers at Lord McLeod's request subscribed a hundred pounds a year out of their own pockets which in all amounts to above £300 a year, not a dispicable thing for a young man. How much it will be augmented in India I can not exactly say ... but have reason to think it will be very considerable ... The climate of India is no doubt not a good one but I have a presentiment that it will agree exceedingly well with me and nothing would distress me more than to hear that the Regt. was ordered home tomorrow. Should our stay in India be but short you need not expect me home unless the want of health should render it absolutely necessary.

I am just as happy as you would wish me having every reason to think that I am Lov'd and respected by the whole corps, in perfect good health and spirits, not in the least in want of money with a very flattering prospect before me in the case I enjoy health and days.

The little Dutch I can speak has been of singular service to me here and has put it in my power to be usefull to Lord MacLeod who thank god is in perfect health and spirits and every man in this Regt. has cause to pray for its long continuance, the day he's gone they lose the best Collonel they shall ever see and I'll lose a father indeed. The particular distinction that his Lordship has been pleased to honour me with has caused some little jealousies among the officers of his own clan of which I never took the smallest notice, it is now pretty much over — these things dies of themselves if one had prudence not to feed them with fuel.

I, however, have been lucky and unlucky on one respect since I came here being almost constantly with Lord McLeod. He had parties every evening of the Field officers and capts. of his own Regt., Capts. of the men of war, Indiamen etc and a good deal of Play was going on. I was in the beginning lucky but upon the whole I find I have lost about £100. The loss of the sum does not, thank god, at present distress me but it has given me a lesson that I'll be the better of all my life which is if I were to continue such practice it might end in my intire ruin. I have now come to a determined resolution never to play but for trifles (I mean by trifles what will give me no concern to lose) and I am certain I'l keep it.

What do you think I have entirely dropt snuffing at the Particular request of a fine woman in England. You see my dear Sir I do not conceal any of my foibles from you for tho I shall always honour and esteem you as my father yet at the same time I should be particularly proud of considering you as my best friend and most intimate companion.

Sandy landed safely in India and in August 1780 was engaged in battle against Hyder Ali, who was in alliance with the French. Hyder Ali, who had usurped the throne of Mysore, was a remarkable man. He could neither read nor write but was an outstanding military commander.

Sandy wrote to Patrick on 30th September, 1780, from camp near Marmelong, India: 'You see by the date of this letter that the Army is in the field. The campaign was open'd the beginning of Aug. under the command of Sir Hector Munro against Hyder Ally who entered the Congeveram with an immense army of 100,000 Horse, 40,000 infantry and 100 pieces of Canon.'

Sandie went on to describe how part of the Army, under Colonel Baillie, became separated from the main force. When the General tried to bring troops to join up with them and then march back to the main force, they found that Hyder Ali's army had cut them off. This ended in a terrible defeat for Baillie's men.

The enemy made a desperate Charge and cut through the line. Our Highlanders as usual, though their ammunition was almost expended, Charg'd through immense Columns of Horse with fix'd Bayonets. The other troops behaved with great Bravery but were at last overcome with numbers. In short the whole army under Baillie were all either kill'd, wounded or taken prisoners, the number killed is not yet known . . . upon the whole nothing equal to it ever happened in this country.

When the General found the Misfortune to Baillie's Army

confirmed he immediately countermarched back to Congeveram that same night where we had left all our provisions and Baggage, where we lay all night upon our arms after marching all day in the scorching heat without any provisions or refreshments of any kind. I myself was almost overcome with hunger and Fatigue yet was obliged to sit up all night dressing the wounded, in short you never saw such a butcher in the flesh market more compleatly bismeared with blood etc than I was at 3'o'clock in the morning without rest or food.

Daylight was not well come in when immense collums of the Enemy's horses appeared everywhere, in front, near and on both our Flanks. Our rear Guard would beyond a doubt have been cut off had not Lord MacLeod, who Commanded the right wing, sent them a timely reinforcement ... Our Flanking parties were frequently beat back upon the line.

A Capt. George Campbell who Commanded a Battl. of Seapoys was shot through the loins, I cut out the Ball upon the field of Battle and he is now in a fair way of recovery. He is from Rosshire and an exceedingly good fellow ...

We were from 3 o'clock in the morning of the 11th until 9 o'clock of the 12th constantly upon our feet, had been for 2 days I may say, without any food, constantly exposed to the intense heat of the sun and perpetually teased by the Enemy's horse, in which time we marched no less than 50 miles.

Sandie went on to tell how he lost all his baggage, medicine and horses. He mourned the loss of half the Regiment; of 1000 fighting men scarce 500 remained. Beside the trauma of losing so many comrades, his financial loss was very great:

Surgeons in this country makes money in Proportion to the number of Europeans they have charge of ... this reduces my revenue to one half, my Kings pay and profits always remain the same but it is so unconsiderable I never hardly count upon it, it does not by any means half pay my servants. But from Lord McLeod's being always my steady friend, indeed more in the style of a Father than anything else, I am still able in some measure to evade the loss I should other ways sustain by the Regt. being so much reduced. In short if I live and enjoy health and Lord McLeod and the regt. remains in this country, in 3 or 4 years I shall still, barring misfortunes, be able to render myself comfortable for life, at least it will assist. The lancet will not bleed a bit the worse of being assisted by the Gold Pagodas of the Carnatic.

I forgot to mention that all the officers lost the whole or part of their baggage. His Lordship lost everything he had, not a shirt or shift, money, plate or other articles remain. His loss amounts at least to 4000 star Pagodas. He does not value the money but the loss of some papers of consequence and very old family plate distresses him much.

Capt. Lamont, his Lordship's Aide de Camp, had a very odd escape when a Rockett, a particular kind of small shell used by the Black Princes of the Country in war, hit Lamont's Hatt and drove it in pieces off his head but he received no hurt but what the Fright gave him. He is a fine fellow and excellent soldier, and in the way of doing soon well. It is a pity that his brother, the Laird of Lamont, and he are not on so good footing as might be wished . . . he swore he would never have any intercourse with his Brother, however I prevailed upon him to write from this Country and I hope all will be well again.

We are to remain here till after the Monsoon and then take the field against our friend Hyder Ally. Give my best love to my father, mother, brother, sister and Aunt. Tell them all that I never was in better health but long confoundedly for a number of good things.

Aftermath of an elopement

Just about the time that Sandie's letter arrived at Dunollie, describing his dangerous life in India, something happened at home which very much hurt and surprised Alexander. His son Duncan, who lived in the district and whom his father had once described in a letter as his 'bosom companion', eloped with Jean Campbell, a daughter of Neil Campbell of Duntroon.

Unfortunately no letters survive describing the actual event but there are some which give a vivid picture of the feelings of the guilt-stricken and unhappy bridegroom after the elopement. It is interesting to remember that Duncan was no callow youth at the time but a man of thirty-seven.

Duncan wrote to Patrick from Dunollie:

14th May, 1781

I met with a servant from my Father with a letter in answer to the one I wrote him from Glasgow . . . He desired I should immediately bring my <u>wife</u> to Dunolly . . . however I think it looks better if she goes first to Duntroon and I can bring her here upon my way home from Islay . . .

My reception here was middling, I shall be out of it as soon as I can . . . I don't know how matters may be in a little time or how they may change, whether to better or Worse, upon Jean's coming here, be that as it may I am determined to discharge my duty to her and the old Folks also, so far as lies in my power.

After Combie and my Father went to bed I had a Conversation

with my Mother. I plainly see she is never to be reconciled to me Cordially, however well she may keep up appearances of a good understanding. I see my life will for some time be a bad one, and my Prospect in general not very encouraging. The severe shock I have given my Father and Mother, who are truely Very much upon the decline of life, Effects me so much that I am certain it will prey upon my spirits.

Oh my Dearly beloved Peter [Patrick] everything appears Gloomy, horrid indeed, but while I'm able to retain, and that you think me worthy of, your Friendship it will be a nourishing Consolation to the poor Girl I have entangled. I don't know what I am doing or writing, my Spirits are quite exhausted, my own disorder increasing, a horrid situation and to my misfortune I must keep all to myself ... I am the Table Talk of the whole World, the aversion of my nearest Friends, except you, and what must destroy me intirely, at war with my own Feelings. Pity me and write me soon.

The next day he felt a little better and wrote again to Patrick:

I wrote you of yesterday's date wherein you'll see I was in a woeful situation, my mind is now something more tranquil ... My indulgent Father came with me the length of Oban and made every thing as easie as I deserved. I find now the whole, or at least a great deal, depends on our own Conduct, as to me I am determined and I trust in the Almighty Jean will be advisable ... It would not be amiss that you drop her a line of admonition setting furth how much it will contribute to our happiness that she be circumspect in her Conduct and subservient to the will of the Old Folks.

Ten days later Duncan wrote to Patrick again. He was just about to fetch Jean from Duntroon and bring her to Dunollie.

You and you alone shall know how much I am to blame. I had a letter from Duntroon in answer to one I writ him from Glasgow. He does not mention any provision for his daughter and I can see from his letter that he has had a misrepresentation of the Story already, and it is my belief we shall only be friends at a distance, I shall take care to keep a respectful distance ... I understand there is a scheme among them of having a new marriage which I'm determined shall be my last Action this side of time, this is my Firm resolution whatever the Consequence may be and I immagine my resolution will meet with your approbation, if not acquaint me.

Meanwhile the two fathers were exchanging letters. Neil Campbell of Duntroon wrote to Alexander:

I hope my conduct hitherto has testifyed my Esteem and regard for you and Lady MacDougall, and I am persuaded that both of you feel sensible concern for any undutyfull step taken by a Child of mine, especially when <u>your own</u> shared alike in the blame, by your son Duncan and my daughter Jean joining hands without asking our approbation.

After the first transport, in my own mind, of resentment at I may say, their unaccountable Conduct had subsided, I considered it best to contribute by all the means in my power to their mutual felicity, since what was passed could not be recalled but especially as I had deservedly a Great regard and firm friendship of long standing for your son, and I doe declare, when I understood that you and the good Lady were of the same way of thinking my forgiveness was perfected and I esteemed you and Her more (if possible) than ever for it.

In my opinion what remains now is to have such settlements made upon them by you and me as are adequate to our situation. I make no doubt that Duncan has informed of all that passed twixt him and me on this subject.

Alexander replied:

Yours by the bearer I have received and let me assure you the step my son took was as surprising to me as it could be to you — a son whom I had with me since his infancie and allways upon the most happy terms. Yet I could not (nor his mother) on account of our particular regard for your family and the small acquaintance we had of your Daughter not but receive them into our family and give all the indulgence in our power. When my son returned here with his wife I asked him if you and he had had any conversation about a settlement to which he answered not a sylable, but as it comes from you to mention I shall be willing any time its convenient for you to have a conferance upon that subject.

Duncan wrote to Patrick:

9th June, 1781

I am indeed a different Man from what you saw me in respect of spirits and I am really resolved what ever disappointments I may meet with shall only be known to you ... As to Duntroon you must lay every iron on the Fire to find out the Contract of Marriage, I deny'd to my Father that he spoke to me at all as I knew that he would be out of all patience at his offer, don't you say anything to my Father. I am sorry to acquaint you that my Prospect of soon heiring the Family is at an end, poor Jean has parted the Grip by a piece of folly of her own, this you need make no mention of, she is still ill and was confined to her bed and room when I left home, but she is now I understand much better than when I parted with her.

This accident happened in Consequence of an over Exertion of dancing at Inverary after I went to Islay.

After this stormy start to their life together, Duncan and Jean settled down to farm at Ardentrive on Kerrera. They enjoyed twenty-six years of married life and had thirteen children.

Family and farming affairs

Early the following year Alexander lost his wife Mary. She had been ailing for some time: one of her sons had written, 'Let me intreat this favor that she desist from that laborious and indefatigable attention she constantly pays to her affairs. It is full time and it is the surest method of re-establishing her health.' After her death, Alexander's sister Annie came to look after him.

Soon afterwards, another event of great importance to the family took place: Patrick, now forty, married Louisa Maxwell, a daughter of Campbell of Achallader. Alexander, who for years had been instructing his heir to get married, now thought fit to send the couple some good advice.

He began with a somewhat daunting message to his daughter-in-law: that she would find it difficult to follow such characters as his late mother and wife. 'If I live to have the pleasure of seeing her here I will make it my Business to afford her all the advice and directions for her future conduct that will suggest to me.' To Patrick he had this to say:

6th May, 1782

I would Recommend to you to make yourself as popular as you can with any that askes for you, a little idle Conversation will please which will Ingratiate you very much with them, your acting this way may be of consequence and will not put a sixpence out of your pockett. I know this method may be disagreeable to you but at the same time it may in time be of more consequence to you than just now you can figure. I would Recommend the same to Maxwell as well as yourself. Your Worthy Mother yet never lost sight of using her own friends and connections with the greatest reguard and Respects. It is a duty upon me not to conseal from you or Maxwell what I think will be for your Mutual Interest.

I am told I need not recommend parsimonie and frugalitie to my Daughter tho' these are very necessary Qualifications, yet let it not be attended with meaness in any Respect, which in my time never entered this family.

It seems from the letters that Patrick was not doing well in his profession of W.S. in Edinburgh. He was constantly asking his father for financial support which, from now on, was going to lead to an acrimonious correspondence.

In a year when everything seemed to happen at once, Alexander's feelings — grief at his wife's death, worry that his cattle would starve owing to the late spring, and joy over Patrick's marriage — were all mixed with deep anxiety for Sandie. Sandie had become ill in India and was said to be on his way home. And then, just as in the case of his brother John, who had died out there, there was silence. It must have seemed as if family history was repeating itself and evidently Alexander feared the worst.

'I see,' he wrote to Patrick, 'ane oyr Packet from India arrived at Limerick in Ireland ... I flater myself we will have some Account of Sandie, my mind with all my other distress is upon the Rack about him. I beg you acquaint me of the first Accounts you get from that quarter.'

A few months later: 'My mind is most Uneasie about Sandie, its most Surprising that there is no account from any of the officers of the Corps he is in. It is folly to conceal anything you know about him it will allways be news whatever time I hear it.'

But soon after this Alexander wrote to Patrick with relief:

> 12th June, 1782
> Last night's post to my great Surprise brought me a Letter from Sandie from Limerick. By his letter to me its amazing how long he lived under the Liver disorder and particularly after the Insition was made upon him and the Liver cut ... The doctor writes me of a widdowed Lady that came home with him in the same ship, who is a fortune of £20,000, in such a Misticale style that one would conjecture he is Buckled to her for Life or to be so ...
>
> I shall be most Anxious till I see him tho at the same time I am much afraid our first Interview will depress my spririts much but seeing him however low as his state of health is most Acceptable to me, its a happyness since parting with him I never expected to enjoy, he has Acted most prudently tho' he had not a shilling in his pocket.

Sandie had met with a terrible shock when he arrived in Ireland. He wrote to Patrick:

> 10th June, 1782
> The day after my arrival here [Dublin] my Uncle informed me of our Mother's death, this unhappy news added to a weak state of health has absolutely almost deprived me of my senses. God knows much happiness did I promise myself and her in meeting her, and when I imagin'd myself on the point of accomplishing it to be thus deprived of her for ever gives such a new turn to my

thoughts that I hardly know at times what I am about, for to me and all of us she certainly was the best and most affectionate mother I have ever had an opportunity of seeing.

I meant to have gone to England and there to have remained for some little time but as I can readily conceive the situation of the good old man at Dunollie I have determined to go immediately to Scotland as I think seeing me will afford him some satisfaction.

Sandie arrived safely at Dunollie, travelling by Port Patrick and Glasgow. Alexander wrote to Patrick:

26th June, 1782

Last night brought me the most Agreeable meating with Sandie who is much better (but far from being strong) than I could figure. I flatter myself that Dunollie Aire will have a good effect notwithstanding. I have reason to thank God for the great & Many blessings I enjoy by the company of the few remaining of my family ... nothing can be more agreeable to me than to have the few happy remains of my family here with me, there are two which I very Much despeired of ever seeing, my son Patrick's wife and poor Sandie but providence has been more kind to me than I expected.

By the end of 1782 Alexander was looking forward to the arrival of the first of Patrick's children. He had written soon after his wife's death: 'I enjoy pretty good health but am much impaired of sleep from my Usual, no help for it. Many happy days I have had of pleasure and health and no wonder tho' there should be alterations.'

It seems however that the happy days were to continue with the arrival of his grandchildren, for the children of Patrick and Duncan gave him tremendous pleasure. He had them to stay at Dunollie as often as he could, which must have been a help to their mothers who were busy producing large families.

He took young Sandy, Patrick's first son, aged two years old while Louisa Maxwell was recovering from a miscarriage and wrote of him to Patrick: 'Sandy is as fine a child as I ever saw, both healthie, lively and goodnatured to a degree. Tho' he is much trouble wt the teething the young spark keeps a good appetite, if it was plain road he would walk without a fall betwixt this and Oban, he sleeps vastly but still not at all cleanly, he is a reall punishment to me for where ever he sees or hears my voice he must come to me and very often in his shirt.'

Duncan commented to Patrick: 'Sandy I saw yesterday at Dunollie ... Whenever he hears the Old Gentleman's Voice he must be there ... He pulls Mattie's [Duncan's daughter] hair and scratches her if she attempts

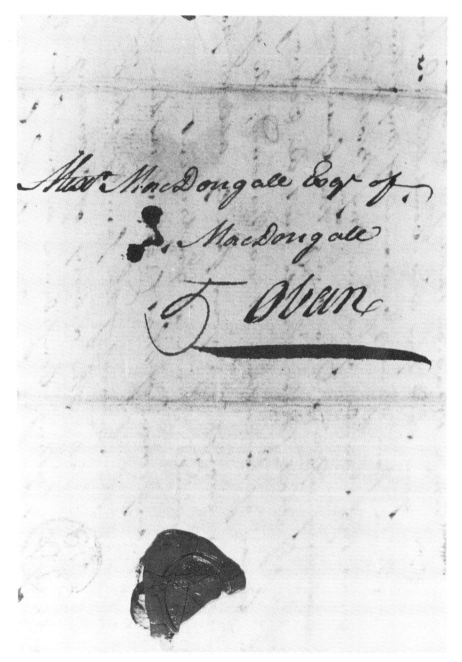

Letter addressed to Alexander, 29th January, 1789

to go near her Grandfather. You never saw such jealousies and the Old Gentleman is quite delighted with it.'

When Sandy was six he was taken ill in Edinburgh and Alexander wrote to Patrick:

> I was very certain when you took him away [from Dunollie] that confinement would not agree with a boy so much abroad wett and cold as he was used to. I parted with him with great Reluctance tho' I said nothing and keepd quiet. I would advise as soon as it will be convenient to return him back to Dunollie which if you agree to I'll take all the care in my power of him and give you no trouble while I'll live, its you that is his father and may dispose of him as you see proper.

Even when he was over eighty, Alexander was still willing to relieve his daughters-in-law of their children. 'Mrs MacDougall Ardentrive [Duncan's wife] has but a slow recoverie, her son Neil is a real torment to her and I intend to separate them for some time.'

When he was eighty-one he wrote: 'I have the easiest managed cargo of Laddies I ever saw. Your Aunt has vastly disscommoded herself by clearing the room above the cellar for them where they all sleep and eat, only the two Johnnies always dines with me, and when night comes I pack them all up there and gives them a fire and candle and is not confounded with their noise.'

However much Alexander was now taken up with his grandchildren his interest in the farming and the tenants had not diminished. He had been distressed for himself and his tenants in 1780 and he continued to complain. '... the distilling is entirely knocked in head. What to make of the farm barly I know not. It is a disappointment of nearly £100 yearly to me, and the poor tennants the boll they had to dispose of will get no price for it. There is no such thing as cash — Duncan is squised to the Back bone for it — as I observed to you before stopping distilling will ruin this country.'

Duncan himself wrote to Patrick: 'This country is in such a dreadful situation by the scarcity of cash that there is no such thing as getting a shilling and the total stop put to the distillery of Whisky has ruined everything. Your father and I don't know under the sun what to make of our Bear [bere: a kind of barley] he is really droll upon that subject.'

Patrick wrote to his father six years later: 'The present Great Distilliaries will not buy scarce a grain of the Bear of this Country but Import from all Quarters at a much Cheaper rate which if not prevented Instantly will ruin the Landed interest of all Scotland.'

In 1794 Alexander was still worried about his tenants: 'This country is in a terrible convulsion betwixt the Landlords and their tennents ... All

my folkes are quite easie not the least complaint or removeall, how long
they will continue so its hard to say but I'll give them all the Indulgence
in my power ... what did them vast Service was those of their cattle I
wintered last season.'

Duncan wrote the same year: 'There is no thing as mony to be got in
this Country and I presume it will Continue so till there is a peace, if so
Many a decent Industrious family will be brought to ruin.'

Since 1793, Britain had been fighting against France in the French
Revolutionary War. The following year Alexander's 'bosom companion'
Duncan, joined the Army. Recruiting for the Fencible Regiments
(regiments for home service only) was going on apace in the Highlands.

According to the letters there does not seem to have been great
enthusiasm for enlisting. Duncan had written in 1794: 'We shall have a
fine Bustle by and by in this Country recruiting Lochnell's regt ... It has
defyd Archie Easdale to make a Single Man upon the Lochnell Estate,
but I'm sure when Lochnell appears in person he will make a good many
... I think he is well out of that Bustle.'

Alexander wrote that same year: 'Recruiting goes slowly in this
Country, even the great Lairds can make but little of it upon their
estates.'

But in January 1795 Duncan told Patrick:

> Yesterday's post brought me an offer from Lord Breadalbane to
> be Captain and Paymaster to his third Batallion of Fencibles.
>   I never applied of any mortal about it and as a further
> encouragement I imagine I shall be allowed an Ensigncy for one of
> my Boys, but of this I am not certain. There is no stipulation
> whatever for men but to recruit upon honour. Indeed as to men I
> don't think if I should exert myself everso I can make half a dozen
> in this country, but it is very ill to judge until its try'd. This is a very
> flattering offer.

Duncan accepted the offer and went with his Battalion to Kells in
Ireland. The United Irishmen, a society working for the separation of
Britain and Ireland and intriguing with the French, were causing
trouble.

Not long after Duncan had left home Alexander received a letter from
Patrick telling of the death of Dr Sandie:

> February, 1795
> Some days ago my wife had a letter from Jean Fisher from St
> Peterborough [Russia] informing that her Husband, my unfor-
> tunate Brother, died at Cherson on 7th Aug last and desiring my
> wife to apply to me to get her put upon the surgeon's widow funds

by paying the arears Due. She says she will soon set out for this country.

This is a matter that requires a little Consideration because we have no evidence whatever she was his wife, he never mentioned it to us in any letter nor do I think the connection is so Respectable as for us to Volunteer in the Allyance.

Duncan wrote to Patrick a few days later:

1st March, 1795

Your letters of 27th and 28th I have received. The former which brings account of our poor Brother's death gives me much concern, at the same time his own folly for many years past rendered him equal to dead to his friends. I some time ago had good reason to believe his unbounded folly had led him to marry Fisher. (Yet he never gave me the least hint of it in any of his letters.) That being the case she is our sister-in-law and of course if indigent will be a plague to us ...

A week later Duncan wrote again:

Last night's post brought me a letter from the Commisary in which he says that Jean Fisher will produce the most unquestionable Document to Establish her Marriage with our Brother, of which from what I long ago heard I have little doubt. What an Infatuate Man he has been, so much so that I could not allow myself, though assured of it by the best Authority, to think he could be such a silly fool. There is no help for it now, God pity the wretched woman. Indeed I never could endure her, but if she's really our foolish Brother's widow I can't help feeling for her.

Then came a further shock: in a letter to Alexander from a Dugald MacDougall, in Guernsey:

I am desired to acquaint you of a Daughter of Doctor Alexr. MacDougall that is in this Island, now staying with her grandmother. The child is anxious to know what is become of her father and so is all her friends here. The good old woman has kept her at school so as her Education is now so far complete as any Gentleman's daughter in the Island, her name is Ann MacDougall she has all the likeliness of the Family of MacDougall and tho' but a natural Daughter she Deserves all the attention her friends may afford.

I as a native of Lorn begs leave to acquaint you of this young woman, which I think it my Duty in such a strange place as this to be partial to any of the name that may be Deserving Friendship.

Ann apparently married, for, many years later, there is a letter from her daughter telling Patrick what she knew of her grandfather, Sandie. She said she knew that his first wife was drowned off Yarmouth during a voyage from Edinburgh to London, and that soon after this he went to Russia to be Physician to the Empress. 'Change of Climate,' she wrote, 'together with different Circumstances, opperated so strongly upon him that in a short time after his arrival he died.'

Very soon after the news of Sandie's death, one of Duncan's sons, John Houston, died at about nine years old. The little boy (often known as Houston) had had an accident the year before but the cause of his death is not known. Duncan had described the incident at the time in a letter to Patrick:

> 7th April, 1794
> I was very near losing poor Houston last week. One of the Plough Horses came near the kitchen door when the fowls had got some potatoes to eat. The poor little fellow went to drive away the horse from the Hens' meal upon which the horse struck at him upon the elbow and overed him in the dirt. There he lay unnoticed till his brother Neil roared out that poor Houston was beat by the Grey Horse. He then got to his legs and came into the kitchen in a deplorable state, his arm hung by his side motionless, his thighs and leggs Black and Blue and complaining of his side. It did not occur to them to send for Mclean to get him bled.

On hearing of the death of his son, Duncan wrote to Patrick from Ireland:

> 16th November, 1795
> Your former letter prepared me a good deal for the shock I felt yesterday and thank God I have been able to Bear the loss of my dear Boy with more resignation than I expected. But my heart is pierced with the Idea that my poor wife should Witness the poor Innocent Lamb's dissolution and me at such a distance from her to comfort her and alleviate her distress. It is however a great consolation to me that you was upon the Spot, and that you think she bore her loss with a proper Fortitude. I have write to her and my Father by this days post.

Early the following year, in his capacity as Paymaster, Duncan was in grave trouble and wrote to his brother in January 1796: 'Since I last wrote a most unlucky circumstance has occurred which with the loss of my son and other circumstances these two years has gone far to overwhelm me.' The letter went on to tell how Duncan had one afternoon left his lodgings to go to the Mess, telling his servant to lock the door. This the servant did, but when he came back later in the evening to make up the fire, he found the lock broken.

My cash box was abstracted from a Chest that lay in an inner room where I slept. The box contained about £300 in Gold, a variety of Accounts, Papers and letters of Consequence, besides private Bills to the amts. of £7 and £300. My surprise and Vexation you may believe was scarce supportable. I immediately sent for the Col. and the Major and every thing had been done to promote a discovery that invention could suggest but to no purpose. Our suspicion is directed against my Landlord and his family, but I am afraid nothing can be brought home against them.

I wrote to Dublin to our agent who has communicated the matter to the Secretary at War. The Agent directs me to give in a Petition to the Ld. Lieut. setting forth the matters of fact and that he has little doubt Government will refund my loss. However I cannot yet flatter myself with success. The money abstracted was the subsistence of the Regt. which must be forthcoming when called for. I cannot in Justice to the Col. omit telling you that he has volunteered every immediat assistance in his power and in the whole business conducted himself in the most friendly manner.

Upon the following Sunday a Woman found the Cash Box in a wet ditch at the end of the Town with the lock picked and the whole money abstracted. I believe they did not take away the papers that were in it, but they were so covered with mud and dirt that some of them were defaced and others (but I believe not of the greatest importance) wanting.

I dont wish this affair to be talked of as it would come to Mrs MacDougall's and my Father's knowledge which would give them great uneasiness to no purpose. If Government will do any thing to re-emburse me its best letting them know the matter afterwards, if not its enough to tell them when it will conceale no longer.

In March, exactly two months later, Duncan wrote to Patrick with relief:

I have now the happiness to acquaint you that this day's post brought a letter from the Commander in Chief to our Lt. Col. acquainting him that his Excellency the Ld. Lieut. has agreed to allow me to Charge the £300 I was robbed of in the Contingent Acct. of the Regt. so that the unlucky business which stood long in suspense is at last settled to my satisfaction and I have still good hope that Ld. Breadalbine will let me have Commissions for my Boys . . . I'm so full of this good news that I can't settle to write you of any thing else.

The following autumn Duncan wrote from Lurgan:

22nd November 1796

I arrived here upon the 12th inst. having marched with the last

Division from Kells. This part of the Kingdome differs very much from the place we left. That Country was much richer in Soil and all marked out in large farms for Corn, Grassing, and breeding Cattle of every description. This corner is all divided in small Farms mostly under Crops and a good deale of Manufacture carried on in the Linnen, Bleaching & Cotton line. The Natives are much better cloathed and look fresher in the Complexion and the women are uncommonly well looked, in so much that they are enough to make an old Man feel Young again.

Yet to live here is hell upon Earth. The County of Meath when we went there was but a joke to what this Country is now [this is the County of Armagh]. No night passes without Murders, Burning of Houses and Barnyard, or killing of cattle.

These Ruffians are Composed of distinct Tribes or Associations. They consist of Defenders (though fewest in number), Orange Boys, Peep of day Boys, United Irishmen and Wacckers, but they are all Bad Boys. The Wretches have dreadful Conflicts amonst themselves and hundreds have lost their lives in their Battles, but they all aim at a Subversion of the Constitution and getting rid of our Sovereign. Religion weighs heavy in the Scale of their discords.

The Protestants Predominate in this Quarter and have Banished 1000 Familys from hence who have taken Refuge in the Roman Catholick Countys to the Southward, and some have gone over to Scotland to save themselves and families from assassination. The Presbyterians lead the Van on savage Barbarity and distinguish themselves in Acts of most Cruel Murders. Few nights pass but we apprehend some Culprits, the Jails of the Kingdome are quite full of one kind or other of them.

The duty here is very severe for our men have one night in bed and the next night on duty, perhaps obliged to puddle on dirty roads 5 or 6 miles in Chase of these Devils that I have described and return at 5 in the morning covered with Clay and mud and without catching any Game.

By 1798 Alexander was eighty-five. He was still in good health, though his sight was failing. Early in the year he sent Patrick a surprising piece of news: 'Soon after you left I lost two of my back teeth in my lower goom but to my great surprise there is two new ones growing in their place, both cut the skin and are somewhat uneasy to me.'

In April Alexander was busy organising a wet-nurse for Patrick's ninth child, Allan. Louisa Maxwell had fed her other babies successfully but was now having trouble. Alexander wrote to his son in Edinburgh:

9th April 1798
Immediately upon receipt of yours I sent for the Miller of Cleugh

[a Dunollie mill about five miles distant, near Kilmore], and his wife who very Cheerfully agreed to go to Edinburgh to nurse your son and settle their own child elsewhere. I told them I would pay the expense for their own child and at the same time wished to know what was the nursing fee she would demand for nursing your child; her answer was she would make no demand but refer it to you. She setts off for Stirling Thursday first on horse back with Duncan Livingstone and from thence to Edinb. in the flay and I have given her direction to your house. I hope she may succeed weel as both she and her Husband were so willing to serve you.

When he was an adult, Allan wrote what he had been told of the Miller's wife's journey:

I was born upon the 2nd day of April 1798 in Thistle Street. I have heard that the Miller at Cleugh's wife, having heard that my mother had given birth to a child and she required a nurse, set out to offer her services. She had never been from home and my mother has often told me that her simple narrative of her journey created great interest in the family. She had never formed any conception of, perhaps never heard of, a four wheeler coach drawn by four horses which she beheld and entered for the first time in Glasgow. On its way to Edinburgh it was upset which would of course not subdue her fears although I have no doubt it quite satisfied her curiosity.

Ten days after the miller's wife had arrived in Edinburgh Alexander wrote again to Patrick: 'Yours I received and it gave me particular pleasure the account you gave of Mrs MacDougall's recovery and how weel your nurse promises to answer your laddie. I sent over yesterday to Cleugh to inform her husband of her safe arrival and you may assure her that her child is doing vastly weele, so weele that his father does not intend parting with him.'

Two months later, at Alexander's request, Patrick, his wife and their nine children, packed up and went to live at Dunollie. Alexander then handed over the management of the estate to his son.

Meanwhile Duncan, who was still in Ireland, wrote to Patrick of trouble in the Regiment.

19th July, 1798

When I writ you some time ago that an unlucky Circumstance has been discovered in the Regt. I was very much alarmed and distressed in my mind. I'm thankful that upon full investigations it has not been so bad as at first supposed.

When our Regt. was dispersed in winter '96 and '97 over the countys of Armagh, Down and a part of Antrim, a great number of our men were in their Drunkenness seduced to take the United Irishmen's Oath, particularly Capt. Stewart's Company who is himself a Fool. We had hints of this before we left Enneskillen but could give no credit to it, at last the whole was discovered Intercepting the letters of one of the Ringleaders to his Correspondent in the Carlo Malitia, who are all united in that Diabolical Society.

We have sent off 5 of these most implicated in the business to serve in the West Indies, the second Class we have flogg'd most dreadfully, the rest are, upon their Confession, pardoned. Many of those sworn in were ignorant of the Consequence for the whole of them were under the Influence of Whisky when they took the Oath . . .

In order to do away with the stain that was left on the Regt. I requested General Knox (under whose immediate Command we were at the time) to order us to the South where the Service was very severe at that time. Knox did so but before the orders arrived the men were without one exception Soliciting to get to the County of Kildare or Wexford and that they would show the World their Loyalty was still unshaken. In the meantime the Rebellion broke out in the County of Down and Antrim and the Route to Dublin was countermanded . . . This Alarming business is now settled and the poor Devils are so sensible of their Error & how grossly they were imposed upon that we have great difficulty in restraining them from Bayonetting every Countryman they meet with. You are not to mention any of this business.

Throughout the correspondence with his brother, Duncan was continually concerned that the fact that he was in danger should be kept from his wife.

In August 1798 he wrote that 'the French have Effected a landing at Killala, County Mayo, on the West of Ireland' and he was about to march against them. 'You will plead what excuse for me you see proper for my not writing to my Wife, according to my promise, as I cannot do it without mentioning to her what is likely at present to happen, knowing it will make her unhappy.'

In this case Duncan later wrote: 'The French laid down their arms in the field of Battle which the Rebels refused to do, which brought the Vengeance of the King's Forces on them and was followed by a Dreadful Carnage . . . This second Rebellion is Compleately finished and I suppose the Country will be pretty quiet till a few more French are thrown among us.'

In another letter Duncan was still worrying about his wife. 'Endeavour to Keep the news papers out of her Way . . . I request of you that in case any thing should happen to me that you pay Attention so far as you can to my poor Wife and young helpless Family all of which must suffer severely. Thank God I'm in perfect health and will be able to bear a good deal of Fatigue of which the troops that are now on Actual service get plenty.'

Meanwhile Duncan's wife was reading the papers avidly and writing letters to other members of the family, relating what she had read.

Of the proposed Union of Ireland with Britain (which took place in 1800) Duncan had this to say: 'The Union with Brittain goes very ill down with the people of Ireland, and I am affraid if its seriously brought forward it will Create great confusion.'

There is a family tradition about an incident which took place while Duncan was in Ireland. It links up with the traditional story about his grandfather Iain Ciar killing the Red Robber and presenting his head to the Earl of Antrim. A grandson of the Robber, the story goes, asked Duncan to dine with him. Duncan's bodyguard, a grandson of the Livingstone who had been with Iain Ciar, went to the house with him: Duncan left his sword on a table just inside the door while Livingstone stayed outside. After a time the bodyguard began to feel anxious about his master, and looking in at a window saw Duncan defending himself against his host with a chair. Livingstone burst into the house, picked up Duncan's sword and rushed to his rescue shouting, 'Captain let me run him through!' To which Duncan is said to have replied, 'No, no, he is in his own house and I'm feared they would hang us if you did.'

In 1801 Duncan came home on leave — and found a sad situation at Dunollie. He wrote to Patrick: 'As to the poor old Man our father — have little doubts of hearing of his dissolution very soon, may the Almighty prepare us all for that awful Change.'

Soon afterwards Alexander died, at the age of eighty-eight. No bill for his funeral remains; there is just a brief mention in an account sent in by a baker, Archibald Wright.

To ¾ peck Plumb Cake for Mr MacDougall's Internment	6/-
To ¾ peck Seed Cake	6/-
To 1½ peck Short Bread	6/6
To 8 lbs Sugar and Spunge Biscuit	6/8
To 8 quarter Loaves Bread	8/8
To 5 lbs Butter	2/6
To 7½ doz. Eggs at 4d	2/3

Family Post

Worries of a Dowager

Mary MacDougall to her son Alexander at Dunollie, from Inverness, 1742

I received the full Contents of your letter, the lord reward you for your good payment for I frankly acnowledge that what I have is better for me for keeping my Credit than if I got hundred marks more and longer delay. Itts the greatest plesurs I have in this side of time to be doeing all the good in my power to my dearest Delights Childrien. I believe there is noe woman bestows less on herself than I doe for I have not bought a goun or coat to my self but what I got from you after my Dearest Life's Death.

My dear I am very well pleased that my Daughter did not come to live with me, I will give you my reson for as good as five hundred marks would goe but in a sober night in this place in gaye way of living or keeping many Company. I know my Daughter is a great scuffer of clothes and oft buying of Clothes will soon drane deep. And when she would run short, and perhaps involf herself in Debt, having but herself and her servant it would be said itt would be supporting me and my family she would spend her monie, and when she would not take my advice it would be a great Cross to me.

God knows I have no need of any additionall Cross as for Johnny he never did aplay to the Latine but he is doing pritty weel to his writing and arthmetick. He is verie impatient to be att sea as he sees many younger than himself going and that of people of Good Circumstance bairns, but I shall doe my best to keep him till his Master says that he is proper for itt ...

(The daughter mentioned was probably Anne who was then twenty-two. Johnny was twelve.)

Short Measure

Rob Arthur, Crawfurds Dyke, to Alexander at Dunollie, September 1746

I am Extramley sorey for the Disappointment of your Ladys Goun. As these kinds are always cutt as to make a goun I never Examined it to the quantity of yards, toke it for granted, its sent to Glasgow to get 2 yards more and shall be sent the first opertunity ...

Advice on a Career

Robert Campbell to Alexander (his brother-in-law) from London, December 1758

Your intention in setling your Boys to business is what I very much approve off, and I am obliged to you for wishing one of them under my care, though at the same time you'l allow me as your ffriend and one who wishes your ffamily well to give you my oppinion very ffreely on that head.

In the first place I have no use for a Prentice and though I had Stirling is the very last Place I should desire you to send your son to learn the Busines of a Mercht. There is no Trade there, no helps to Push a young Man Properly into the World. I know this to be the case from experience, and am so sensible of the Truth of it that was I to Begin Life, and capable to judge for myself, it is the very last Place I know I would settle in. Its true I made shift hitherto to scramble through, but sure I am that was I to be at the same pains in Edin. Glasgow or here I should have had a very Different Tale to say. My business though I live in Stirling don't in the least Depend on the place, if it did I would not live by it.

If Duncan shapes to be the Mercht. I would Advise you to settle him in Glasgow as the only place in Scotland that knows anny thing of Trade, and don't Fix him with a shopkeeper there, but with a Forreign Mercht who can instruct him his Busines in a regular Plan and, if he likes him, can push him on in the world when his Time is Out. You must not stand to give £100, £150, or £200 Prentice fee to such a Man if Insisted on, for I Assure you it will be the Ruin of your Boy if for the sake of a small Prentice ffee you affix him with low People, let him have a ffair chance in his first setting out in Life and leave the rest to Providence and his own industry.

All Perish

Hugh MacLean to Alexander, from Glasgow, November 1761

Your namesake Robert McDougall, Brother to James late of Greenock showed me a letter from you to him advising him to be ruled by me respecting his Claim on his Brother's effects, but before yours came to him he had entered into ane Agreement with the widow by which he got £50 str. in full. With this sum he, his wife and two of his children returned to Ireland but unluckily on their passage they and the Vessell in which they were perished, which finnally ends James effects and relations.

The Isle of Man

James McLagan to Alexander, from Belfast, December 1771

If you conclude from my not writing you sooner that I have forgot
the kindness shown me by you and your Family, I can with a good
conscience assure you of the contrary. The truth is I waited till
something should occur worth the troubling you with, tho' you will
find that it is not the case even now.

I had in particular an Intention of visiting our people in the
Isle of Man, and of consequence the Island itself in which some of
your ancestors .had once great concern. This Design I have
sometime ago Accomplished — when there it was Natural for me
to Desire an Acquaintance with the History of that little Kingdom.
In it I found that in the year 1156 Sommerled fought Goddard the
Norwegian King of Man with 80 ships. That in 1158 he attacked the
Isle of Man with 58 ships, Conquered and added it to his Kingdom
of the Isles.

This Island probably had its name of Mona (in latter times
corrupted into Man) from Mona a Hill and with propriety too, for
excepting the two Extremes, it consists of Mountains and Vallies.
Two of its Hills are so high that from the Tops of them one may,
from the same spot, see Scotland, England, Wales and Ireland.
The Face of the Isle Resembles many parts of the Highlands much.
It is about 30 miles long and in some places 10 or 12 Broad. With
respect to both soil and climate it is fitter for Pasture than Corn.
Notwithstanding, they generally have Bread enough for themselves and Plenty of Flesh of various kinds, and great Abundance
of Herring of which they bring in sometimes to the value of from 3
to 500 pound per Night. The Produce of the Isle is cheap, but their
Imports are Dear and their Trade almost gone since the Island was
sold.

There are lately opened a Lead and a Copper Mine that promise
well and will I hope turn to Advantage to the Duke of Athol who
otherwise does not draw £2,000 per Annum from it instead of near
£10,000 that it yielded to him in the Days of Yore. There are several
gentlemen on the Island who have estates that yield one half of
what he has from the whole, and the greatest Number of the
Farmers have the property of their own Farms for ever paying the
Duke only a kind of Feu Duty.

On this Island are 4 Towns all lying on the sea coast. Ramsy
towards the North East has nothing Remarkable. Douglas, on the
East, is the largest and fitted for Trade, but in Decay like the Rest.
Castletown in the South is the seat of government. In it stands
Castle Rushen the Norwegian Palace: Large, Dark, high, well built
of rough hewn grey Limestone. It is surrounded with a Ditch and

Rampart within which are the Barracks and courts of Justice. The House of Kees, or Members of Parliament is without. Peel is on the west side, near it is a small Island on a Rock that contained a Cathedral, the Bishop's Palace, a seminary of Learning, a Prison and a number of other buildings now in Ruins. Each Town has a kind of Harbour but none of them good. The only good one in the Island is Derby Haven, but they never improved or built upon it.

Near Peel is Tinwald where the King or his governor convened the People at Certain Period, to consult the Interest of the Nation. It is a small artificial Hill, consisting of 4 different steps. The King or his Representatives on the Top, and the subjects on the Different steps or Flats around him, the first in Rank next him and so on to the Bottom. They say it is a Norwegian word signifying an Inclosed Places. But as the Original Inhabitants must have had some such place before the Norwegians knew it, and as there is an old Tinwald to the Northward of the Modern one, I suspect it is rather a celtic or galic word derived from Teine Fire and Bal, a Name the Celts gave to the sun, to whom they offered sacrifices on the tops of Mountains and particularly on Important occasions like this convention of the States. In the galic Fire of Bal would write Teine Bhail and sound Teine val or Teighn vail. How easily this might be corrupted into Tinwald is quite obvious. This conjecture is also supported by our Baltein or Beathuin, a Feast now kept by the Herds only on May day when the sun approaches and his genial Heat Cheers the Face of Nature. Both consist of the Same Radical words and Differ only in the order they are placed in.

The Language of the Island is a Dialect of the Scots Galic to this day, which, (considering that we are separated from each other for 1,600 years at least) Differs surprising little and that little consists mainly in the Pronounciation. A Highlander would soon be master of it. They still Preach and Plead in galic, have translated several Books into it and are now translating more. I got a copy of most of them from their worthy Good Bishop who tho' an elderly man before he left England knows a deal of the Language. There is no great Difficulty in understanding them, tho' they differ in their orthography from us and the Irish.

Bad Season

Alexander to Patrick, from Dunollie, 24th April, 1782

We have had a very cold, dry, parch'd Season for man and beast, no vegitation of any kind. Black cattle holds it out surprisingly in this country, but if provinder is all gone I am obliged to enter upon the Hay Stack.

Alexander to Patrick, 6th May, 1782

The weather is such here that everything will go to ruin. I durst not as yet stir a beast from their winter Quarters, they'll starve where they are and sending them to the Muirs is not better.

Duncan is a sufferer in Glenketellan by the loss of sheep, and the horses there will not do after my trouble and expence in bringing them here in time of the great snow, and since they were returned they are so much reduced that we were obliged to send equale to four Bolls white oats for them. The foals dye as they are dropt with cold and hunger. Your Brother dares not stir a beast for England as usual, they would starve upon the Road. My Byred cows and stirks are weel as still I have plenty to give them, a remainder of Provender I do not expect for as I am certain I'll have no out pasture for them, lett the weather answer never so weel, for four weeks to come.

Family Piper

Duncan to Patrick, April 1782

My father is just by me and has his Young Piper playing to him in the passage, to whom he seems reconciled and desires when you return to Breadalbane that you apply to Glenlyon to get him for some time with his piper. If Glen. agrees to this know from the Piper upon what terms he would receive a rising Genius of his own profession for a year or two. My Father desires to acquaint your Maxwell that a Piper must always be of her Household and hopes she'll Contribute to the Expence of his Education.

Infanticide?

Alexander to Patrick, from Dunollie, May 1782

There was Munday last ane Infant child found burried in the sand at Oban side of my March Dyke at Corran; the moyr [mother] is taken up and sent to Inverery. She owned her bringing to the world the Child but that it was still born. She was servant maid to the old Lady Dunstaffnage and a Collonsay woman, this is the second Instance of the kind in my memorie in this country.

Alexander to Patrick, April 1791. Copy of Advertisement enclosed.

Sale of Black Cattle

There is to be sold by Publick Roup at Dunollie in Argyleshire upon the 11th day of May next the stock of Black Cattle upon the said lands and Soroba consisting of Tydie or Milk Cows, Farrow

Cows, 4, 3, and 2 year old Hyfers and stirks, 3 and 2 year old Stots [bullocks] and Stirks [heifers] and several good Bulls. There are few Stocks of black Cattle on the West Coast of Argyllshire of a more fashionable stamp and they as wish to plant their Grounds with a Breeding Stock will not easily meat with a better oppertunity of being served in a true Breed. Trust till Martimas on Good Securitie or discount of 5 pr cent for readie money.

Shipwreck

Alexander to Patrick from Dunollie, 12th January 1796

Since Sat. last was little rest upon this coast from Luing to the extreme point of Lismore, the coast of Mull from Cregan to Duart gathering the wreak of a Liverpool outward-bound to the West Indes loaded with a cargo of dray goods suitable for the West Indian Market such as soap, candles, butter and immense quantities of muslins of all kinds, cloaks, shoes, boots, medicines.

She was broak at the entrance to Loch Speil: yr [there] was a vast number of boats for severall days gathering part of the cargo floating upon the surface of the sea betwixt all the way from Easdale to the point of Dowart and great quantities were cast ashore all of which has been pilfered by the people . . . My Kerrera Ladies will be so decked wt muslin I'll not know them. What of the wreak came ashore the people picked up in the night time with lantrons . . .

5th February 1796

We have had a Justice peace Court at Oban these 10 or 12 days . . . deponing [taking evidence from] the people that was thought to have a part of what was thrown a shore, got floating upon the surface of the sea, or drag'd out of the wreak.

The tennants of Kerrera were . . . willing to give upon oath what they got or had in there custodie ych [which] would not be received unless they gave up what they know oyrs [others] got ych they would not do, they were ordered to be sent to Inverery [the County Jail was at Inveraray] which accordingly was done with a party. But the Judges thought proper to send ane express after them and return them.

12th February 1796

The Oban Congress only broak up yesterday after being together 14 days. They will collect a great deal of goods. Sandie Cadelton at Inverery has got a power from the owners to be sole manager of the whole of the subjects recovered. The Ferryman's servant at Port Kerrera was impris'd in a Garet in Oban, and fettered for being unrulie and sent from Oban for Inverery under a Guard of

the Volunteers and still fetter'd . . . but returned. You'll inform Mrs
Mac that I employed Mrs John Stevenson to purchase a piece of
muslin for her, and ane oyr for Bess MacDowell, at the Oban Roup
of the goods saved of the wreak.

PATRICK

1742-1825

Patrick MacDougall, 24th Chief (1801-1825)
(also known as Peter)

PATRICK, 1742-1825 *m* LOUISA MAXWELL CAMPBELL, 1782

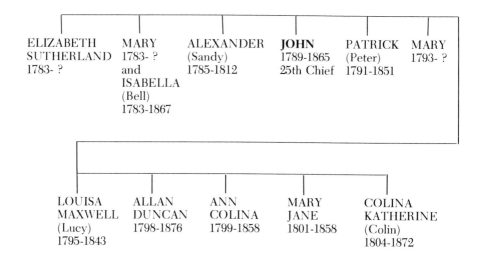

ELIZABETH
SUTHERLAND
1783- ?

MARY
1783- ?
and
ISABELLA
(Bell)
1783-1867

ALEXANDER
(Sandy)
1785-1812

JOHN
1789-1865
25th Chief

PATRICK
(Peter)
1791-1851

MARY
1793- ?

LOUISA
MAXWELL
(Lucy)
1795-1843

ALLAN
DUNCAN
1798-1876

ANN
COLINA
1799-1858

MARY
JANE
1801-1858

COLINA
KATHERINE
(Colin)
1804-1872

The family of Patrick

His father: Alexander, 23rd Chief, married Mary Campbell, died 1801.

His mother: Mary, third daughter of Patrick Campbell of Barcaldine. She married Patrick in 1737 and died in 1782.

His wife: Louisa Maxwell Campbell, born 1761, daughter of Campbell of Achallader. She married Patrick in 1782 and died in 1841.

The children

Elizabeth Sutherland: died at nine months.

Mary and Isabella (Bell): twins. Mary died young. Bell eloped in 1810 with Neil, the son of her uncle Duncan, Ardentrive. He was killed fighting in Spain in 1813, leaving her with a son, Neil, and daughter, Louisa (Missie). Bell died in 1867.

Alexander (Sandy): was in the Army and was killed at the storming of Ciudad Rodrigo, Spain, in 1812.

John: succeeded as 25th Chief in 1825. He joined the Navy at thirteen. In 1826 he married Elizabeth Sophia Timmins, daughter of Captain Timmins of the East India Company. He became an Admiral, and was knighted. He died in 1865.

Patrick (Peter): went into the Army and reached the rank of Colonel. He died unmarried in 1851.

Mary: died young.

Louisa Maxwell (Lucy): died unmarried in 1843

Allan Duncan: became a W.S. in Edinburgh and died unmarried in 1876.

Ann Colina: married Patrick Campbell of Baliveolan in 1827. He died in 1830, leaving a son, Donald. In 1840 Ann married George Lock: they had a daughter, Louisa.

Mary Jane: married Charles Monro in 1827 and lived at Ingsdon, Devon. She had several children and died in 1858.

Colina Katherine (Colin): died unmarried in 1872.

4

Patrick

Patrick, like his father, was no adventurer, and his concerns were peaceful and domestic. His adult life, almost until he became chief at the age of sixty, was spent in Edinburgh following a legal career. What emerges from the letters is a fascinating picture of his change in character after he settled at Dunollie. Described by both his father and his son as having led a somewhat dissolute life in the city — indeed, driving his father almost to distraction with his extravagance — Patrick now became unsociable and frugal to a fault. His strict economy, tiresome as it was to his protesting family, did, however, help to leave the estate in a less tottering financial state when he died, than it had been in for some time. His independence of mind had prevented him from following the current fashion of apeing the lifestyle of the English gentry, without sufficient means.

Patrick, like his father before him, seems to have been an affectionate if somewhat heavy-handed father.

He was born in Dunollie Castle on 19th June, 1742, the fourth child of Alexander (Alastair Dubh) and Mary Campbell of Barcaldine. The family pattern of infants at the time of his arrival was girl, boy, girl, boy and there were eleven more babies to come. Three years after Patrick's birth, the family, now increased by two more infants, moved to the new house built by Alexander below the Castle.

There is no mention of Patrick as a child in the surviving letters, except that his occasional childhood ailments are indicated on the doctor's bills by such entries as 'to Patty a dose of purging powders'; 'to Patty a vomiter'; 'to Patty eye water and eye salve'; and 'to Patty a blistering plaister'.

During his childhood Patrick is said to have been fostered in Morvern by a man of the name of MacCulloch, who had formerly been a miller near Oban. There is no mention of this among the letters, but Lord Archibald Campbell mentions it in his book *The Records of Argyll* (1885):

> The child was reared for several years in this family where he would hear no language but Gaelic, or see manners other than

those of the Highland peasantry. When the time arrived for his return home MacCulloch sent him with 13 head of cattle, including a bull, on condition that the father would add an equal number of them to form a stock for his son. When they were landed at Port Mor, below the Castle, MacDougall was highly gratified.

Patrick's life, as far as the letters record it, can be divided in two: the years in Edinburgh as a Writer to the Signet (W.S.), and his life at Dunollie, where in 1798, at the age of fifty-six, he joined his father.

Patrick in Edinburgh

It was in 1776, when Patrick was thirty-three, that news of the death of his elder brother John came from India. Patrick was now the heir and his father wrote to him: 'My dear Patrick, your Burthen is now, as my eldest son, much More than being as you was. The appearance of a subject [estate] to inherite is good, and I flatter myself you'l endeavour in all respects to use your endeavour to regulate your conduct in all respects worthie to represent your Brother in holding the greatest reguard for this place, family and dependents.'

Alexander also told Patrick he must get married: 'You are now to your shame 33, Grey Haired, Bauld headed without either grace wife or married children [children of a marriage] tho I know there are others in abundance to your Honour be it said.'

This letter had no immediate effect, but from a letter written four years later by Patrick's brother Duncan, it is clear that the family were still concerned:

> 18th April, 1780
> I am sorry you seem to despond in the Scheme we were talking of, at the same time it surprises me that in such a wide field you cannot please yourself, the more especially as there is some sort of necessity for it, it is a shame for you. I do assure you the longer you postpone that affair you'l find yourself the more indifferent about it. However you may do as you think proper. But I think its extraordinary if you can't find one with 3 or 4,000 gns. otherwise to you mind that will venture to pass her life with you. But if your Belly was less than it is, which it will never be till you eat and drink less than you do, you would not find the matter so difficult.

Unfortunately, although Patrick was not doing well in his profession, he had involved himself in Edinburgh's lively social life, and so needed to ask his father for money. Alexander was displeased:

> Your letter ... has given me a picture of your situation that

Portrait of Louisa Maxwell (1761-1841), wife of Patrick

amusement at Edinburgh has been dear bought, so very dear that I
wish it may not end in our mutual ruin.

It is idle for you to mention to me in the jocular way you do that
Company is either inducible to health or Business, nor can I
conceive, or is it possible, that any man can attend to Business and
Company at the same time ... I am 63 in tollerable good healthe
which I very much impute to the strict Regime I have observed all
along, do you follow my example both health and business will
flow upon you.

From the letters it seems that Patrick and Duncan were very close.
When Duncan eloped in 1781 and was suffering from guilt and remorse
at upsetting his parents, Patrick gave him much support.

Duncan wrote: 'How can I ever, my dear Patrick, repay my debt to
you on this occasion. Your conduct throughout the whole affair has been
such as scarce can be instanced. I can only say that while I retain my
senses I shall with gratitude remember your kindness.'

In another letter he expressed his feelings even more charmingly:
'The consolation of a Friend's advice is the most Comfortable refreshment I ever met with but when I meet with the advice of Brother joined
with that of a Friend in the same person it gives that sort of relief to me
that I may say saved me from distraction.'

Next year Patrick himself took a wife, Louisa Maxwell (never
referred to as Louisa, but as Maxwell or Louisa Maxwell). A daughter of
Campbell of Achallader, she was twenty, half Patrick's age, and judging
from her letters, became a woman of character. Her portrait shows a
mischievious twinkle in her eye, which is borne out by the traditional
story of how she threw their first-born baby out of a top window,
shouting 'catch' to Patrick who was standing below. Patrick with a
frantic effort caught it, only to discover that what he thought was his
precious child was just a bundle of shawls. He was not amused so the
story goes. Maybe the fact that his bride was so much younger
accounted for their different ideas of humour.

Patrick's father was disappointed that the Bride had not brought a
larger dowry. However, his son refused to be bullied beyond a certain
point, and justified himself in a letter written a few months after the
wedding: 'My marrying was your constant theme, to please you I did, so
you say you were disappointed in money, it is true more might be got
but you must allow I was to live with the Woman and not you'.

A long and angry correspondence soon ensued between them. Alexander insisted that he could not give the financial support that his son
now demanded, Patrick accused his father of breaking promises of help
made at the time of the wedding. Alexander has painted a harrowing

picture of his son trying to starve him in the 'decline of life', Patrick has painted one of his wife and children being starved, and he himself being allowed by his father 'to rot in a debtors Dungeon' if money was not forthcoming.

Patrick wrote to his father: 'I do not know but it was the most grievous circumstance of my life my brother's Death. It certainly was so far so that it appears the unnatural misunderstanding betwixt you and him seem to be transferred to me, for what cause God knows unless it is ordained that whomsoever is your representative [heir] must have your displeasure.'

After the correspondence had been going on for some time, Patrick's two brothers, Duncan and Sandie, joined the argument. Realising to what length matters would go unless their brother showed more respect, they wrote in alarm to warn him of his danger.

In November 1782 Sandie wrote: 'You in my humble opinion write him [their father] unkindly ... Now my dear Patrick in this you are certainly wrong, there is great allowances should be made for an old man and particularly for a parent. The case is literally this ... he will strip you to the last penny ... nor will he allow you a penny while he lives ... I would by all means recommend writing your father a kind letter.'

Duncan then added his persuasions:

I have perused the foregoing letter as also the letter you wrote your father on the same subject, likewise one you wrote him formerly ... which by the by, was not more impudent than it was indelicate. I should reckon myself deficient of my duty to my Father and you did I not suggest to you both what appears to me will inevitably be the Consequence of your Discords — utter ruin. By the humour he appears to be in at present you may depend upon it you'll be Stript of all that is possible and tho' I may naturally expect some share of the Spoils I don't wish to enjoy them without attempting to put you on the right Track. By this I mean that you should be more Condescending to his requests.

After this the relationship between Patrick and his father seems to have improved and the letters take on a more genial tone.

Early in 1783 Patrick's first child was born, Elizabeth Sutherland. There was great rejoicing, for at forty-one Patrick was said to have married 'late'. His friends and relations seem to have been nervous as to whether or not his marriage would produce offspring. His brother-in-law wrote: 'To be free with you this same Proof of your prowess was more than many of your friends expected, but you have been lucky in getting a fendy wife.'

Patrick's sister Mary, who had married MacNeil of Oronsay, wrote:

Pincushion for a first baby, Elizabeth Sutherland, daughter of Patrick and Louisa Maxwell, who died in 1783 aged nine months

'When you are Blessed with half a score of Daughters you will then think what a Follie it was in you to marry at your advanced time of life.'

(As it happened, Patrick and his wife only missed by two the predicted half score of daughters. Of their eight girls, not all of whom survived, the last was born when Patrick was sixty-two.)

At nine months old Elizabeth Sutherland died of smallpox. There is still a rather touching memento of her kept in the Family. It is a pincushion, with her own and her parents' initials, the date, a heart and the words 'Sweet Baby' all picked out in pins.

Patrick's friends and relations sent letters of condolence on the death of his 'amiable child', which were, as was the custom of the day, more full of advice than sympathy. 'God giveth' they wrote, 'and God taketh away, there is nothing in this world to be depended upon so we should all be resigned.'

A brother-in-law wrote: 'I hope you have more sense than to be Cast Down for a misfortune that you know Poor Mortals are always liable to.' He went on to say in effect that if the bereaved parents didn't die themselves they could soon replace the child.

This was written in October and in November Patrick wrote of his wife: 'She is very big and unweildy more so than a week before her last delivery, at present she thinks she has upwards of two months to go.' On 16th December twin girls were born to Louisa Maxwell and so Elizabeth Sutherland was more than replaced.

Duncan wrote to Patrick: 'I am happy to understand that Mrs MacDougall is in so good a way and that the little things are thriving, yet their life is very precarious, the loss of them is less to be regretted when they are Young and that the Mother is safe. I think my friend you have not much to say now against me for getting Daughters. I dare say the next Birth will be three Daughters.'

Duncan's pessimism was only partly justified: one of the twins, Mary, died young. But Isabella (Bell) lived to the age of 85!

Patrick's father was disappointed and in one letter he is reported to have said that he'd far rather it had been one son than two daughters. However it wasn't long before he was comforted by the arrival of a grandson who was named after him, but was to be known to the family as Sandy.

Patrick continued to lament his poverty, and wrote to Alexander: 'The only means that now appears to me at present to save our subject is leaving Edinburgh with my family and residing with you ... A man servant and a horse is all I want at my own command and a reasonable allowance for my wife and also for pocket money and clothes.'

Alexander's answer unfortunately does not survive, but can be imagined: Patrick remained in Edinburgh.

The following year, however, his father wrote suggesting another solution:

13th July, 1787

I am of opinion you are not ignorant of your situation that it is absolutely necessary for you to put all irons in the fire to endeavour to procure something or other that will assist your living in your present situation; you should likewise consider that my funds are exhausted one way or other. There is for certain a Custom House to be erected at Tobermorie in Mull, being a collector there would be no despicable affair, if it would suit your wife in any degree you should lose no time in making all the interest in your power ... there is ane oyr office spoak of in this country it is a Sherrif Substitute in Mull and ane oyr in Isla and each to have fifty pound sterling.

Patrick, however, stayed in Edinburgh, and his letters continued to be peppered with gloomy prophecies of starvation and financial ruin, reaching their zenith rather pompously with: 'I have faught the Battle keenly and long but I fear at last that I shall be overcome which may happen to the Bravest.' It is puzzling to note that during this period he was living in no modest dwelling, but in Lady Stair's House, a large and elegant house in the Old Town which is now a museum. When it was put up for sale in 1825 by a subsequent owner it was described as 'that large Dwelling house sometime belonging to the Dowager Countess of Stair situated at the entrance to the earthen mound.' [The Mound, as it is now called, runs up the hill from Princes Street to the Royal Mile.]

It was just before Patrick left this house in 1787 that an incident took place which shocked the family. Duncan, who was farming at home on the Island of Kerrera, wrote to Patrick of their brother Sandie and his wife:

> It was only since I returned here I came to the knowledge of the Skirmish that happened in Lady Stair's Close about a month after I left Edinburgh. It is a hard case if Poor Sandie must, in Consequence of the Connection he has made, fall out with all his nearest friends . . . Even suppose my wife being perfectly Guilty of what was alledged — behaving with Insolence and offering Indignities to Mrs MacDougall [Sandie's wife] — it was not a proper Mode of Correction for a Woman in her Situation [she was pregnant] to Bully her with Clenched Fist to her Teeth . . .
>
> [Duncan went on to describe how he thought the incident should have been handled.] In short whether my Wife was to Blame or not her correction was beyond what was necessary and should the ladies have differed upon any point he [Sandie] should have allowed themselves to settle it, or write me it was necessary they should part for peace sake. This I would have managed without it being known to any Mortale but you, himself and me. But when all the servants in the House were perfectly acquainted with the dirty Broil it must soon have reached the ears of the Publick. I am tired of this dirty subject, I shall never mention it again on paper.

After leaving Lady Stair's House, Patrick and his family moved to the New Town to a house (now demolished) in Thistle Street, which one of the sons described later as a genteel residence. It was bought by Lady Gordon when the family left it.

Duncan did his best to supply Patrick and his fast growing family with country produce: 'My wife is just now very throng gutting a Turkey and a pair of fflowls for you, they were only killed this day but I think by the jolting upon Hugh Bane's Back, joined to the Heat of his body by walking, you'll find them pretty tender by the time he Arrives in Edinburgh.'

'My wife sets out tomorrow morning for Glasgow,' he said in another letter, 'and is to carry with her a pair of Fowls, some ffresh butter in a white iron Jug and a Turkey which she will forward to you by Gabriel Watson the Carrier. I think the Turkey large and will probably Scruple the Carriage of it, at any rate you will receive the Fowl and Butter. My wife desires to inform you that she sent you by another Conveyance this day week 9 prints of ffresh Butter in a stone Mug and about 15 days ago 4 small rolls of Butter in a Box which she hopes went safe.'

In March 1786 Duncan wrote to Patrick:

> I hear you and Mrs Mac. are to come to this Country so soon as the season is over. I am happy to hear it as Mrs MacDougall will before then have finished her Nursing. I think she may spend a considerable part of her time here. I have this day put up a good Large Pig to be fattened. I hope he'll be fit for the Hot water by the time you arrive. I have a sow that I think will in the Course of a few days produce a strong Family of Pigs. I have plenty of Fat hens and Lean Geese, Potatoes without measure, but if you insist for Mutton you must apply to the Old Gentleman [their father]. I have not yet finished my Bill of Fare, I have got a fresh stock of Capital Whisky which will intoxicate you into Drunkeness and not a headache in a Tun of it, and small ales as good as ever was tipt.

'There is shipped on board the sloop Dunstaffnage, bound for Leith,' he told Patrick on another occasion, 'for your use one Barrel containing Oatmeal and half Barrel Containing Excellent whisky and a Cheese weighing one stone weight (16 lbs to the stone). My mother desires that you return the half Barrell with a good Biscuit and the little Keg empty, as its very usefull in the house and can be of no service to you.'

While Duncan took the trouble to send Patrick food, Patrick was always willing to do shopping for him in Edinburgh.

> You are such a good hand in the Line of Commissions [Duncan wrote] that it would be a pity not to employ you in that way, and I dare say you would take it ill if I employ'd anybody else. Therefore I wish you to send Cloth for a pair of Riding Breeches of the best and strongest kind. I find flimsie low priced stuffs don't stand me one journey decent. It will occur to you to send all the necessary furniture. I likewise want a decent Riding Vest, pretty dark in Colour and of the very best Woollen Stuff, with Buttons and other furniture. You know my mode of dress is different from people in Town for I'm always best drest when on Horse Back, by this you'll Guess the Stuff that suits me. I find the best stuffs become Cheapest to me in the end.

There were further requests:

I hinted to you before you left the country that in course of the season I should wish to have a piece of cloath to make me a wearing, half short, half long coat. The last you sent me was the very best I ever had, but now its beginning to break in different places. Send me any durable colour you please but send as much cloath as will face the coat and make lapells. You'll observe that I mean to have Buttons of the cloath which of course will consume the more. Send silk thread, linning for the sleeves, Buckrum etc and direct the parcel to the care of Mr Gilvary to be forwarded by the Oban Carriers.

I wish you would take the trouble of endeavouring to find me amongst the Goldsmiths ½ a dozen of second hand silver table spoons. You know I have but a dozen and when there are 3 or 4 people here besides my own family some body must want a spoon or there will be none for Gravy or any other purpose. If you fall in with them they will be got nearly for the price of Silver Bullion. Get any mark that may be upon them neatly erased and cause put the Crest and motto in its stead which is all I have upon my own spoons. I am plagued with the Breaking of Chrystal salts and at this moment I have but 2 remaining. Will you let me know what I could get 4 Good Silver Salt pits for.

Two years later Duncan was in need of a greatcoat.

Will you remember to carrie me home as much Green and White plaid of the Sheppard kind as will make me a Great Coat. Straight bodied and a velvet neck of the same colour, and as many hair Buttons as will be necessary and green tape of the same colour. This you'll think a most uncommon Garb but I think it will be light and comfortable in the summer time. [Later he mentioned that seven yards were needed.]

Then came an urgent plea:

I am almost naked, you must Credite me with some strong kind of Cotton stuff for Breeches. I think a drab Coloured Corderoy such as you see Collensay wear is the most durable of any, a dark Drab colour is the best. I'm equally in want of all other Articles of body cloathes but I think I shall leave them alone till May or June, but by all means send me the Breeches by Hugh Bane, otherwise I may keep my bed.

Duncan's wife wrote to Patrick's wife with her own request: 'If this overtakes the sending of the Box please take the trouble of sending me a 100 needles of different sizes, a pound of pins and a paper of Tiffney pins and a plain edition of Sherlock upon Death.'

In 1795, when Duncan joined the Breadalbane Fencibles serving in Ireland during the Revolutionary War, his requests for clothing were of a different kind.

> 9th April, 1795
>
> Upon a new Arrangement of our Regimentals the Bonnet is laid aside and small Hats like Horsemen's Helmets substitute in their place with a Bear Skin over the crown of it and a Yellow Feather on the one side, a narrow silver lace binding and a silver cord and tassel round the crown below and above a Cockade of course. . . . ? [page torn] on the North Bridge furnishes them, you will see the Pattern at the shop. My reason for saying anything to you about it is that it will, from the largeness of my Caput, be a difficult matter to find a Hat what will fit me. To obviate that as much as possible I have on the other side given you the Exact diameter of a Hat that will fit me, and you'll take the trouble of procuring me one of that size.
>
> The Bear skins are black, let mine be of the best quality, I mean the Bear skin as black as possible. When the Bear skins are not of the best they loose the hair in a very short time and become useless, but when they are of the best I am told they will serve for 2, sometimes 3, Hats. You will direct the whole trimming.
>
> It will be necessary that you get a Box made for it to convey it here safely. You know the least friction would destroy it completely. I wish to have it as soon as possible that I may appear in it at the Inspection.
>
> You may send me a Couple of Pairs plain Raw Silk Stockings and two pair Cotton. If you send the Cotton ones ribbed let them be of the smallest ribs you can possibly get, and if you can't get them of that Description send them plain ... The stockings may come in the Hat Box which dispatch immediately by the quickest and surest Conveyance.

Nearly three months later Duncan wrote: 'I have received my Hat, the hat is a most ridiculous piece of dress but it will catch the Eye and that is enough.'

At the end of the year he wrote again: 'Lord Breadalbane has now agreed at the application of the Regt that we should assume the Highland Dress and has given direction accordingly for next year's Cloathing. Will you let me know what the price of Tartan hose stockings is at Edinburgh.'

However, during the next year his request was for something which didn't sound like Highland dress: 'You'll send me as much Scarlet cloath of the best quality from Mason and Thomson on the Bridges as will make me a Regimental Coat and as much white cloath as will make me a vest and pair of Breeches.'

With all Duncan's concern about his own clothes in Ireland, he didn't forget the ladies he had left behind. Whether he was being as tactful as he thought is questionable!

> Give my sincere good wishes to Mrs MacDougall when you write her and tell her I have purchased 3 Poplin Gowns, 1 for her, 1 for Dr Peter's [Gallanach] wife, and 1 for my own Lady. They are all of the same pattern to prevent jealousy among the Ladies. But God knows how I'm to transport them to Scotland, I fancy they must remain till I go myself for I can get nobody to venture on them for fear of seizure. However they will be New Gowns whenever they arrive.

Meanwhile, because of the war, food was becoming more expensive every year in Scotland. Patrick wrote to his father in 1798: 'The coarsest bit of Butcher's meat that last year cost me 3d. pr. lb is now 5d. and bread is rising fast so that I must somehow borrow a little more money or starve for there is no alternative. So much for being forced to live here. Adieu, this is an unpleasant subject.'

Patrick at Dunollie

In 1798 Patrick and his family moved to Dunollie to take over the management of the estate from his father, now eighty-five. Alexander, despite having long looked on his son as extravagant and pleasure-loving, had decided that the time had come to hand over. He died three years later.

When Patrick succeeded his father in 1801 he had eight surviving children, with one more to come. Four were boys and four girls, of the following ages: Bell eighteen, Sandy sixteen, John twelve, Peter ten, Lucy six, Allan three, Ann two, and Mary Jane who had been born that year.

Much of the correspondence of the time, and for years to come, was on education, settling the boys into careers and, once that was done, trying to get them promotion.

In the eighteenth century Patrick and his brothers had attended the local school before going away to finish their education. (Dr Sandie's school bill came in from the local shop, and was sandwiched in between '5 pints of the best tar and a boll of meal'. It came to forty shillings for the year.) Now, however, Patrick was to employ tutors to teach his boys. This was becoming a fashion among the local lairds, but in Patrick's case he may have been influenced by the following letter from Duncan:

31st December, 1795
My wife sends Sandie to Mr Warwell's who has a good teacher for

his own children. Indeed there was a necessity for his leaving
Oban for the Villain McFarlan (the Minister schoolmaster) Beat
the poor Boy most unmercifully. I would not regret his whiping his
Backside but he cut his head frequently with a Ruler in so much
that he has almost lost his whole hair. Did you ever know anything
more Barbarous for, laying aside any partiality one can suppose on
my side, he is one of the most inoffensive Creatures in the World.

But tutors do not seem to have been a success and Patrick later wrote
to his son John: 'You and Peter suffered much from private teachers in
the Country of which I repent greatly.'

A naval officer wrote of John at the age of thirteen: 'I am sorry to find
he is so very backward in his education, his Tutors could not have done
him any justice as he cannot work a common sum in the rule of three.'

John was the first of the children to be settled in a career. In 1800
Patrick had written to a cousin, Captain Patrick Campbell, when John
was eleven: 'My second son John, since he could almost speak showed a
strong inclination to go to sea and still continues in that Opinion.'

Captain Campbell replied:

> I receiv'd yours of the 1st and am sorry to say it has not yet been in
> my power to get your son a situation there are so very few ships at
> present in commission and so many young men who have serv'd
> during the war out of employ that it is a very hard matter to get any
> one appointed especially who has not before been at sea. I have
> however got one of my friends to keep the first vacancy that
> should happen for him, in the mean time he should be going on
> with his navigation.

Two years later Patrick received an urgent message from Captain
Campbell, telling him to send John south immediately, in order to join
H.M.S. Cruizer, a brigg. The following year, 1803, the Napoleonic War
broke out, so John was soon involved in battle.

Meanwhile, Patrick was trying to get Sandy into the Army.
Commissions at that time had to be bought and D. MacDougall, an
Army Agent in London, wrote to Patrick.

'I was in hopes of being able to procure a cheap Ensigncy for Mr
Alexander, but after all my endeavours I cannot procure one under
£380 — and indeed there are very few to be had under £400 in old
Regiments stationed at home, Ensigncys in Corps stationed in the West
Indies sells for £300. gns.'

Of Patrick's suggestion of an ensigncy in the Foot Guards Mr
MacDougall wrote: 'the heavy expenses you would be at in order to
support Mr MacDougall as other Ensigns are would cost you in a few

years as much as would purchase him a Company in a Regiment of the line. The Guards are not so desirable as they formerly were.'

At this time Sandy was studying in Edinburgh and boarding with the family man of business, John Young, who wrote to Patrick:

6th April 1803

You will expect I should make some remarks on Sandy now that I know him, and without meaning to flatter you, or to say one word I do not think, I cannot resist congratulating you upon having such an excellent and superior young man for a son, superior to any I ever knew. He has a great portion of natural and useful sense, he has a prodigious stock of intelligence from observation, he is assiduous in his studies to acquire knowledge, he is obliging and sweet tempered, he is funny, jocular, and shrewd in conversation, he has no ill habits of any kind that I can discover, he wishes to appear like a Gentleman without any extravagant ideas, he is shocked by every kind of profligacy and idle folly, in short he does everything with a consideration and wisdom that would do credit to the most experienced, all of which is truth as god made me.

With regard to Sandy's board I am not inclined to take anything, but if you will not be beheld to me for that we can fix something for it at any time. No person could give less disturbance in a house than he does, nor could any body be easier to please, of which he himself will reap the benefit if he is ever upon a Campaign. The Army is a poor business and will every day become less in repute, yet Highlandmen do contrive to get forward in it.

Soon after this Sandy joined the Army. John Young wrote a warning to Patrick: 'You must lay your account with doubling his pay while an ensign. I hold it to be absolutely impossible for the most carefull to live near like a gentleman in a moving army upon single pay.'

The following year Sandy — by now in the 69th Regiment — became a Lieutenant and soon after was writing to his father of buying a captaincy which was for sale for £500.

7th September, 1804

Although the sum no doubt is very inconvenient for you at present still I have no doubt but you will agree to the measure, as a step of that kind to me at present would be of the greatest Consequence for my future advancement, and would throw me entirely off your over burthan'd shoulders ... I am very sensible of the low state of your finances at present and Confident of the difficulty it will be your giving such a sum ... I am happy to hear you never had so good a season and I hope the crops will turn out as well. Do you think the Cows look as if they would get me a company? I am sorry to hear you have got your hands in mortar, it will be a barrier in my way — but you were very much in want of a new stable.

Nothing seems to have come of this and a few months later Sandy wrote again suggesting a company costing £950. Nothing came of this either, although Patrick said he would try and borrow the money.

Sandy wrote from Horsham, where his regiment was now stationed:

> Since our arrival here we are informed that we are on our way for Jersey. We thought we were to remain here all winter however we are going to a better Quarter for a soldier where I understand a doz of good port wine can be got for 12/- and famous at 18/- instead of this place where the only good house in the whole town, alth'o its one of the County towns, is the Jail any room of which is far superior to the best room of our Barracks.
>
> You cannot conceive the expence that officers are liable to in travelling through England, the March here of three days came to near £3 when we paid for dinner and wine each day at an average of 12/- and 2/6 for breakfast.

Sandy had a three day march from Horsham to Portsmouth, where he was very impressed by the fortifications: 'the strength of which surprised me much together with their extent, also the Docks where they make Cables, anchors etc. In fact I saw the first navy arsinal in the World.'

Having arrived in Jersey he wrote to Patrick:

> 9th December, 1804
> We are sent to the most disagreeable part of Jersey, nearest to the coast of France. It is so near that with the assistance of a Prospect Glass I saw yesterday the french troops upon a sand beach and taking away pieces of a Gun boat that was driven ashore some weeks ago by our Cruisers. We were inspected yesterday by General Gordon who seemed highly pleased with the appearance we made so much so that he intends to send us to St Hillier, the chief town of the Island where he resides.

On Christmas Day, 1804, he wrote:

> Your letter of the 28th I received enclosing your letter to General Gordon ... I was engaged to dine with him upon the following Wednesday which day being very cold, he being much afflicted with the Gout, together with the dinner not being ready in time, and the house smoking, the old hero scarcely spoke a word to any person.
>
> We had a dreadful storm some days ago. It drove a 44 Gun ship, the Severn Commanded by the Duke of Bouillen on a rock in the centre of the Bay. We expected to see her go to pieces every minute as the sea Broke Compleatly over her and of course every soul must have perished before our eyes without being able to

render them any assistance. What made it more dreadful was we saw them hoist their best boat over and the moment it was out it was stove to pieces and several boats that we endevoured to get out to them were swamped. I foolishly went in one of them and got a most compleat ducking. However they at last succeeded in getting a boat to swim and brought 260 men, women and children ashore. When the tide began to flow, as it was then ebb, we expected she should go down but wonderful to say she was thrown off the rock and drifted ashore without any injury than her keel being broken off and full of water. There was not a life lost.

During this year the last member of the family was born, a girl christened Colina, but always known as Colin. Patrick was at the time trying to get his third son, Peter, started on a military career, and wrote to a friend, A. Ross:

30th April, 1804

I presume so much upon an old acquantance as to adress you on behalf of one of my sons to get him upon the list of Cadets at Woolwich, having a throng family I have used this freedom with you to solicit your good offices on behalf of my son Patrick [Peter] which I hope you will not deny me, flattering myself from the situation you hold in the Board of Ordanance you may accomplish my wish. His age is 13 years, my oldest boy is in the 69th Regt., my second a midshipman in Doris Frigate and I have another boy besides Patrick with several Daughters. All this is a serious Charge upon a small Highland property which I have retired to some years back.

Ross replied that he could not do anything until the boy had entered his fifteenth year and even then didn't think he had much influence.

In 1806 Sandy at last became a Captain. In March he wrote to his brother John from Peterhead: 'On 19th Dec. last I was thro' the interest of that worthy man the Duke of Argyll promoted to a company in the 72nd Regt. by purchase, on account of this I left Jersey ... I set out from Dunolly to join the 2nd batt. 72nd Regt. which are quartered here, a tollerable pleasant sea port town, in summer a great watering place. Take care of your health, apply yourself to such studies as will enlighten your mind and improve your profession.'

Sandy was not the only one to tell John, who had been engaged in battles at sea with French and Spanish ships, that he must keep on studying. Education for boys who joined the Navy at an early age could be almost non-existent, depending entirely on whether or not the ship had a schoolmaster on board. Patrick gave John the following advice:

15th June, 1806

I believe there may be some Teacher on board ... if so I entreat you to take every advantage of that kind that is in your power for, my dear Johnie, this is the greatest disadvantage you lye under, and although you are a Young Man of 17 years old, do not think of neglecting any opportunity for Improving yourself that may come in your way. Idle fools may Spurn and Ridicule these things but never mind their Remarks and nonsence for now or never is the time for you, and if you neglect the opportunity you'll repent it all your life. None is too old to learn.

The following year Patrick suffered a great blow: his brother Duncan died. Duncan had come out of the Army in 1802, after the short-lived peace with France had been signed, and had continued to farm on Kerrera. That year he and his family had gone to Skye, where he was to be factor to Lord MacDonald. Louisa Maxwell, writing to John, painted a rather macabre picture of the way they heard the news of Duncan's death.

The distressing account of your Uncle Duncan's Death arrived by his corpse landing at the shore, we only having heard the day before of his being Dangerously ill, his family had only gone to Skye this summer and had just been 5 weeks there when he died of a locked jaw of a few days illness, brought on by over fatigue being too fatiguing a business he had engaged in for a man of his time of life.

Patrick wrote: 'He has left a widow and 12 children and I am Deprived of my best friend and Brother.'

In 1808 Patrick succeeded in getting an Ensigncy for Peter in the 72nd Regiment, but this was not without strings. In January General Stuart, the Commanding Officer, wrote: 'The Usual Numbers of Volunteers procured from the Militia to obtain an Ensigncy is Twenty Five, if however your Friends in Argyleshire can prevail upon twenty to Volunteer for the 72nd I have not a doubt of His Royal Highness's appointing your son to an Ensigncy.'

In March General Stuart wrote again: 'I have the pleasure to Acquaint you that His Majesty has been pleased to appoint your son Patrick [Peter] to an Ensigncy in the 72nd Regiment under my Command. I hope your son will continue his exertions in getting men for the Regiment and that you and his other Friends will afford him your influence and support in promoting this desirable End, which may lead to further preferment.'

Patrick had evidently changed his mind about recruiting — a few years back, with regard to Sandy, he had written: 'I might be successful in getting some men for my son but for less than a Company I would not embark in so Disagreeable a business.'

Meanwhile John was doing well in the Navy. Patrick was getting good reports of him, and wrote encouragingly:

> Long may you continue to deserve the Esteem of your Superiors and all Ranks you Serve with: it convinces me you have paid attention to what I wished you to fulfill: to be Attentive to your Duty upon all Occasions and Submissive to your Commanders. I have likewise to remark with Satisfaction that you have Improved in your writing Spelling and Diction, in short you write much better in every particular and not so small as you used to do which spoiled your hand of writing.

Patrick was now considering the education of two more of his children: Allan, aged ten and his sister Lucy. Allan was sent to Perth. His father wrote 'Allan Goes soon for the Grammar school at Perth there being no good situation in this Country for his Education.' The following year Lucy, by now fourteen, was sent to a school kept by a Miss Jane Fraser in Edinburgh.

Lucy's school bill introduces a lighter aspect among the letters and conjures up a picture of a gay social life.

	£	s.	d.
Coach to and from the concert		1	
Bombazett for a Petticoat		10	
Chair to Lady Abercromby's Rout		1	6
Returning from do. at a late hour.		3	
Chair from Theatre with Miss McKay		2	6
Do. from Mrs Pattison's Rout.		1	3
Do. to & from Mrs Fergueson's		2	6
Hansels to servants, post, and beadle.		7	6
Hair dresser 1st practising		2	
1 pair Corsets	1	1	
Coach to and from Mrs Gordon's		2	6
Ticket to Theatre @ 4/- Coaches 1/-		5	
Flower and sash for practising	3	6	
Do. for breast 1/3 Sash 4/-	5	3	
Coach to and from the Ball		1	6
White beaver hat & feather	1	4	6
Cleaning a feather		1	6
Coach to and from Mrs Gilmour's		2	6

From this whirl of gaiety the bill moves on to 'carriage on a bag of nuts, 2/6' and then sobers up with the entry, 'seat in Church for 6 month, 6/-'.

The bill for Boarding and Instruction for the six months came to £20, additional charges being made for most subjects taught. In the section of the account headed Education it is interesting to note the item 'ticket to Ball'!

	£	s.	d.
6 months writing	2	8	
Do. French by a private teacher	3	3	
Do. English do.	3	3	
4 months Music	8	8	
3 months at 12/-	1	16	
Ticket to practisings		10	6
Ticket to Ball		10	
Needlework	1	1	
Use of Musical Ints.		10	6

Then came the amounts owed to various shops. The most expensive of the accounts is from an exclusive-sounding Habitmaker named Schultze for £7.13.6. The rest are from Apothecary, Dressmaker, Hairdresser, Milliner, Shoemaker, Stationer, Hosier and various Haberdashers.

The whole bill for everything, including education and board, comes to £80.11.4. Miss Fraser has added to the end of it a letter explaining why so much has been spent upon clothes:

> March, 1810
>
> Sir, I was favoured with your letter of the 26th & agreeable to your request have transmitted Miss Louisa's [Lucy's] Accotts. with the vouchers under 2 franks. The Accots. for cloathes may seem high but really they could not be wanted considering the many genteel familys she had occasion to pay visits to in the course of the winter. The Pillesse [mantle] in particular may appear so but this was got by the express orders of Capt. MacDougall and will turn out thrifty in the end as it will last her three winters.
>
> I flatter myself Miss Louisa is much improved since she came to town and I cannot help thinking that it would be attended with loss were she to be taken away too soon, but this entirely rests with you and her Mama. She is already so well provided in cloathes that very little addition will be required during the current quarter, and with regard to the schooling matters are so arranged that they can be given up at any time you please.
>
> I beg leave to offer my most respectful compliments to Mrs MacDougal & family and have the honour to be sir your much obliged humble servant Jane Fraser.

As expenses mounted, Patrick became infuriated with Peter's demands for more money. (Peter was now with his regiment in Ireland.) History was repeating itself, with the son demanding money from his father just as Patrick himself had done. Although in every generation money appears to have been in short supply, Patrick seems to have been more obsessed by the lack of it than anyone else. If he felt himself to be on the brink of starvation before succeeding to the property, he could not have felt much better after he had succeeded, when he was weighed down by the financial burdens of the estate, as well as by the needs of his very 'throng' family. The older he became the larger the spectre of ruin loomed. Worry, however, does not seem to have affected his health: in March 1806, when he was sixty-seven, his son Sandy wrote of him to his brother John:

> I am happy to say that he at present enjoys very good health and is surprisingly stout for a man of his time of life considering the dissipations of his youth and the crosses he met with in life.
>
> May God grant him still a long enjoyment of this transitory life and whoever shall happen to succeed him in the charge of the family may his footsteps be a trail for them to follow, or if it falls to my lot it is a great satisfaction for me to observe you all vying with each other in promoting the comfort of us all.

Patrick wrote to Peter's paymaster about his son's extravagance and received the following answer:

> 2nd January, 1809
>
> I am not aware that his pecuniary embarrassments proceed from any particular imprudence. The terms of the Regimental Mess at present are rather extravagant and such as an Ensign's pay cannot well afford, but I understand from his Brother Officers he incurs as little expense there as possible. If he does exceed at all in point of expense I can only account for it by his having for some time lodged with a Capt. Gregory of the Regiment who I believe is a young man of fortune and from the Guards where of course he could not learn much frugality.
>
> I have spoken to your son upon this subject and gave it as my opinion that however desirable it may be for a young man to keep the genteelist company he, I conceived, by living with Capt. Gregory must either subject himself to greater expense than he can afford, or else lie under obligations to him, neither of which are commendable but Patrick [Peter] assures me it is not the case.

Sandy visited Peter and wrote to John, who had not seen his brothers for seven years: 'Petter is with his Regt. at Belfast still an Ensign but I hope will soon be promoted, he is a very fine lad, not very quick but a good appearance, stout and good looking, rather handsome about 5ft 6inches, very fond of Dress, inclined to expense but I hope will become more prudent with years & I have no doubt but will make a good officer.'

But later in the year Peter's hopes of promotion were dashed. He wrote to Patrick:

> 9th August, 1809
>
> It is with painful feelings that I inform you of the loss of my

Lieutenency, however there is no help for it. I find the only way in the World is to content oneself and be always prepared for the worst, notwithstanding this disappointment I am advised by all my friends in the Regt. to lose no time in getting one in some other corps.

Dear father I hope you think it unnecessary for me to express the affection I have for you and I know it is your wish to do everything that is reasonable for me, still you must make allowances for one at my time of life if I do go a little astray. [Peter was eighteen.]

The following year, in 1810, family history repeated itself once more. It will be remembered that Patrick's brother, Duncan of Ardentrive, eloped with Jean Campbell. Now Duncan's son Neil eloped with Patrick's eldest daughter Bell. Extremely upset, Patrick wrote to John:

> 25th August, 1810
>
> I mett with a Circumstance on my Return that hurt your Mother and me not a little ... Neil Ardentrive who is a lieutenant in 75th Regt. was in this country for some time upon leave of absence and passed the greatest part of his time here. He and your sister Bell formed an Attachment for each other which perhaps was of some standing. They were privately married some time ago and she has gone to Dublin to her husband.
>
> Bell could not have been guilty of a more Imprudent step for Neil is not worth a shilling having spent all his Patrimony and much in Debts, therefore ruin must be their fate. Had Neil thousands he would throw it away, I cannot, nor will I, support his Extravagances and giving him money would be Idle folly. I have every Reason to think the Connection Bell has formed for herself will turn a very bad one. Her friend Neil wants both steadines and prudence and what is worse he is a Begger without principall, unfortunate Creature she has Distressed us all in no small degree.

Patrick now had further anxiety: Sandy had gone to fight in the Peninsular War, where Wellington was in action against Napoleon's French troops in Portugal. Sandy wrote to John from Portsmouth:

> 13th March, 1810
>
> I am thus far and on my way to join the Army under Lord Wellington in Portugal, having exchanged from the 72nd Regt into the 5th Regt, the second Batt. of which is there and I must join, which I must say is my wish although I cannot say that I look to any good result from that army ... When I was ordered to join the 1st Batt. of the 72nd Regt. in India I was advised by all Battery friends who have served in that country not to go on any account as the promotion there is very slow and the great difficulty and expense of getting home should I at any time be inclined.

The following July he wrote from Portugal (on the banks of the River Coa near Pinhel)

> The army here are at present on the frontiers of Spain ... Lord Wellington with the Headquarters of the Army have been moving about very much of late. I went there the other day to see Colin Melford [a cousin] who is Commandant at headqrs ... I remained to dine with Lord Wellington ...
>
> The enemy are at present pouring an immense force into Spain and have a large body of infantry and Cavalry before Ciudad Rodrigo [a frontier fortress] which has made a most noble defence — but I am afraid has fallen as no firing has been heard today from that quarter. We are only about 25 miles away. Lord Wellington would have attacked them but for their immense superiority of Cavalry. But I am in hope they will still be kept out of this Country owing to its Mountainous Rock Barrier where a small force can act against a greater. Because of the bravery of the Troops and the Confidence they have in their General, to make use of Boney's own words, should he come with the wings of an Eagle we shall meet him with the Roars of a Lion.

Meanwhile Peter was acting as Aide de Camp to his uncle, General Archibald Campbell, in Ireland. This caused his father extra expense and the Paymaster had written to him on the subject:

31st December, 1809

> Just the time I received yours your son Peter was asked by his Uncle General Campbell to spend a few days with him at Amagh upon which occasion the General told he intended recommending him for his Aide de Camp ... Peter received a letter last night from General Campbell by which he seems to think everything is now settled but your consent to advance the money necessary to fit him out which the General says will come to about fifty pounds. This although you may consider it too large a sum to advance for the occasion will not (as it happens at present) be much more than you'l find it absolutely necessary to advance for him very soon at any rate in consequence of the Change of Uniform the 72nd Regt. is ordered immediately to appear in of which he has got no part as yet, waiting till this matter should be raised. I am convinced it will take £25 st. to provide the new Regt. uniform. It is certainly worth your while to let him have the £50 considering the great many advantages getting upon the Staff may prove to him ... I beg to mention that in the event of Peter being appointed Aide de Camp almost all his appointments would be of use when he is ordered back to the Reg. & his horse he could of course not lose much on so as I Really think it is worth risking.

Patrick evidently paid up the £50 and Peter wrote to his brother John at sea giving him the news:

> 24th March, 1810
>
> I am glad to inform you I was appointed Aide de Camp to our uncle General Arch. Campbell about three months ago. He is a most excellent man and gives me very little trouble. I have ten shillings a day exclusive of my Ensign's pay and 7/6 a day for keeping of three horses ... The Army is a bad profession for making money. I am pretty well off at present, I have near a pound a day ... Your old flame Jane Melfort is married to a Major. It was a most extraordinary choice, he wants an Arm, eye and is quite deaf.

The beginning of 1812 brought great grief to the family when the news reached them that Sandy had been killed. According to family tradition his mother, Louisa Maxwell, saw him standing by her bed on the night that he was killed, but when she spoke he vanished. Another tradition tells how a mysterious light was seen on nearby Maiden Island that night. Suddenly it went out.

Patrick wrote to tell his son John, still at sea. 'It is a most melancholy event for me to inform you that your valuable Brother Sandy fell when Storming Ciudad Rodrigo ... His death is a severe loss to us all but God's will be done.'

Louisa Maxwell also wrote to John:

> 4th May, 1812
>
> How you must regret not being better acquainted with your excellent brother whose death is not only regretted by his family and friends but I may say by the country at large, for he was most universally esteemed, respected and beloved by all who knew him and even those who heard of the uncommon good character he bore. His excellent dispositions and warmth of friendship gained him the love and esteem of all who knew him, and his abilities of late years appeared to be far above what we ever imagined. Perhaps in short there is no better test of a young man's character than that which he bears amongst his Brother Officers and by all accounts he stood Very high indeed with his former associates as well as with those with whom he lately served.

The MacDougall piper, Ranald Mor MacDougall, composed a lament in Sandy's memory — 'Lament for Captain Alexander MacDougall — and the family planted a memorial tree, a Scots Pine, which still stands on a mound in the Gean Tree field behind the house.

By now John had been away from home for ten years. Patrick wrote to him:

*Scots pine planted in 1812 at Dunollie in memory of
Alexander (Sandy) who was killed at the storming
of Ciudad Rodrigo*

17th February, 1812

This distressing misfortune makes it absolutely necessary you get home with as little delay as possible and I have written to your Cousin Capt. P. Campbell to precure you permission by making the proper application to that effect. My very advanced period of life and diseases and misfortunes that Old Age is naturally subject to makes my time of this life most precarious & cannot be supposed of a very long duration. Many other Considerations Regarding this afflicted family and the situation that providence has been pleased now to put you in, makes your presence here highly proper.

(Patrick was seventy at the time. Despite his fears, he lived to the age of eighty-three.)

Louisa Maxwell wrote: 'Your father is very anxious you should try and get home however short a period as we are, I may say, entire strangers to each other.' John had been thirteen when he left home.

Four years later Patrick was to write to John that perhaps sending for him at the time of his brother's death had interfered with his career, but he continued: 'My distress of mind at that time urged me to recquire seeing you to alleviate the suffering I laboured under at the loss of your valuable Brother.'

The year after Sandy's death the news came that Bell's husband Neil had been killed fighting in Spain. Bell was living at Dunollie at the time, together with her two small children, a boy and a girl.

Beside the family news both Patrick's and Louisa Maxwell's letters are full of the state of crops and cattle. There is a delightful bulletin about the cows written by Louisa Maxwell to Patrick, who was away at the time. 'Three of the Cows are Bed since I last wrote.' (Ladies of that time were described as being brought to bed when they gave birth.)

Patrick, like his father, took a keen interest in agricultural improvement and a letter survives summing up some of his ideas:

> Most of the land lords with us pay too little attention to the breed of their cattle by having proper Bulls, a proper kind and properly stocked. Every man, I am satisfied, must attend to his estate as he does to his family, especially small heritors. If the production of the lands are capable, they should be suited to the crops and articles for which there is a demand. Therefore two principles I would lay down, moderate rents, and keeping the land in good heart.

Patrick's latter years

Louisa Maxwell, who was so much younger than her husband, seems to have become increasingly exasperated as Patrick grew older with what she looked on as his meanness. Having been left behind at Dunollie when he went on a jaunt to Edinburgh, she wrote to him in no uncertain terms: 'Much do I regret your not taking me to Edinr. for all the triffling additional expense it might have much more to the benefit of my family than any dirty little saving here in looking after bannocks & herring!'

Later, writing to John, she ended her complaints with this diverting picture: 'We had a visit of Lady Melford on Tuesday in her carriage, servants etc. and your old mother traveling about in a Dung Cart, for the Gig has not been run since you were here.'

Another visitor, this time on foot, was Walter Scott (not yet Sir Walter) who paid a visit to the castle. But owing to Patrick's grumpiness, caused possibly by gout, the great man did not get inside the door of the house.

Louisa Maxwell wrote to John: 'I met Walter Scott, who was visiting the ruined castle to get atmosphere for his poem 'The Lord of the Isles' and would fain have asked him in but durst not. However I walked down with him to the march burn and was very pleased with his conversation. Little did I know he was writing of this family.'

Bell wrote to John the following year: 'You must read the Lord of the Isles by Walter Scott Esq. then you read enough of the Lord of Lorn and Dunolly Castle, it only came out last winter ... you will get it for 12 shillings and we really should have more than one were it only for the pretty tribute he pays to poor Sandy's memory in one of his notes when mentioning this present family.'

The note referred to was: 'The heir of Dunolly fell lately in Spain, fighting under the Duke of Wellington, a death well becoming his ancestry.'

Of the castle Scott wrote: 'Nothing can be more wildly beautiful than the situation of Dunolly. The ruins are situated upon a bold and precipitous promontory overhanging Loch Etive and distant about a mile from the village and port of Oban.'

And he said of the family: 'The story of the MacDougalls affords a very rare, if not unique, instance of a family of such unlimited power and distinguished during the middle ages surviving the decay of their grandeur and flourishing in a private station.'

Louisa Maxwell was a great admirer of Sir Walter, and on a later visit to England, was indignant at what she found to be the English attitude towards him. She told John:

28th January, 1828

They will scarce allow him any religion which provokes me. I tell them he does not kneel, stoop or stand as often as they do — for our blessed and pure form of worship is pure, simple and from the heart, without parade or show therefore he made no parade in his writings. They likewise accuse him of being fond of money I should be glad to know who are fonder than they are of everything which lends to their comfort, neither did he make money to hoard it up but unfortuneately his taste for improvement, like many, was beyond his means and his colleagues were shamefully extravagant.

Soon after Scott's visit Lord Mountjoy invited himself to stay at Dunollie. He had married Patrick's niece Mary, the daughter of Dr Sandie, and she had recently died. The preparations for his Lordship's visit caused a flurry of correspondence, there being a difference of opinion between Patrick and his wife and children as to whether or not the family's standard of living should be raised for the occasion.

Patrick was obsessed with the idea that comfort and ruin were synonymous: times were bad during the Napoleonic War and some of his neighbours had been forced to sell their properties. 'So much' he wrote in one letter, 'for elegant houses, fine furniture and living that was called Comfortable, those that assumed that stile must now assume the contrary system.'

Louisa Maxwell wrote in distress to John about his father's attitude to Lord Mountjoy's visit: 'You will no doubt ere now have received your father's and Bell's letter acquainting you of the death of poor Lady Mountjoy ... He [Lord Mountjoy] is quite determined to come here against summer having written to your Father and Bell so repeatedly and surely he is paying us the greatest compliment he possibley can.'

In her agitation, she broke into a breathless sentence of a hundred and forty words:

> 25th February, 1815
>
> I only regret exceedingly to think I fear very much he will leave us with very different idea of this family from what he had at present, not so much in regard to our wealth as to our meaness and vulgarity which I am sorry everthing about us has but too much the appearance of, nor do I think there will be the smallest change made for the better in any respect which is rather provoking and distresses me to think that so very honourable a connection, and one who seems so very desirous to keep up the relationship with this family, should get a disgust at our seeming so indifferent to rendering him any thing tolerably comfortable, say even that we denied it to ourselves, I know of nobody else but would stretch a little point on such occasion.

John tried to intervene by writing to his father: 'My mother in a letter mentioned that Lord Mounjoy meant to pay you a visit this summer which I am sorry for as you have arrived at a time of life and in that state of health which will prevent you from paying that attention to him you would wish & I am convinced he expects and certainly merits from his kindness to the family.'

One of Lord Mountjoy's kindnesses had been the paying of an annuity to Bell, since her husband's death had left her in an impecunious state. For this reason she was as anxious as her Mother that proper preparations should be made. She reported progress to John:

> 2nd August, 1815
>
> You may believe when his Lordship mentioned to Peter and I his intention of coming to Dunollie we did not picture it out as the finest and most comfortable place in the World, he knows our

Father's age and state of health and I am sure will expect no more than he will receive at least I hope so. We have got the house cleaned and some little articles it required, a <u>Cook</u> from Edinburgh, Wine etc — so if your times answer I'll not be surprised tho' you shewed Lord M. here yourself.

As the visit drew nearer Louisa Maxwell was still in a state of worry and fret, and wrote again to John:

30th August, 1815

Bell had a letter from Lord Mountjoy from Paris which he is to leave Sunday last so will be in London before this reaches you & still talks of coming here. I hope you may come with him which will be a great relif to me.

His accomodation is what I am at the greatest loss about, for meat and drink I have plenty to give him. Your father has got a little madeira and I believe Bell has got a little claret privately and what with old mutton and poultry I am not att a loss for table, but we have an awkward table boy however if you come you could hire a man in Edinburgh or Glasgow even for a few weeks. I know a person myself in Glasgow that would answer, but the purse, the purse that is the great loss ... As your father won't give up his bedroom I think as the blue room is so very small I had better give him mine, and yours for a dressing room as there is a door of communication. Let me have your opinion, it is no doubt dark, damp and noisy and your Father's would be much more suitable, but I will make all as comfertable as I can.

The madeira provided by Patrick was a triumph but the awkward table boy was still a worry. In September Bell wrote to John:

I write these few hurried lines in hopes of their reaching London before you set out for Scotland. My mother would inform you of my having a letter from Lord Mountjoy from Paris and that he proposes coming this month ... I suppose you will both travel together ... My mother wrote you I believe about a man servant. If you brought the one from Glasgow I would go halves with you in paying him for the time Lord M. was to be here, Peter Robertson no. 237 Gilmours Land Glasgow, only hire him by the week or month and let him bring good coloured clothes ...

I got in the Summer a supply of <u>wax candles</u> for him [Lord M.] as he feels uncomfortable sitting in a room with tallow ones, but as the nights are now longer we will not have enough. Would you bring down a <u>paper</u> of wax candles that is a dozen and half in each paper — we would be the better of 2 more silver decanter slides the same as you formerly brought as we will have Claret and Madeira, and one dozen white Ivory handled dinner knives (without forks) and carving knife and fork. I have already bought one dozen but it will be too few. I merely mention the pair bottle slides and knives to bring as you find convenient. The wax candles we must have tho' his Lordship should only be a few nights here . . . I enclose a £5 note.

Unfortunately there is no description among the letters of the actual visit. Lord Mountjoy later married again and on the death of his father became Earl of Blessington. When he died in 1832 he left Bell (at the request of his first wife), £100 a year for life.

Soon after Lord Mountjoy's visit Louisa Maxwell, who had just received 'a small pension', wrote to John: 'I get what Sandy's widow would have been intitled to £50, most opportunely for poor I who would otherwise have been ruined by the things I got for the house when expecting Lord Mountjoy and no butter or cheese to sell now partly owing to our good old brown Katy having last summer fallen over the Castle Rock and been killed.'

Louisa Maxwell was at this time much concerned with the education of the three younger daughters, Ann, Mary Jane and Colin. She told John:

> I have parted with Miss Robertson & got a highly recommended young woman who teaches French, Italian, Music etc etc, she has a high salary but I trust they will be much benefited by her as she seems to have a good method & is very attentive, their education is above all things what I am most interested in ... they are often reminded how anxious you are for their improvement & how disappointed you will be unless you see a great change to the better which I really hope you will.

The new governess, a Miss Kinaird, was a great success, Louisa Maxwell informed John later: 'I have been most fortunate in an excellent Governess and from the very great progress the girls are making your father need not grudge her salery ... She was quit sorry how very ill Colin's letter to you was written but she said it was all owing to her Trembling with anxiety to do it well.'

Next year Louisa Maxwell and Patrick had an argument about the girls attending a dancing school in Oban. In May 1816 Louisa Maxwell wrote to John:

> Your Father has agreed to let Colin go twice a week to the dancing school at Oban at which she is quite delighted. I could have wished the other two could get down once a week to the practising to dance reels and country dances they have almost forgot, for be assured however beautiful or well informed a young lady may be

unless she can acquit herself at least tolerably in a Ball room she will
be quit neglected. Surely now we have the opportunity that we
have of getting that little accomplisment at so easy a rate — but
I must rest contented.

Louisa Maxwell was worried that her daughters were 'dull and
heartbroken' with the uneventful life they led at home and wished that
they could sometimes get away. Patrick, convinced that he was on the
verge of bankruptcy, would not supply the necessary money. In 1817,
however, he did have the chance of allowing his children to pay a visit to
their aunt and cousins in Colonsay at no extra cost to himself.

He wrote to John: 'It was one of my Agreements with the tennents on
the Mainland to give them shell sand for manure. I freighted a vessel at
Oban to go to Collonsay and Peter, Lucy and Mary Jane took the Benefit
of this conveyance to see their friends eight days ago.'

Mary Jane told John:

I had the good fortune to be allowed to go to Colonsay with Peter
and Lucy. I enjoyed my voyage very much and I was not in the
least degree sick and you may believe was quite charmed with
Colonsay. Aunt MacNeill is now very frail and never rises till
twelve o'clock. I don't think she will live much longer. Mr & Mrs
MacNeil were very kind and attentive in entertaining us, we had
an abundance of dancing driving and sailing on the lake.

Towards the end of the same year Louisa Maxwell wrote to John:

21st September, 1817
I hope your Father may find it convenient to send Anne and Mary
Jane to Edinburgh this winter as they are now so old and so big that
they never could go to a Boarding school at any future period
indeed they have been fitted as much by Miss Kinaird as they can
reap from any Governess, some little time of Good masters and to
see how other genteel Girls conduct themselves and to see a little
more of the world than they can at Dunolly is what they require
now. I trust their improvement will compensate for the expense.

Ann was now nineteen and Mary Jane seventeen. Patrick evidently
found their proposed sojourn in Edinburgh convenient, for a few weeks
later Louisa Maxwell wrote again to John:

30th November, 1817
I have been very busy since I received your last letter, indeed more
so that I ever was, in the first place getting the girls all in order for
going to Edinr. for which place you would no doubt have heard
we set out five weeks ago. We passed two nights at Killin where the

Girls were very much amused & pleased at visiting Achmore, Killin, Fintary etc we like wise passed a forenoon at Stirling where they saw the Castle & everything that was worth seeing and set off at two o'clock in the afternoon for Newhaven in the steam Boat.

As the day was uncommonly fine, it was beautifull passing down the banks of the Forth close to a number of Gentlemen's and Noblemen's seats, in short nothing could surpas the Girls surprise except the pleasure they enjoyed at seeing scenes so new to them. We directly took Lodgings in Edinr upon our arrival there & I immediately commenced my inquiries about the fittest school for placing them at.

My arrival in Town was no sooner known to my numerous friends & relations than they all flocked to see us & parties made up for and invitations came pouring in upon us from every body we knew, indeed it is impossible for me to express the attention we received from every body that I could possibly expect it from, none were behind hand. After stopping a week in lodgings till I got the Girls things in order, I determined to fix them with a Mrs Beaton in How Street who has the genteelest school for grown up Girls in Town.

In December Ann wrote to her brother from Edinburgh:

I will, my dear John, give you an account of our different occupations as I am still sensible how anxious you always are for our welfare and improvement. I will first tell you the different classes we attend. We have a righten master three times a week from nine till ten, Reading mistress comes on the same days from ten to eleven, we then practise from eleven to twelve, from twelve to one we write our French versions and prepaire our french lessons from one to two, we walk from two to three.

Twice a week we go to the Periase painting, this is a new sistom of teaching drawing on wood, glass, or satin it has a very beautiful effect, the rest of the week at the same hour we go to the landscape painting with oil from three to four, we have our French master three times a week from four to five, we dine at five, we then go to the schoolroom where we have waltzing and quadrilling till eight. Fortunately our dancing master comes three times a week. I think he is the master who is made most welcome. For the days we are not at the academy we have also a master for arithmetic and english grammar.

She also said they were being taught music by a new 'sistom' of teaching which she didn't think suitable. 'I intend to ask permission to get another master or singing mistress.'

Mary Jane wrote: 'Every moment of my time is occupied, Satterday

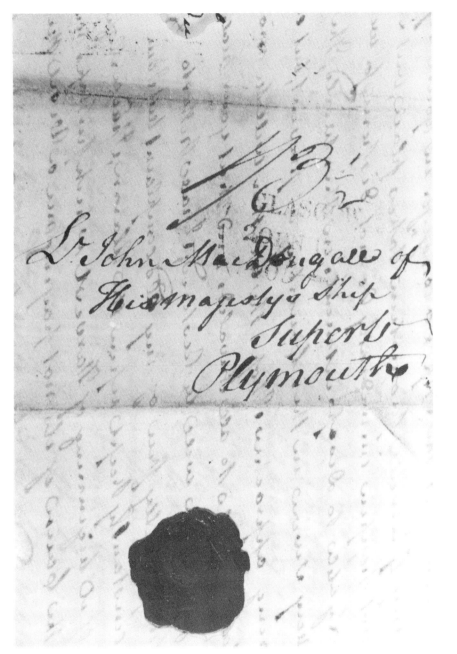

Letter to John, 17th July 1817

is the only day we are allowed to write letters, make calls and shopping. On Sunday we go twice to Church and read sermons after we come home, and take notes of what we hear in church so you see every day of the week is well employed ... We pay all our letters and coach hire which runs away with a great deal of our small allowance.'

Later their mother wrote to John that the money spent on them had not been wasted as they were much improved. But Patrick fumed away that he had been obliged to borrow money to pay 'the very large sum they foolishly expended'.

If he had to borrow money for this purpose, it does seem that Patrick was not just mean but was suffering, like many others at the time, from real financial problems. In 1816 he had written to John:

> The situation of this country is truly distressing, I have not touched £5 since you left and want near £400 that my tennents should have paid me before this time, and the demands upon me are now beginning to be rather serious and little prospect as yet of any relief. The Produce of the Lands yields nothing and every degree of Circulation is vanished and the distress is not confined to this particular quarter but is most generally felt. Although little retrenchment seems to be very little adopted in my quarters yet I am determined to put it, as far as I can, in practice now.

The next year he wrote:

> 4th July, 1817
> If country concerns does continue long in their present situation this country must be ruined. The People are starving and neither money or Credit is to be found ... Not only our tenentry are Bankcrupt but the Proprietors are little better. Barcaldine has sold half of his landed property. Combie has sold all his unentailed Estate even his place of residence and many others equally destroyed. The greater Part of the Island of Mull has been or will soon be in the Market. So much for being comfortable and living in splendour ... My expenditure and Income does not by any means Correspond and a perseverance in present Conduct must in the end prove ruinous.

Among his other financial worries, Patrick was plagued by what he considered the extravagance of his son Peter, by now a Captain. Patrick had borrowed money to buy him a commission and the arrangement was that this should gradually be repaid. No money had been forthcoming. Disgusted with his son when he came to Dunollie on leave, Patrick had written of him: 'Peter is the Idlest and most useless fellow I Ever knew but in great Condition so much so that all his Clothes must be made wider.'

His sister Colin wrote: 'Papa has been laid up with a fit of the gout for this fortnight past and Peter spends the whole day in chewing and smoking tobacco which you may be sure he would not be doing if the Laird were about.'

Patrick wrote to John:

> 18th September, 1818
>
> Peter has certainly acted most ungratefully to me and surely his conduct to me deserves a much harder appelation, you say you would not wish to hurt his yearly Income but you seem to have no hesitation in distressing your Aged Father with Infirmity born down of the burden of a family unprovided. But this Agressor must rest assured I shall use every legal means to recover the £500 due to me without delay, be the consequences to him what it will ... He is certainly not Entitled to any Lenity from me which he will find shall not be shown. His conduct has been most Undutifull and Ungrateful.

Less than two weeks later, Peter wrote to Patrick:

> 28th September
>
> In reply to your letter of the 20th Aug. I beg leave to state that I am about £100 in debt to the trades people and I declare to you that I have not in the world at this moment £10 in cash ... Your demand is I acknowledge extremely reasonable, it is my change from one regiment to another that has embarassed me so much ...
>
> I am afraid nothing but a trip to the East will enable me to pay all but I cannot bear the idea of parting with you at your time of life, and more particularly as John is going to so unhealthy a climate [the West Indies].

Patrick wrote to John:

> 20th October, 1818
>
> From two letters I had from Peter I fear little relief is to be expected from that Quarter at present and it is like daggers to my heart to Compel him to sell out of the Army yet his ungratitude and folly is most Provoking, his Arguments in Vindiction of himself does not deserve notice and in consequence I have not Acknowledged his letters. He must act in a Different Manner that what he has hitherto done before I have much Communication with Him in the shape we should stand with each other.

Patrick's next expense was sending Colin, now fifteen, to a boarding school at York, kept by a Mrs Charlotte Howard. Here the bill for instruction and boarding was £40 for a half year, with an entrance fee of five guineas. French, Geography, Dancing, Drawing and Music were extra. Copy books, pens and a slate came to ten shillings.

Colin wrote saying she was much surprised that the young ladies at
the school were allowed to break the sabbath by playing on the harp and
piano, as well as playing games.

Louisa Maxwell commented to John:

> 14th November 1820
>
> I daresay she may not altogether like the confinement & close
> attention to lessons but she must now if ever make up for her long
> idleness here and unless she makes use of the opportunity she now
> has it is all over as to education, she will have plenty of time
> afterwards for triffling. I beg of you to talk seriously to Mrs
> Howard for I know all Colin wants is application and exertion. I
> am not afraid of her progress in music but I am truly anxious that
> she should apply to French & Geography. Pray if you can spare it
> give Colin a guinea or two from me & I will repay you. I did not
> give her a farthing when she left this ...

Meanwhile, at home, Patrick, whether from worry or gout, seems to
have become crusty in his old age. His own letters remain genial, if
complaining, but in letters from the family to each other there are hints
that he was not always easy to live with.

Louisa Maxwell told John: 'Your Father never appears in better
health than he does just now but the present scarcities of money with
him, as well as every other person, does not improve his Temper, but
unfortunately for him bad humour won't fill his purse otherwise he
would be rich indeed.'

Mary Jane, (of whom Peter had written 'there is a kindness and
sweetness of temper about Mary peculiar to herself'), wrote of her
father with aggrieved resignation: 'He is in his usual humour and I
generally get a repremand ..: but My dear John, he is our father and we
are obliged to take whatever God alots for us, though some times I think
it very hard to suffer.'

In 1820, after much argument, Mary Jane and Ann were grudgingly
allowed to go to the County Meeting at Inveraray. 'I must now tell you,'
wrote Mary Jane to John 'of our Inverary meeting which Papa did not
determine to let us go to till very shortly before it took place.'

Louisa Maxwell wrote:

> 31st October, 1820
>
> Indeed it cost them very little except the frocks which I paid and
> the Laird their tickets ... The girls were perfectly delighted as well
> they might be as they never were so much noticed or made much
> of. They were constantly at the Castle when not at dinners or Balls
> ... There were a great many genteel young men there but few
> Ladies which made them in great request, in Short Staffa told me

the meeting never would have gone on without the Misses MacDougall and told your father he need not expect to see them return with that name.

Mary Jane wrote with enthusiasm: 'There never was such an assemblage of rank and fashion there before so that it would have been a pity if we had not gone as we enjoyed it very much. I never saw anything so beautiful, so many elegant appartments lighted up and filled with company. We danced till near seven in the morning!'

She went on to say that there was horse-racing and different amusements during the morning, and that the festivities went on for five days. They sailed on the loch; had lunch with the officers ('genteel young men'), in a Naval ship, the *Nimrod*; took tickets in a lottery, and watched a balloon go off — 'quite a new sight'. One morning when they called at the Castle it came on to rain, so they stayed there all day and were well amused by the playing and singing of a band.

This was the year when Peter went to join his regiment in Australia. He and his father parted on good terms.

Louisa Maxwell wrote to John in February 1820: 'I cannot express how much both your Father and I are affected at Peter's going to such a distant clime at our time of life, we have little chance of ever seeing him again and what adds much to our painful feelings is he appears much averse to it himself, indeed it will be a very unpleasant duty going out in the same ship and with the charge of such a cargo.'

The cargo was convicts. That month Peter wrote to Patrick:

> Harlow Convict Ship,
> Deptford
>
> In my last to you I noted my having been ordered to join my regiment at New South Wales and the sum it would take to fit me out for so long a voyage. My dear Father I wish you had mentioned the sum that you intended to give me … for I was told by the Agents of Transports here that we should sail in a few days. I of course had not time to correspond with you and was obliged to ask Greenwood and Cox if they would advance me £150, which they agreed to do on my giving them a bill on you at ten days sight.
>
> Now my dear father I hope you will not be offended at this, what could I do … I now beg and entreat of you to accept of the Bill if not you will ruin me, this is my last request of you. You do not know the feelings that one has at parting with their nearest and dearest relations particularly those at so advanced a period of life as you are. I can assure you I do not despair of seeing you again & would not leave the country with those ideas.

In March he wrote to his father from Cork:

30th March, 1820

Since I read your last welcome letter to me of 29th of Feb. I feel my heart glow with affection to you and I am sure all you state is perfectly just, I hope you know my disposition to even think that I could wish to deprive any of the family of their rights. Since my arrival here I have insured my stores and wearing apparel to the amount of £200, the policy is lodged with James Mitchell 6 Great Winchester Street London, so if any thing would happen to this ship you will receive the above mentioned sum, the assurance cost me £6.17. I hope you think I have done right.

This my dear Sir will be my last to you for some time. We expect to sail about the 2nd of April. The Convicts are very quiet. We have 150. My guard consists of one Sergt., 30 men & about 30 of a crew well armed. This is force enough to guard 500 men with both legs ironed as they are. I have recognised some old army acquaintences among them belonging to my late corps 11th Regt ... I Must now bid you adieu my dear Father, you have a large share in the affection and prayers of your Truly affect. son.

Allan, Patrick's youngest son, wrote to his father: 'I have written to and heard from Peter since he got to Cork, he has called up his best spirits for the Voyage. I expect yet to see him the Banker to the family, your letter to Colonel McQuarrie will be useful. Men going out to Botany Bay have sometimes Prejudices against them which require the best introductions to overcome.'

Peter arrived safely and wrote to Patrick:

Sydney Barracks, New South Wales
1st September, 1820

Here I am safe and sound in the land of Convicts and Kangaroos. We arrived here on the 5th August and sailed from the Cove of Cork on the 2nd of April which is reckoned a good passage, in adding up our log we sailed nearly twenty thousand miles.

The convicts were very quiet during the voyage and any disturbance that takes place on board these ships I am now satisfied must be through great neglect and mismanagement.

This is the first opportunity that I have had of writing to you as we made a direct passage, and were not so fortunate as to fall in with a Homeward bound ship. This is a delightful country and climate, it is our winter at present which is about the temperature of the month of June in England. All European Fruits and Vegetables grow here in great abundance, the Pears and apples are the finest I have ever ate. The Pigs are fed with Peaches, you see here cart loads of them going through the streets.

I have met with great attention from the governor and Mrs MacQuarrie, it is thought that they will go home soon. I can assure you he does not sleep on a bed of roses here: he has a sweet set to deal with. Robberies of course are commit'd here every hour of the day and night, stone and lime will not keep them out, as to locks they are of no use, but Murder very seldom. We are not very scrupulous about hanging them, there has been 6 or 8 executed since I landed. The officers of the Army sit as jurymen at all the Criminal Courts which is a very unpleasant Duty.

Peter was over twenty thousand miles away, but now Patrick's youngest son, Allan, was in debt and clamouring for money. Allan was in the office of Mr Young, Patrick's man of business in Edinburgh, where he was training to become a W.S.

Patrick wrote to John: 'Allan is still with Mr Young, some times they agree well at other times the Contrary, Money the Father of all Disputes is at times the cause. I wish that mettale had never Existed but there is no wanting it ... Allan I think is a most singular character, I do not know what to make of him, he does not want abilities but they are most singularly placed and it difficult to say how he may come on in his profession.'

Louisa Maxwell wrote: 'Allan does not want good sound sense altho' odd in some things but he is very affectionate and good tempered.'

During this year Allan wrote his father a letter which was not well received.

16th November, 1820

Now that you have placed your affairs in that state which a few but the most prudent can accomplish, that our Mother has been spared to you and most of your family along with her, what should distress your mind or bear hard upon it? Nothing, my dear father but what you or I cannot avert. It but remains for you to look and enjoy your gratifying view and doing so you will find your health and spirits hourly advantaged. Take care of my Mother's health along with your own, live easily for your circumstance will allow it, and above all do not harass yourself to make or save a few pounds which perhaps some of us may yet misspend.

Patrick was not only displeased; he refused to stop worrying. He wrote to John:

4th December, 1820

My outlays of late have been most absurd and inconsistant and I am sorry to say too much persevered in which must be put a stop to, should the remedy be unpleasant ... Black Cattle have fallen much in price which I fear will make ill paid rents ... Bear [barley] is a great Article in my rentall which I have not yet disposed of. Last year's I have not had as yet an offer for. There was a heavy Duty laid upon Malt last year which is the Cause of the present depression upon that article. I fear I will be a sufferer of at least £70 ster. in that article. Indeed, there is no demand for it and the Tenantry, unless they can get theirs disposed of, will suffer infinitely more than I do.

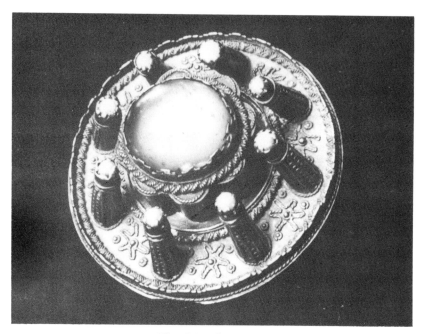

The Brooch of Lorn

One comfort was to come: in his old age Patrick had the pleasure of having the Brooch of Lorn returned to the family. This brooch had been taken by the MacDougalls from Robert the Bruce at the Battle of Dalrigh near Tyndrum: Bruce and the MacDougalls were on opposite sides because Bruce had murdered the Red Comyn in a church at Dumfries. The murdered man was related by marriage to the MacDougall chief of the time.

In the Covenanting Wars the brooch was stolen during the sack of the MacDougall castle of Gylen on Kerrera. It remained in the possession of the Campbells of Bragleen until the widow of one of the family, who had many children to educate, sold it to Campbell of Lochnell.

In 1822 John received the Brooch on behalf of his father, and wrote to him: 'I have to congratulate you on the return to the family of the Brooch taken from the breast of Robert Bruce.'

I am indeed indebted to Lochnell for its restoration and the manner it was presented to me by the Duke of Argyll one day after dinner [at Inveraray Castle] was most gratifying to my feelings. I hope soon to have the pleasure of presenting it to you.'

But by now Patrick was failing in health. Peter, on the point of leaving Australia for India where he hoped to make a fortune, and so pay his debts, wrote to John: 'It grieves me very much to hear that our Father has been so long confined to his bed and room ... My dear fellow what can we expect at his advanced age it is true, but when I think of all his kindness to me, I may say from my Birth, and the very little prospect that I have of ever seeing him again it distresses me very much.'

The following year John persuaded his father to send Mary Jane and Ann to Cheltenham so that they could have some social life and Mary Jane could recover from her recent serious illness, in a warmer climate. John had several naval friends living there who had offered to chaperone the girls. When they had been there some time and were due to come home, Mary Jane wrote to her father:

4th August, 1824

I have been slowly gaining strength since I left home but to restore my health and strength completely I would require a few months longer in this delightful climate and I hope my dear Pappa you will gratify me by acceding to my earnest wish, as from what I have already suffered I dread the winter at Dunolly untill my strength is fully restored. You may believe how very reluctant I am wishing to be so long absent from you in your present distressed state of health but nothing but my late severe sufferings would ever have induced me to have made such a request so contrary to my feelings in your very precarious state at present.

John had written to Patrick about the two girls: 'I have reason to suspect they have some admirers but this I intreat you will keep perfectly silent and in due time I will give you every information when necessary, poor things they have been very economical.'

Patrick evidently gave his daughter leave to remain in Cheltenham and Mary Jane wrote to thank him: 'Your very kind letter I have just received. I can never forget your great goodness in allowing me to remain here, be assured I shall be as economical as possible. It greaves me exceedingly when I reflect the enormous sum I have cost you but God's will be done.'

Patrick had by now handed over the management of the estate to John, who was without a ship and home on half pay. A cousin wrote: 'I am happy to hear that your worthy old father has at length disencumbered himself of all cares by giving up the Management of the

Property etc. to you and I have no doubts it will be the means of prolonging his life and of passing the latter days of it without that care and anxiety that is unavoidably attendant on those concerned at any time of life in worldly affairs.'

In spite of this it seems Patrick had not handed over the purse strings, for Allan wrote to him in February 1825:

> I received a liberal education and entered a liberal profession. This you all did and then your hand stopped ... I now wish to establish myself as a man, a gentleman and a gentleman's son in fulfilment of the education I have received and the profession I have entered. I am without the means, this is my situation. My situation is just the often ridiculed one of a poor man's son who has received a good education but he has not money to begin a profession suitable to his education, and his education unfits him for the situation of his humble birth. But a poor liberally educated gentleman is by the circumstances of his birth in a worse situation of the two. From vexation alone I cannot add a word more as my heart is full.

Soon after this letter was written, Patrick died.

Family Post

Smuggling

John MacDougall, Lunga, to Patrick in Edinburgh, February 1776 (John MacDougall asked Patrick to get testimonies of Kilmory's bad character.)

> He [Kilmory] came to the Customes at Oban at my Return from the fishing to condem my two vesseles as he alleged that we ship'd a great Quantity of Rum among the Barley when we sailed for the fishing but, I thank god for it, 18 men swore against him. He is a very great vilan ...
>
> The Comisioners ordered the Colector at Oban to examine all the men of the Dunollie [boat] that helped the Irish man to send some of his rum to Morvin, unknown to the Master or me, the time we lay wind bound here and they declared upon oath that they went themselves without the master's leave or mine.
>
> I do not know but the Comissioners will endeavour to stop the bounty for this boat but it is hard that I should suffer and that I did not know of their going with the Irish man. Sailors will do anything if they get plenty to drink which smuglers seldom spares.
>
> I beg you will not neglect anything that can be done in regard to Kilmory. You can get a number of gentlemen at Edinburgh that knows Kilmory's character and I am sure any honest man will not scruple to give it in who knows him and his behaviour to me. He

give up to the Colector that I had a cask of rum in every barel I sent north, but you see by the mens' disposition that he is a lier. Its hard that I should suffer by such a villan that lived upon lies these 16 years past.

I am very ill used, the man the Rum belongs to threatens me vengence for asisting the Colector in keeping the Rum after it was taken possesion of.

Smuggling Prevention Service

Patrick to his son John, 1817

I am sure our friend Capt P. Campbell advised you properly in dropping the smuggling interference business, it would not be very respectable in this Quarter in particular.

A Watch for a Wedding Present

Pat Campbell, from London, to his brother-in-law Patrick MacDougall, July 1782

Your Wife's Watch which is ordered from one of the best makers in Town will not be forwarded before the middle of Aug.

It is a very difficult matter to get an iminent Watchmaker here to undertake to make a good Watch at so short a notice, many of them require a Twelvemonth, some two years, and the famous Mr. Mudge, to whom I applyed, would not promise one in less than three years. The second rate Gentry in the profession have enough of showy ready made Watches but I have found to my cost that they are not to be depended on which has been my reason for not purchasing a watch at once for you, so Madame must just have a little patience.

Pat Campbell from London, 17th September, 1782

The watch for your Wife has been finished and in my possession about a fortnight during which time I found it to keep time remarkably well. It has 2 cases a common Shagreen one [a kind of untanned leather, dyed green], and an Enamelled one for Days the last is the very pink of the Fashion, it is really very elegant and much admired by judges to whom I have shown it. You must caution Maxwell to be carefull not to let it fall which might be the death of it.

Besides the long Shagreen Case in which the Watch and glass are packed there is also a small Black one to hold the Enamelled Case when out of use. The whole is put up in one packett directed to your wife and sent to Edin. a few days ago by the Young Laird of Glenfalloch who was so good as to take charge of it and promise to deliver it to my Wife but incase she had left Edin. before his arrival he promised to carry it to his Father's and from thence to Achmore.

I have not send any Trinketts as baubles are not fit to wear with so good a Watch, and handsome ones would come higher than the price you mentioned. The Watch itself with the Charm and Shagreen Case have cost £31.6.0.

> New Jewelled Gold Enamelled Watch by John Holman London No. 6554 Including a Green Shagn. case, 2 black ones & a high polished blue and black Charm.
> 31.6.0.

Clothing the Army

Henry Galaway from Mount Carron, to Patrick, 1783

I expected in the course of this year to have had it in my power to have paid you. I am sure this was my inclination. But as soon as the Peace came to be thought of Seriously a Stop was put to the clothing [of the Army] which rendered my plan abortive.

I had also fixed, as I thought, Col. Humberstones Regiment in the East Indies, having got the Interest of the Gentleman who manages his affairs, but on applying to the Agent he said that the Highland Regiments there neither gott Plaids nor Bonnets, they not being proper for that Climate. They wear a sort of straw hats in place of Bonnets, what they use instead of Plaids I don't know so I was much disappointed there also ...

Fire at Oronsay House 1784

John MacNeill to Patrick, 1st December, 1784

You would certainly have heard of the fortunate escape which Colonsay had with his life very lately.

I had no account of it from himself, but Mr McGibbon who came from Islay some days ago informs me that Colonsay [Colonsay was Archibald MacNeill. His uncle was Alexander MacNeill of Oronsay, married to Patrick's sister Mary.] was sleeping alone at his Uncles's house at Oronsay. The house took fire in the dead hour of night, and the flames proceeded so far before he awaked, that he hardly had time to tye the sheet on his bed to a chair which he put cross the window, and bring himself to the Ground by the end of it. I am told the house is totally demolished.

Archibald MacNeill to Patrick, Glasgow, 5th December, 1784

I came here last night and received your letter. I am confined with a cold having never thoroughly got the Better of having been so long without Clothes in the air when my Uncles house was Burned. I am heartily glad it was Ensured.

Alexander MacNeill to Patrick, St Andrews, December 25th 1784

I beg leave to offer you this trouble wishing to know what resolution the under writers have come to as to the misfortune of the house in Oronsay. I mean whether they pay the insurance money or put the house in as good order as it was in without loss of time. I am obliged to you for the offer you make me of money.

Duncan to Patrick, from Ardentrive, December, 1784

This accident prompts one to Insure my own House. Suppose the House Furniture and wearing Apparell £400 what would be the yearly expense?
(Duncan had built a new house at Ardentrive the previous year.)

Washing Machines

Duncan to Patrick, February, 1791

I see an advertisement in the news papers about a new invention machine for washing. There is one by McKinner and another by Mr Bullrewark agent for Coats & Hancocke. If they answer the description given of them they are a valuable piece of furniture. Will you be so good as to inquire minutely about them and let me know whether they give satisfaction or whether you think one of the lowest price will in a small degree answer the purpose.

John McNeill to Patrick, Oronsay, July 1791

Dear Uncle, I beg leave to offer you the trouble of purchasing for me and sending by the canall a washing macheen fit to wash 14 shirts at once.
    Direct it to the care of Messrs Arch. & Dun. Campbell Greenock and let it be carefully packed.

Agitated Father

Patrick Campbell to Patrick MacDougall, from London 1798

My dear Sir,
    I am sorry to have occasion to trouble you on a subject which naturally interests Mrs Campbell and myself much and gives us extreme uneasiness.
    My son, I find, has been your guest for some time. He was always a great admirer of female Beauty and rather apt to fall in

love with every pretty Girl he sees, but we never had reason to apprehend anything serious till now that he writes his mother about marrying your neice who he saw in Edinburgh and now at her mother's.

For heavens sake try by every means which your friendship and good sense can suggest to prevent a slip which would most assuredly entail a great and irreparable misfortune on your brother's family and on mine. I need not I trust be more explicit with you. I have wrote to the young Gentleman himself on the absurdity of a Boy of his age years entertaining such thoughts and the wretchedness in which he would inevitably involve himself and the young lady, for whom he professes a regard, by such a step.

I have also directed him immediately to set off on his Return to London and given him leave to visit Inverarary on his way. If he is with you or in your neighbourhood I entreat you to hasten him hither without any delay and favour me with a line to intimate his departure. He will require a guide in going the Cross road to Inverarary which I request you to procure and direct him what to pay. He will find his way from Invererary according to the rout I have given him.

I beg of you again to excuse the frequent trouble I have of late given you and that you would by return of post favour me with a line which I hope will sett Mrs Campbells mind and my own at ease respecting this most foolish affair which gives us more anxiety that I can well express.

     With kindest regards, I am my dear Sir your affect. Br.
     Pat Campbell.

Un-neighbourly Exchanges, 1799

Angus Campbell to Patrick MacDougall, from Dunstaffnage October 1799

Dear Sir, As the Season for shooting Wood Cock is commenced I beg leave to shoot on your ground and may perhaps through this winter take a day after the Roes. All here join me in best respects to Mrs MacDougall, you and family.

     I am, dear Sir, your most obedient Servt.
     Angus Campbell

Patrick to Angus Campbell

I do not wish any person should sport upon my grounds unless I am of the party, when I return from the Low Country will be happy to take a day Cocking, or any other beside, with you that this place can afford.

Angus Campbell to Patrick, 28th October, 1799

> Dear Sir, Your not wishing any person to sport on your grounds
> unless you are of the party is to me, I must say, an awkward kind of
> permission and any gentleman who does not chuse to give me
> liberty to hunt on his grounds by myself may enjoy his Sport alone.

A Debt Repaid After Thirty-four Years

Donald Stewart to Patrick, 1800

> I take the Liberty to inform you that Mr Donald McLeron in his last
> will gave me orders to pay forty pounds sterl. to Peter
> MacDowgald Esq. of Dunolly near Obane in Argylshire in
> Scotland, or to his heirs, for brandy and green tea Bought from the
> said Peter McDowgald about the year 1766. The said Mr McLeron
> lamented was not paid Long before this as that money was the
> means of him taking the Brewery from the Earl of Dunmore at
> Dunmore Park near Caron iron works, but he said man may
> propose but god is the disposer of all things.

Brotherly Concern

Duncan to his brother Patrick at Dunollie, December 1801

> I cannot restrain myself from puting you to the Expence of this
> letter which I hope will overtake you before you set out for Edinr.
> My reason for writing to you on this occasion is to beg you may not
> think at this season of the year and the state of health you have
> been in of Undertaking the Journey on Horse-back, should you
> happen to get wet in the feet the Consequence may be very serious
> to yourself and not less so to your Family, a few pounds saved at
> the Hazard of endangering ones health is the worst of all
> Economy.

Starving Child?

Duncan to Patrick, December 1801

> If you go by Stirling to Edinr. or return that way I beg you may (if
> you have so much time to spare) see the Masters of the Classes
> Sandy is Attending and endeavour to learn what progress he is
> making. I know he has a Voracious Appetite, endeavour to learn if
> he gets enough to eat, I don't mind the Quality if it is Wholesome
> Food, but its terrible that a growing Boy should be the least
> pinched in his Food.

Opinion of Inveraray

John Young to Patrick at Dunollie, October 1803

> Sandy would inform you what an agreeable journey we had to

Inveraray and how charming a day we had to see the place, which
is indeed wonderful. I had no idea of such a quantity of fine timber
trees, the situation of the place, the woods, the hills, the rivers, the
loch, all forming a one that is truely magnificently grand. I never
saw such a pretty view any where as from the top of the hill above
the house.

The Loch part of it was in reality what I have seen painted for an
Italian Landskape, but the Dukes buildings were to me mortifying
— without taste or judgment (the bridges excepted), the soil
miserable and the corn hanging upon pins like old wigs was
laughable.

Journey from Inveraray to Glasgow

John Young to Patrick, 1803

I proceeded to Cairndow, thought a good deal of Ardkinless, have
since been informed that there is there one tree larger than any at
Inveraray, got a herring dinner so rich that I became sick on the
way, was really terrified of going up Glen Kinless and down Glen
Crowe, got to Arrochar before night and found myself happily put
up, surprised some Greenock men with Fife jokes and extra drink.
The hills and Loch Long very pretty and wild (romantic does not
apply to that country). Proceeded next day to Luss a fine day and
Loch Lomond very pretty, hills still magnificent and the woods
grand. Luss I think one of the prettiest Gentleman's residences I
ever saw, met Sir James travelling home.

The coach quite full of people, two drivers, two men besides on
the Coach box and two more on the top. I thought at first it was a
stage coach covered with hangys, as they call whom the drivers
take up on the road.

Proceeded to Dumbarton thro' the most populous and busy
country I think I ever saw and hundreds of Gentlemen's houses in
view all along, got a shabby dinner and poor attendance. Went to
the Castle which is a great Curiousity, but not so high nor pointed
as I expected, and caste out with folks of the house for bad
attendance, dirtiness and want of every comfort, so took horse at
night with the intention of stopping at a ferry to go to Paisley, but
the house was so full and it was dangerous to ferry horses in the
dark so proceeded to Glasgow very tired I assure you.

Fashion for Castles

Louisa Maxwell to her son John, 1814

Dougald Gallanach is building a great edifice in the form of a
Castle, it will outdo everything in this part of the World, he has
bought the furniture of his principal bedroom at a sale for £120

guineas, its original cost was £300 guineas so if every thing will be in proportion it must be a fine affair . . . Coll's family are at Bath, he is at home <u>turning his house</u> into a Castle which is the present <u>rage</u>, the Barcaldines manouvring their old house which is neither castle or cottage. I suppose when you Build, which I think will depend a good deal upon prize money, to differ from them all it must be in the form of a Man of War.

Peat and Commissions

Louisa Maxwell to Patrick, staying in Edinburgh, 1814

We have had two days of eleven carts and one day of twelve carts at the peats, I never saw them in better order. I am quite angry they did not begin sooner to lead them & they might have been all in in excellent order last night, however if the weather permits they will be all at home this week . . . I am not idle I assure you being up every morning by five o'clock.

Sunday evening. No letter tonight. I suppose you are so taken up with <u>feasting</u> or else offended at my list of commissions in my last, that you don't chose to write, it is of little consequence whether or not you bring them for I believe few or none of them were for me, but for the house which I assure you I would much rather deck if I could than myself.

Death Foretold

Lady Mountjoy to Isabella MacDougall, her first cousin, July 1814 (Lady Mountjoy was Dr Sandie's daughter Mary)

July 1814

My dear Bell, Nothing you may believe could have caused my long silence but inability to write. Since last Feb. I have been on a sick couch hovering between life and death. Repeated attacks on the lungs with the medecines I have been obliged to take, and the constant bleedings, have so reduced me that you would never recognize the Mary your partial eyes admired. I am fast I fear hastening to that Bourn from whence the traveller returns no more. I believe myself to be in a confirmed decline. My cough is eternal. Nothing has any effect on it, and the pain in my breast had drawn me quite double. I tell you all this, my beloved friend, to prepare you for an event which must happen. Nothing can arrest it, my race is run.

I have not seen my children since I left Ox. in the beginning of March. Oh death where is thy sting! You are a mother, think what my feelings must be at the prospect of leaving four infants unprotected for alas! what can a Father do for young children, but these subjects only weaken my mind which I ought to fortify . . .

Miss Gardiner has been staying with me all this sad dreary spring and summer. Ld. M is quite subdued and like a man beside himself but cherishes hopes, and the Drs encourage him. They fancy I am about two months gone with child. If it were so I might recover, but I have no idea that it is. In short my mind is resigned to leave as much happiness as ever fell to the lot of woman. It is the expiation of my transgressions, and I dare not repine.

Value this scroll, dearest friend, for I have not written to anybody, nor dare I to you were not Ld. M. gone to have his ride, as I am positively forbidden all exertions.

I often dream of being at Dunollie those happy scenes of our guiltless youth, which I shall behold no more. I fancy that the fresh air revives my faded form, and then awake to pain, thirst and heat.

My poor unconscious children are to be brought up to town that I may see them again next week. May God protect them. May they live to be a comfort to their Father or die in innocent childhood.

Give my tender love to my dear and kind aunt, present my respects and duty to your Father, and now my dear, very dear, friend and companion of my youth, Adieu, think of me, pray for me. Remember me when I am gone and be assured that I am to the last your attached M.C.Mountjoy.

I shall write to you again if able. I have a plan for you and your children if Ld. M. will agree to it.

Note: Lady Mountjoy had two children by Lord Mountjoy while her first husband, Captain Brown, was in the West Indies. When he died Lord Mountjoy married her and two more children were born. One was a son and heir, born in the November before this letter was written. In September 1814 Lady Mountjoy died.

A Burrow

Louisa Maxwell to John, September 1817

The village of Oban is now a burrow, having a provost and magistrates.

Good Harvest

Patrick to John, 25th October 1817

As good a season as this I never remembered to see. All the Crops in the Country is got home in good order and they appear to be very Fertile. I have near Double the Quantity of Oats and Barley that I used to have upon the same sowing and my potatoes are excellent. We have had no rain for a month past which is a new thing in this country and the weather is uncommon mild at this season.

Death of Princess Charlotte
(Daughter of the Prince Regent, later George IV)

John to Patrick, from Plymouth, 16th November, 1817

What a serious loss the Nation has sustained by the Death of the amiable Princess Charlotte, if every individual in this quarter had lost a near Relation it would not occasion a more meloncholy gloom on their counterances & I may say the Navy have lost a sincere friend and in this port they have paid the most devoted respect to her memory by all going into the deepest mourning. If she had survived with the Child this letter might have informed you of my Promotion.

Louisa Maxwell to John, 30th November 1817

A few days before I left Edinburgh the whole city was overwhelmed with the deepest sorrow upon hearing of the unlooked for and most affecting intelligence of the Princess Charlotte & her infant's death. Old as I am and hardened you would think with many sorrows I could not refrain from shedding tears at hearing it. We are short sighted mortals but at present it certainly appears as a great national calamity ... We must just console ourselves with the Christian Maxim that all things are ordered for the best by the wise disposer of all events.

John Urie's Scrape

Patrick to John, 1818

John Urie, who is at present with me, thought proper to grapple with our Cook maid and get her with Child and so to Crown his misfortune has since married her. I am truly sorry for poor Urie getting into this scrape for your Mother and I was very much pleased with his Conduct here — being Strictly sober and Honest.

Steam Boats

Patrick to John, February 1820

The Conveyance in this Country is much improved by the steam Boats. One plyed from Loch Crinan at the Canal to Fort William during the harvest untill the beginning of Dec. and passed just below the Castle. It starts again in a month hence so that you may Breakfast here the second day from Glasgow for a Mere triffle of Expence.

No Christian Forbearance

Allan to Patrick from Edinburgh, 1820

> The Christian Knowledge [Society in Scotland for the Propagation of Christian Knowledge] have no christian forbearance and are beginning to enquire for their cash.

(Patrick had borrowed money from them.)

Celtic Society

William McKenzie to Patrick, 3 Castle Street, Edinburgh, 8th May, 1820

> By desire of the Committee of Management of the Celtic Society, I beg leave to enclose to you a Copy of its Regulations, from which you will learn its objects, and be enabled to judge how far they merit your support.
>
> This Society, it will be observed, has been formed for the purpose chiefly of promoting throughout the Highlands the general use of the Ancient Highland Dress; and its object is proposed to be accomplished by distributing Premiums, in the different Highland Districts, to the Highlanders habitually wearing the Tartan, and by the influence and occasional example of the Members connected with the Highlands.
>
> It appears to the Gentlemen of the Society to be of the utmost consequence that the Highlanders would continue to wear this most ancient and characteristic Dress of their country. It is known to have a material effect in cherishing the martial spirit of the people, and the powerful influence of the 'Tartan', and the associations combined with it, on the general character of the Highlanders and on their conduct, when in the field, is universally acknowledged. That the Dress has of late years fallen much into disuse is no less true than generally regreted; and there is too much cause for apprehension, that unless encouraged now, it may, at no distant period, cease altogether to be the garb of the Highlander.
>
> Should this Institution for preserving it then meet your approbation I shall be happy to propose you for admission and at any rate shall be obliged by your communicating any information connected with its object and proposed measures.
>
> I have the honour to be, Your most obedient Servant,
>
> > Wm. McKenzie Sect.

No War

MacDougall of Soroba to Patrick December 1822

> As a soldier I fear there is an end of any probability of a war ... This is a bad lookout for your son and myself but we must only pray for better times.

JOHN
1789-1865

Sir John MacDougall, 25th Chief (1825-1865)
(known as The Admiral)

JOHN, 1789-1865 *m* ELIZABETH SOPHIA TIMMINS (Sophy), 1826

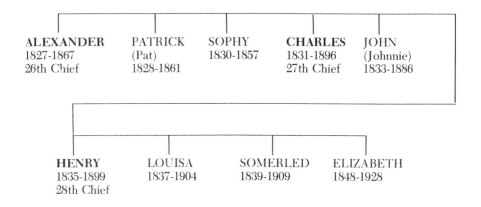

ALEXANDER
1827-1867
26th Chief

PATRICK
(Pat)
1828-1861

SOPHY
1830-1857

CHARLES
1831-1896
27th Chief

JOHN
(Johnnie)
1833-1886

HENRY
1835-1899
28th Chief

LOUISA
1837-1904

SOMERLED
1839-1909

ELIZABETH
1848-1928

The family of John

His father: Patrick (Peter), 24th Chief, married Louisa Maxwell Campbell, died 1825.

His mother: Louisa Maxwell, youngest daughter of John Campbell of Achallader. She married Patrick in 1782 and died in 1841.

His wife: Elizabeth Sophia (Sophy) Timmins, born 1806, only child of Captain Timmins of the East India Company. She married John in 1826 and died in 1881.

The children

Alexander: succeeded as 26th Chief in 1865. He was in the Royal Artillery and reached the rank of Captain. In 1867 he married Anna, daughter of T. Barclay of Ballartney, Co. Clare and died seven weeks later.

Patrick (Pat): was in the Navy and reached the rank of Commander. He died unmarried.

Sophy: married Sir Angus Campbell of Dunstaffnage in 1852 and died without children in 1857.

Charles: succeeded as 27th Chief on the death of his brother Alexander. He married his first cousin Harriette, widow of Donald Campbell of Balliveolan. They had no children. Charles was in the Indian Army and reached the rank of Colonel.

John (Johnnie): worked for a time at the War Office and then in various jobs in the West Indies where he frequently got into scrapes. He eventually came back to Britain and became a clergyman.

Henry: succeeded as 28th Chief on the death of his brother Charles. He qualified as a doctor in Edinburgh and joined the Indian Medical Service, reaching the rank of Deputy Surgeon General. In 1871 he married Caroline, daughter of James Forsyth of Glengorm, Mull. On his death in 1899 he was succeeded by his eldest son Alexander.

Louisa: was a good amateur painter, founded St John's School, Oban, taught there and showed keen interest in the children. She also did much social work in the town and played the organ in St John's Church.

Somerled: was in the Navy and reached the rank of Commander (said to be the youngest Commander in the Service at the time). He retired very reluctantly at the age of thirty-four — with the rank of Captain — owing to an illness contracted in the Gulf of Persia. In spite of this he outlived all his brothers.

Elizabeth (Kitty): was the delicate member of the family but she outlived them all by many years. She was interested in social work and was musical. She died at the age of eighty-six.

5

John

Life in the Navy

John's intense loyalty and dedication to the Hanoverian Navy of his time echoed his Jacobite great-grandfather's commitment to an army fighting to put the rival Stuart dynasty on the throne.

A dangerous and often uncomfortable life at sea took John all over the world. But his devotion to the Navy did not detract from his love of his Highland lands or his wife and family. His children's welfare was an unceasing concern and he seems to have ruled over them with a lighter hand than many a Victorian father.

John himself was born at the time when Patrick and Louisa Maxwell had lost two of their four children. Patrick wrote with delight of the stoutness of the new baby, who was then nine months old: 'The smallpox did not reduce my sweet laddie in the least degree. He is a fat boy ... my little lass is well but an arm or leg of Johnnie's is as thick as two of hers.'

John chose his profession early. His father, it will be remembered, wrote to Captain Patrick Campbell when John was eleven to try and get him into the Navy. 'My second son John since he could almost speak showed a strong inclination to go to sea and still continues in that Opinion.'

Two years later, on 8th November, 1802, Captain Campbell (a nephew of Louisa Maxwell), wrote to Patrick that he had got an appointment for John, who should be sent to London immediately. He continued: 'I think you had better let him be supply'd here with every thing except Linnen and he must also have an allowance not exceeding £36 a year as for the first three or four years he will receive little or no pay. Let me be wrote to when he leaves Leith that I may look out for him.'

John was soon dispatched, and his elder brother Sandy, who was in Edinburgh at the time, wrote to Patrick on 15th November:

I have just arrived from Leith after seeing John on board the Berwick merchants under the charge of Captain Turner who promised to see him safe with one of his cousins before parting with him. Poor fellow he seemed very sorry at parting but there is no fear of him by several examples before I parted with him. As I understood that the midshipmen supplies themselves with bed and table linnen I got two prs of sheets, two table cloths and two pillow slips for him here a great deal cheaper than it would have been in London ... I might have got him off on Tuesday in a Post chaise but as the expense was so great (£14) I thought it was better to send him by sea which he seemed more inclined to himself.

Captain Campbell wrote from London on 1st December:

Your son arrived here yesterday afternoon, I really think him as fine a Boy as ever I saw and make no doubt but that he will turn out well. I am setting about getting him rigg'd out and hope by the end of the week to get him afloat. You have given him a very good proportion of Linnen for the present and I'll take care he is supplied with everything else that is proper ... You maybe assured I will be as economical as possible in his outfit and will request his Captain to take charge of his money.'

John wrote the next day: 'My dear Father, I arrived here safe upon Tuesday the 30th after a passage of 6 days, from the little I have seen of the sea I think I will like it, I was only a little sick for the first 2 days, my cousin is just now getting clothes for me ... I hope I will here from you soon ... I will write Mama soon and I remain your affect. Son John MacDougall.'

While in London John lodged with a clansman, D. MacDougall, who wrote to Patrick on 8th December:

Knowing you will naturally have an anxiety about your son Mr John MacDougall who left this for Sheerness on Monday last in good spirits and health accompanied by his cousin Captain Campbell of the Navy. I was happy to have it in my Power to show him any attentions whilst in London that I Possibly could and indeed he deserved any thing that can be done for him; every Person here who had seen him with me seemed to be quite astonished at his fortitude in not shewing the smallest symptons of uneasness at being at such a distance from his friends; I wish him every Prosperity in his undertaking; and I am Confident if he is spared that he will be some day or other an Ornament to Society and of great Pleasure to his Relations; I can assure you that during the short time he was here he gained so much upon my affections that I was quite sorry in parting with him. I desired him when ever he came to London again not to go to a Coffee House but come to my house; where he can always have a spare bed etc ... Anything I can do for you and the family here I shall be extremely happy to take the trouble. I have the honour to be sir your most obt. servt.

On 11th December, Captain Campbell wrote:

> I left your son on monday last on board his Ship and Capt.
> Hancock promises to take every care of him and I make no doubt
> of his doing well. I left with Capt. H. £20 for his use and gave
> himself 8 Guineas to begin with. I did not purchase him a watch as
> you mentioned — it would be better to give him a little idea of the
> life he had enter'd on before he was entrusted with any things of
> value. I find on writing up my account that you are indebted to me
> £25.16s. so that his outfit has not been very extravagant.

So John began what was then a very tough life in the Navy. He was not
to see his family again for ten years. When he first went to sea Britain
was enjoying a short spell of peace after the French Revolutionary War.
But in May 1803 the Napoleonic War began and John was soon pitched
into battle. A friend in Edinburgh wrote to Patrick:

> 27th October, 1803
> As I was resting my bones on top of my bed who comes in but your
> John, a fine conversable fellow as in the king's Service, vastly
> intelligent I assure you and well looking. He says it is worth ones
> while to board a French ship for the fun of it in getting on board, it
> is devil take the hindmost, fire their pistols, throw them in the teeth
> of the French and cut them into collops cursing them dreadfully all
> the time. Then taste the Frenchmans' liquor and sherry and receive
> the caresses of their shipmates on getting into their own ship.

John wrote a less lurid account of this action: 'engaged an armed
Schooner and Brigg and after an action of an hour and a half we
captured them both.' This was off the north coast of France.

In 1804 he joined his cousin Captain Patrick Campbell's ship, the
frigate *Doris*. Early in the following year the *Doris* was wrecked. John,
writing later of his career, put this incident on a par with his wounds:
'was three time wounded and I was wrecked in the Doris in Janry 1805'.

After the wreck he was transferred to *H.M.S. Hero* under the Hon.
Captain Gardener. He took part in the Battle of Cape Finisterre on 22nd
July. 'The Hero,' he wrote, 'led the fleet under Sir R. Calder in the action
of that day against the combined fleets.'

Patrick wrote to John after the battle:

> 10th August, 1805
> Your very Acceptable letter of the 24th July relieved us all here of
> the Anxiety we were in regarding you after the Action of your
> Fleet with the Combined Squadron of the Enemy [French and
> Spanish] upon the 22nd and I pray God my Dear Boy that you may
> be equally fortunate in all your Conflicts thereafter with them in
> Escaping unhurt. Your Gallant Captain and his Ship made a very

conspicuous appearance and if our news papers are Correct his good conduct was the means of bringing the Enemy to Action that day. I hope if you have a second Brush with them their Destruction will be more compleat. Had the day been more favourable no doubt you would have given a better Account of them, but it is very well what happened. It will convince them our Superiority upon unequal numbers and that nothing can resist the British Tars.

Louisa Maxwell wrote the same day:

Last Tuesday morning brought us the papers giving an account of the Battle off Cape Finisterre and as their was no names mentioned of those that suffered and were hurt you may believe I slept but little that night. However Wednesday night brought your most welcome letter. I cannot express my Dearest boy how much I think of your attention in writing so soon which took such a load off my mind to find you were unhurt for which I hope you are thankful to God considering the great chance you all ran it is meraculous how few were hurt.

In 1806 John was once again with Captain Patrick Campbell. During the next three years he served under him in the Mediterranean and in the Adriatic. During this time they stormed batteries and forts, fought desperate actions in large and small boats, boarding and capturing French privateers and other enemy ships. Sometimes they fought against heavy odds: once, off Corfu, John commanded one of the ship's eight-oared cutters which was chasing an armed French Privateer. 'After a pull of 3 hours and a sharp engagement the enemy boat was captured.' John had a crew of eight, while the enemy had thirty-six.

Most of the actions John described were successful but one must have been a big disappointment. He was in command of some boats sent into the harbour of Trieste, which was protected by two batteries. 'After boarding six vessels under a heavy fire of Grape and Round and musquetry we were obliged to abandon them as they were all found to be made fast to the shore by Cables from their mast heads and their rudders unshipped.'

John evidently did well under Captain Campbell. His father wrote to him in September 1808:

Your very pleasant letter of 22nd June arrived here lately giving me the satisfaction of your being well and that you and your worthy Captain were fortunate as to make so many Captures without receiving the smallest injury from the enemy in the contest ... It is particularly gratifying to me to understand the opinion that Capt. Campbell has of you, which he has communicated in the most flattering terms to our friends in this country; and his anxious desire to forward your views in Life is Clearly shown by his appointing you to officiate as acting Lieutenant in his ship before your time as Midshipman was Expired.

But the following year John found himself bound by Admiralty red tape when the time came for his official promotion to lieutenant. It appeared that he would have to go back to being a midshipman, because he had not served long enough in that capacity; his time as acting lieutenant didn't count. Both he and his Captain were disgusted. In order to serve his lost time as a midshipman John joined *H.M.S. Ville de Paris*, the flag ship of Lord Collingwood.

'I assure you,' he wrote to his father, 'it was a great change to me joining this ship as a midshipman after being Acting Lieut. in the Unite for so long, and parting from one who had always treated me as a son and from a worthy set of messmates who from a long and intimate acquaintance I was attached to as a brother.

Once in the *Ville de Paris* John met with an unpromising situation: there were many young midshipmen waiting for promotion who, he wrote in despair, had been 'recommended to the Admiral by the first men in the Kingdom and it is always his rule to appoint them first.'

Despite his despondency John soon overtook the nine above him awaiting promotion, by volunteering for and taking part in a dangerous expedition in boats to attack and board a French armed convoy in the Bay of Rosas, Spain.

He told his father:

We got in sight of the convey about three in the morning and signalled our division to board the store ship, the others to attack the Armed merchantmen. On the signal being made to attack we gave three cheers and were answered with a tremendous fire from their heavy Batteries and ships.

Nothing could resist our brave tars, it is astonishing the bravery they will Display when put to it. The enemy fire was now nothing to what we had to encounter when we got along side of them. We had to scramble up their sides then get over a netting which they had put round their rigging. All the time we were annoyed by musquet fire and pikes but when we got on their Decks we soon made way.

On account of their being fast to the shore, abrest their Batteries, we suffered very much after we got possession. I had a very narrow escape. A frenchman made a thrust at me with a pike which went through my trousers and grazed my knee. I was at this time in the net struggling like a fish to get out of it, but thank God I got clear safe and sound. It is astonishing the few that suffered considering the tremendous fire that was kept up.

I have this moment received my commission. (2nd Lieut.)

On John's promotion his father, who had suffered much from his son's letters railing against fortune, saw fit to give him some paternal comment and advice.

> 5th January, 1810
>
> You must not, my dear John, despond should your view not always succeed. Surely it was a Galling circumstance you being ordered to your old situation as a Midshipman in the Ville de Paris after being placed in a higher situation by your worthy cousin but when you consider the change as correct and Consistant with the Rules of your profession you had no reason to complain. And think how this was compensated on the other hand by your good fortune in prize money while acting lieut. which might have been otherwise.
>
> If you live long in the Arduous profession you have chosen (and I Pray God you may <u>long and happy</u>) be assured you will meet with many Vexatious Occurrances which you must endeavour to surmount with fortitude, good sense and toleration. Very few indeed in this world but have such tryalls frequently. Now at the age I am of I have got great access to know the Vicissitudes of Life, therefore I must in some degree Judge of them to be the fate of all mortals.

On his return to Britain Captain Campbell wrote to Patrick of John's prize money: 'He has between 5 and 6 hundred pounds which he means to lay out in Government securities, so that he has not done amis in the prize way, and has been careful of what he got.'

John's brother, Sandy, wrote:

> It was rather hard your being obliged to serve longer as midshipman but nothing, I see, is to be shared over in the navy and I hope soon to see the Army in the same footing, till then we shall never be well officered, but we are improving daily. I was much gratified to understand that you had sent home from £500 to £600 with your Captain which I hope is only a beginning to an independant fortune . . . as you can expect but little assistance from an Estate Burdened with debt, & a large Family to maintain which is my Father's case & will be mine should he be called upon to pay that Debt to nature which I hope is far distant . . .

In 1812, when John had been away from home for ten years, he received a letter from his father telling him that Sandy, the heir, had been killed at the storming of Ciudad Rodrigo, while fighting in the Peninsular War. He begged him to get leave and come home.

Patrick continued: 'Your Mother's Grieff is Very Great and she has had much cause to be so, he was an attentive and dutifull son and would

have proved a Father Protector to the Children when I was no more.
Your task is now great and I have no doubt but you possess his goodness
of heart and kind feelings.'

John's mother wrote:

> 4th May, 1812
> Oh my dearest John you can easier imagine than I can describe the
> overwhelming misery into which his irreparable loss plunged us
> into. Nor can I yet restrain my feelings when I think of the dear
> valuable son I have lost ... As you are now, my dear John, placed
> in a different situation, altho I sincerely believe you deeply lament
> the cause, your Father is very anxious you should try and get home
> however short the period as we are, I may say, entire strangers to
> each other & should anything happen to your Father, which from
> his advanced period of life there is more reason to dread, you will
> have a very heavy charge with so throng a family and very small
> funds ...
>
> You rejoice in war but alass little do you know what your poor
> mothers and Fathers feel, but we must trust in Almighty God. 'Tho
> his arm is strong to smite it is likewise strong to save.' May God
> almighty watch over you my dearest Boy in the hour of Danger. I
> trust Allan [John's youngest brother] will be neither Soldier or
> Sailor. You need not wonder, my dear, that our late severe loss
> should make us all have serious thoughts ... Oh my dear John what
> a heavy debt lies upon your warmth of heart & affectionate regard
> before you can fill dear dear Sandy's place. Alas it cannot be
> supposed that you, who are such a stranger to us, can, however
> willing or well inclined.

This last observation, rather daunting to a young man of twenty-three,
Louisa Maxwell softened a little by adding that she thought John had a
natural good disposition and wrote affectionate letters.

John returned home. After some leave, he was applied for by Sir
George Collier as first lieutenant in *H.M.S. Leander*. Britain had been at
war with America since 1812 and the ship was ordered to North
America. Louisa Maxwell wrote in July 1814:

> Your letter to your father acquainting us of your safe arrival at
> Hallifax Nova Scotia gave us all sincere pleasure ... We see in the
> papers an account of the prodigious Isdelands of ice you fell in with
> which must have been a very tremendous and awful sight. I am
> astonished how you and your convoy escaped so well ... We are all
> peace and quietness now in Europe & I hope will remain so at least
> during my Life, the news papers will give you a better detail of
> these matters than I can. With the prodigious armaments that have
> been sent out to America I suspect they won't attempt to cope so

that I hope we will soon hear of the Leander being ordered home which I am convinced will be no acceptable piece of intelligence to you but will I assure you save me from many anxious thoughts on your account so that I hope you will be content to make up your mind to turn your sword into a plowshare.

The peace was signed in January 1815, but those on *Leander* didn't know of it until March and continued to chase enemy ships. John wrote to his father the following May:

We left the American Coast in chase of the Constitution and Congress on 24th of December . . . Since December the Leader has visited Faial [Azores] San Miguel [Azores] Madeira, Teneriffe, St Jago [Cape Verde Islands], Barbados, Dominique and Gaudaloupe, and although we followed the track of the Enemy I am sorry to say they have returned safe into Port.

We were off the Island of St Jago for some days and on that unfortunate day, the 11th of March, made the Island though it was still very foggy. On the fog clearing away a little three men of war were observed ahead and looming very large in the haze. We soon made them out to be the Enemy and all sail was immediately crowded to close with them, in an instant we were clear for Action awaiting the happy moment to convince Mr Yanki what we can do on equal terms. Unfortunately the wind favoured them and it came on very foggy that we lost sight of the hindmost ship the Constitution, the other two proved to be her Prizes the Czane, Capt. Falcon formerly of this ship, and Levant; the later we captured. On our return into St Jago next day with the Levant we heard of the Peace.

(Later John wrote to his father, 'the Loss of the Constitution annoyed me excessively.' Having failed to capture this ship he feared he would not now get promotion to the rank of Commander — in fact he was not promoted until five years later.)

On his way home, he wrote to his father from the entrance to the 'British Channel' saying that he would not have time to write for a few days after their arrival.

July 1815

We have under our Convoy 57 sail of transports having on board the 1st Division of the Army that were employed in Upper Canada amounting to upwards of 9000 men. We left Quebec on the 11th June. I was much delighted with the River St Lawrence, Quebec and the Country round and consider myself very fortunate in visiting that part of America. I made a point of seeing all the natural curiositys and the spot where the immortal Wolf fell, indeed America of late has been a grave for several such Heros and

Britain will always suffer in that country until an other mode of Warfare is addopted and the country cleared of wood.

We are all astonished at the state of Europe since the escape of Bonapart from Elba, we boarded an American Ship a few days ago who informed us of the glorious Battle of Waterloo, he had a paper with the Duke of Wellington's Dispatch, it has been a most bloody affair.

The following year John joined a naval expedition to Algiers in *H.M.S. Superb.* Algiers was, at the time, a hot-bed of piracy. One of the reasons for the expedition was to release three thousand Christian slaves captured in the Mediterranean, from ships of all nationalities who were being held in appalling conditions by the Turks. Louisa Maxwell wrote to John on the eve of his departure:

July, 1816

I am writing a few lines to convey my blessing and prayers for your safe return which I trust will be in a few months and that your forminable appearance will bring those raskaly Moors to proper submission without the necessity of even a shot at the wretches, the news papers are full of your expedition.

I am afraid my dear John you will be much at a loss to fit yourself out for this expedition even though you get the little your Father has allowed, how I regret you not having your Glass and silver spoons and forks but there is no help for it ... I see by the papers there are many offering their services to go upon your expedition and that a number of the powers in Europe are arming aginst the Algerines so trust you will have little to do.

Louisa Maxwell's hopes were not realised. A battle in which both British and Dutch forces took part was fought in a violent thunderstorm. John was wounded but, towards the end of the battle, had to take command of the ship as his superior officers were more seriously wounded. He wrote a full description of the Battle of Algiers (see page 259).

After the battle John received a letter from his eldest sister Bell:

8th October, 1816

I sit down to congratulate you on the most providential escape you have lately made from falling in Battle ... I trust your wounds may be healed ere you reach England unless you have made them at first appear slighter than they really are.

You can conceive what a state we were all in from Thursday till Saturday night — expecting a list of the killed and wounded after hearing 800 had suffered. My Father and mother sat up till the post came in and when the bag arrived no one could hardly open it ...

I really have no news to write, nothing is heard of or talked of but the Battle of Algiers and its Brave Heroes. You will be so much

made of on your return to England that it will make you <u>too Proud</u>
... Adiew my dearest John I hope you never will put yourself in
such Danger again or give us all such a Fright.

John's sister Ann wrote: 'How thankful we all feel my dear John for the
wonderful escape you made at Algiers, where so many brave men lost
their lives. I shall never forget the state we were all in that night when the
dispatches arrived none of us for a considerable time could venture into
Papa's room to read the list of the killed and wounded we were so
agitated.'

Next year, when John was at Plymouth, he received a letter from his
father suggesting: 'The best course I think you can make and the most
certain to promote your interest is if you could get a Good Lass with as
much money as could make you and her live comfortably independent
of me and my succession for some time, and it would be the happiest
step you could take but for God's Sake make a proper choice for other
wise you may tumble over a Dreadful Precipice.'

John replied with enthusiasm:

6th January, 1817

I perfectly coincide with you that my best plan would be to get
hold of a good lass with as much cash as would keep me
independent. I have had my eye on one for some time, she
possesses very good qualities to make a man happy and is of the
first family in this quarter, and I know will have an independent
fortune, but my dear Father in my present situation it will be
impossible for me to lay seige to such a prize ... before I can
continue my visits I must have a little cash, in the first place I want
a horse, and with a little addition to my pay I would be able to keep
up a respectable appearance.

But Patrick apparently refused to assist and John wrote back with
admirable resignation:

21st January, 1817

I am sorry it is not in your power to supply me with what is so
absolutely necessary in this Life, I am aware how much you must
be pinched from bad payment of Rents etc and God forbid that I
should be the means of Reducing your funds more. From having a
debt of £300 and only 6 shillings a day (my full pay) to support
myself I have frequently weighed in my mind the propriety of
increasing my income and I know of no way more conducing to
my feelings or likely to promote my Happiness, Comfort and
Respectability than uniting myself to a woman of respectable
connections and sufficient to be independent, her Disposition
amiable and her person far from being Displeasing. These were
my reasons, My Dear Father, of Requesting your aid to execute

my views, but since it is impossible I must hover about until a better opportunity offers of carrying off my Beloved Prize.

While John was worrying about matrimony he was also concerned about the quiet life his sisters were living at Dunollie, at an age when they should be making more social contacts. He had been urging his father to send them to Edinburgh for a short time and, on hearing that his advice had been taken, wrote:

> 16th November, 1817
> I was much gratified to hear that you had sent Ann and Mary Jane to Edinb. I am aware of the exertion you must have made in their behalf, considering the large demands you have lately been obliged to answer. Keeping them longer at home without seeing a little of society I should think would be greatly to the disadvantage of both (particularly Ann). They are sweet warm hearted creatures and I am convinced you will be handsomely remunerated for the inconvenience and trouble you must be put to by sending them together this winter, a twelve monthes delay would be of serious consequence to them. The satisfaction of having the Girls around you finished in their education must afford infinately more pleasure than the Reflection of being a few hundred pounds in debt can possibly distress you.

In 1818 Admiral Donald Campbell applied for John to be his flag lieutenant in the *Salisbury* sailing to the West Indies. While there, John was much concerned about his admiral's health, and wrote: 'the Admiral has not been so well of late, he had a very severe attack at St Thomas indeed the surgeon gave him over, however he has recovered most astonishingly, as he does not wish the state of his health be known to his friends don't make this public.' Captain Patrick Campbell wrote to John, 'You must take great care of the worthy old Admiral and not let him slip his cable while abroad.'

The *Salisbury* was involved in a severe hurricane which hit the island of St Thomas. Mary Jane wrote to John:

> 22nd January, 1820
> We were quite shocked when we saw in the papers of the dreadful hurricane at St Thomases and that out of an hundred the Salisbury and three more were all that escaped. What a state you must have been in witnessing such distruction and I dare say every moment expecting to be driven ashore if you were on board, and if ashore to be destroyed. We are much disappointed at not having heard from you since and would be more so had we not heard of you.

During the hurricane John rescued three seamen 'off the bottom' of an upturned Danish ship after fruitless attempts had been made from the shore. For this he received the thanks of the King of Denmark.

In 1820 the old Admiral died. John was sent home with dispatches, and was soon afterwards promoted to the rank of Commander. At the time promotion was difficult to obtain without the help of influential people. Many letters had been written by John and his parents to anyone who might possibly help.

At one point Patrick had written to John summing up the situation: 'I fear any interest we may apply to will avail little for the truth is Everyone has their own near Connections in the Army or Navy and Political influences, of which we have none, is the surest to succeed.'

Louisa Maxwell, nothing daunted, had tried for the influence of the Duke of Wellington. She wrote to her brother, Sir Alexander Campbell, who replied:

> I should feel real pleasure in forwarding your son John's views if it were in my power but the thing at present is quite out of the question. Whoever tells you nonsence about my influence with the Duke of Wellington deceives you & although no man is more obliged to His Grace than I am I never asked him a favour for myself although he has conferred many on me this gives him a right to expect my devoted services but gives me no claim on him. Your sons are like many thousands of other meritorious young men thrown back upon their friends by the peace, few men feel it more than I do for I had a most agreeable situation which I lost by the termination of the war.

However, John was promoted before long, and in 1822 wrote to his father from London: 'Since I came here I have been presented to his Majesty and had the honour to kiss his hand, it is customary on being Promoted to Commander, he looks well and in high health.'

John was to see the King again that year. A few months later he paid a visit to Edinburgh, and John, representing his father, took part in the celebrations held to welcome His Majesty. He wrote to Patrick:

> 10th August, 1822
>
> You will feel a little surprised at my not having wrote you before this but really I have been so constantly employed that my meals interfere with my military duty. The Celtic Society are formed into four companies McLeod, McDougall jr., Sir E. Macgregor Mury and Clanranald and are to mount guard at the Holy rood Palace during the King's residence, the Archers in the interior of the Palace. We are constantly at drill and I think will make a good appearance.
>
> This town is in quite a Bustle it is said His Majesty leaves London

Portrait of John MacDougall of MacDougall (1789-1865)

today and probably will be here on Tuesday morning. Every person far and near are gathering. It is said a thousand Highlanders will be in the procession. There was a meeting of the County Gentlemen and an address is to be presented. I am one of those who are to have the honor. I believe the Duke is not to be here. The girls [John's sisters] poor dears, are happy and delighted at every thing they see and hear and a little stir does not displease me.

In a letter written after the King had arrived, John told his father: 'The girls poor dears have been gratified beyond expression. Mary has been at the Drawing room and the Ball and has been kissed by his Majesty which she is very proud of. I received his Majesty with a guard of forty Highlanders at Holy rood Palace.'

Although he was now a Commander, John had no ship and, like many naval officers of the time, he was put on half pay. For the next decade or so he was to lead a completely different life.

Life on Half-pay at Home

John came back to Dunollie and took over the management of the farm and estate from his father, by now in bad health. Farquharson of Invercauld wrote to John:

> 20th October, 1823
> You are extremely well employed on the Management of your Estate as your Father's very advanced age and infirmities render him unfit for it and I think the life of a Country Gentleman the pleasantest of any as it is evidently the Most Natural one to Mankind. Mrs F's uncle Lord Gardenstone used to say 'we are all naturally Farmers, or born to superintend the production of the Soil, all other Professions, Trades, & employments have arisen from our wants, occasioned by the State of Society.'

The following years, until John went back to active service in the Navy, were to see many important family events, including marriages, births and a death.

In 1823 Mary Jane, John's favourite sister, became seriously ill and the doctors despaired of her life. However, quite unexpectedly she recovered and — as related in the last chapter — John took her to Cheltenham to convalesce. Ann went too, and the family hoped this visit would prove a step towards matrimony for the two girls. Ann was by now twenty-five and Mary Jane twenty-three and it was considered high time they found husbands. From Oxford, John wrote to his father of their journey:

18th July, 1824

If ever I enjoyed visiting England I have reason to be delighted with this trip from the astonishing improvement in my dear Mary Jane's health, she has gained strength daily since I left Dunolly, the change of air & scene has proved a blessing to her. We left Liverpool upon Wednesday last & went as far as Trenthem (62 miles), at dinner Mary eat a little fish, leg and wing of a fowl & part of a Beef steak, after that walked through part of the Marquis of Stafford's grounds & his house & at night slept like a top. The following day left Trentham for Birmingham at 11 o'clock (42 miles) where she dined & slept equally as well, this morning at 10 we left Birmingham for this beautiful City (64 miles). Ann and Mary insisted on travelling outside to see the Country few ever beheld a richer one, & I am satisfied there never were two young Ladies more delighted & I hope happier. Mary is now busy writing her journal which she is to amuse you with upon her return. I intend taking my charges to London tomorrow as both are anxious to see the great metropolis.

Four months later John wrote to Patrick from Cheltenham:

I arrived here the day before yesterday & found the young ladies in great spirits & Mary much improved indeed I may say in looks and manners & what is still more surprising Ann considered a beauty. They have got acquainted with several very Respectable families since I left them & their conduct has been most examplay other wise they would never have got introduced & been on such intimate terms with so many people of Distingtion in a place where they are so particular with strangers. I begin now to think there is a prospect of your Daughters getting settled in Life, it is my duty to watch those who are particular in their attentions & if gentlemen & possessing the means of supporting my Sisters as Ladies I have no right further to interfere provided they are satisfied.

John's Courtship and Marriage

It was at Cheltenham that Mary Jane met a young man named Charles Monro, of whom much more is heard later in the letters.

And in Cheltenham, John at last found himself a bride. The story goes that a naval officer friend, knowing he was interested in building, took him to see a Captain Timmins of the East India Company, who had just built a new house — Oriel Lodge. Afterwards, when asked by his friend for his opinion of the new building, John admitted that he hadn't noticed it: his eyes had been only for the Captain's daughter Sophy!

Early in 1825 John wrote to Captain Timmins saying that he wanted to marry Sophy: she was then seventeen. He had not yet consulted his own father. Captain Timmins replied at length:

28th January, 1825

The Happiness of our Dear Child is now the only hope her parents have for any enjoyment or Peace in this life; her own inclination must solely guide her in the choice of a future friend and Partner ... Her mother as well as myself would prefer having her mind more strengthened by a mixture in Society than it is now, prior to her making so important a determination, and for myself in particular I must confess that many causes arise in my heart for bitter reflections and useless regrets for neglect in my pecuniary concerns and merchantile pursuits, which have been unfortunate in the extreme, so that I am not left the power to make that present provision for my daughter which my fond inclination would prompt and deserve.

Painful as you will believe it is to my feelings I find it my duty not to conceal from you my present circumstances ... and inform you that it is out of my power to make any settlement upon My Daughter but that to which she must by Law Succeed to when her Mother may be no more: her future provision during the life of her parents must depend upon the good will of Fortune in the strenuous endeavours of her Father to obtain it. Do not think, my good Sir, that my being thus explicit implies a suspicion that pecuniary concerns would be any temptation to your forming a connection for life; I believe they would not ... but I take the liberty to suggest the propriety of your giving this matter the test of Absence, and reflection of some time, before you take any further steps: as a friend I advise this to you <u>Most earnestly</u> and as a Father I wish it for my Child's sake.

Your natural affection will also prompt you to require the advice and sanction of him whose place you are to take when it shall please the Almighty, and the course of Nature, to remove him from being the Protector of his family; but these are considerations which I am sure you will always bear in mind.

[Of Sophy herself he wrote] — I have never in one instance of her life had to complain of the disposition of a child whose whole conduct from infancy has been a source of comfort and honest Pride in her parents. She has benefited by the anxious care of an excellent and prudent Mother and cultivated by her own Industry and Natural Talent every accomplishment that can adorn a Female. I may confidentally affirm she possesses all that is admired in Polished Circles or that is valuable in any Society. A sound and descreet mind is tempered by Virtuous and Religeous Principles.

Eighteen months later, Captain Timmins wrote:

It is my Duty to suggest that a Moderate Settlement be made by you on my Daughter and such Children as she may probably have, and I shall be ready to make over the possession of our Property after the Death of myself and My Wife, which is the Utmost I can in justice to either undertake.

I cannot suppose that what you have seen of the habits of my Family has led you to think my dear Child would be happier by riches and I affirm, for my own part, I should prefer an independant Commpetence to extreme Affluence for her; if she can live as she has been accustomed, in ecconomy and genteel comfort it is all that can be required; I am sure she has no other wish, nor ever had any other expectation.

In 1826 — the year after his father's death — John, now thirty-seven, married his Sophy. She was, judging from her portrait, a very beautiful woman. The wedding took place in the South and Allan, John's brother, wrote:

This twenty second day of August, one thousand eight hundred and twenty six I hope you, my dear Brother, and your amiable Sophy will long live to remember as your happy Bridalday. This is a day of much anxiety but to unite ourselfs to an amiable and intelligent partner for life is surely the happiest and best spent day of our lives. This I believe to be your lot for, together with her form which nature I believe in her fairest mould hath cast, I believe Miss Timmins to have other no less attractions and more lasting qualities; then am I mistaken in calling <u>this</u> your happiest spent day. I don't know that I am mirthful for I believe my pleasure is softened by the distance from its source and appears to me in pleasant revery ... Since writing the above I have dined with our Mama and sisters and have dedicated a <u>full bumper</u> to all that can give you pleasure ... All here joins me in wishing you and your 'Pussy' a safe journey — you need not tell her that I take such liberties with her <u>own</u> name for you know even kittens can scratch.

After the wedding the bride and bridegroom travelled by coach to Dunollie. Sophy was evidently enraptured by her first sight of Highland scenery. Allan wrote:

7th September, 1826

Yours from Arrocher giving so delightful an account of your sweet Lady's feelings upon first viewing our mountain scenery, delightful for the pleasure she received and the proof that a chiefteness may be found many miles South of the Tweed. The smoke will yet curl over the old trees at Dunolly many more months of the year than those who only know that your <u>fair</u> partner is from under a more Southern sun are perhaps inclined to admit.

Portrait of Sophy (1806-1881), wife of John

[The newly married couple arrived safely and Allan wrote again] The reception you met with must have indeed been very gratifying and I am glad to find your journey so prosperous, and that you even had a few fine days. I am sorry there was not an eminent reporter of the scene at your landing for we should have it in print.

Louisa Maxwell and the girls moved out of Dunollie and went to live in York in a rented house. Louisa Maxwell was a reluctant dowager and soon quarrelled with her son on the subject of money. In December Allan told John:

Your letter to our Mother has certainly nothing unreasonable in it and why she will not reply to it is best known to herself ... From all I have remarked and heard I shall only say that I feel if I were your Mother and sisters I would act differently towards you than they do — were I your Mother I would not war with my son because he will not gratuitously add to my income. I think my pride would revolt from it. Our family tradition says a Mother's pride led her to give up a great part of her own & return to obscurity that her son might live in a greater state ... I regret on many accounts that I have not open free communication with my Mother upon her own or my own matters but when ten minutes conversation brings you under language that, now-a-days at least, is unsupportable it is better to avoid words ... Avoid, my dear John, quarrels — they are Mother and sisters. We are men and would gain little in warring.

However, quarrels were soon forgotten with the arrival of John and Sophy's first child, Alexander, the following year. Louisa Maxwell wrote to John with delight:

28th August, 1827

It was with the most heartfelt pleasure that I this morning received your letter with the truly happy tidings of your dearest Sophy having presented you with a son and Heir, upon which joyful event your sisters and I beg to congratulate you and your dear wife, and most sincerely hope that both she and the young gentleman may continue to do well, of which I beg you may acquaint me from time to time until she is perfectly recovered.

Your ride from Glasgow was certainly very astonishing yet for all your speed the young chief thought proper to step into the World without even, I believe, one of the Clan being in Dunollie at the time to welcome his arrival. Is Mrs MacDougall able or has she wherewith to suckle the little fellow? I hope she had all her necessary attendants with her upon the occasion.

Allan wrote to John: 'I hope you may yourself feel no bad effects from your late and long ride.'

Three months later, John, who had allowed neither battles, hurricanes, plagues nor any other hazard of life in the Navy to alarm him, was alarmed for what seems a most peculiar reason: his baby son was breathing quietly. He wrote to his mother for her advice.

Louisa Maxwell replied: 'I don't think you need be in the least alarmed at dear little Alexander's quiet breathing if he is otherwise in good health, digests his food and his bowels are in good order. I suppose he has your short neck which it may be partly owing to, at the same time I don't approve of too much spoon feeding if he has plenty of his natural breast food.'

The Courtship of Mary Jane

It was during this year that Mary Jane was in trouble over her romance with Charles Monro, whom she had met at Cheltenham. In her distress she turned to John as head of the family. It appeared that, two years before, when Mary Jane was twenty-four and Charles nineteen, they had made a secret arrangement that as soon as he was twenty-one, and came into his heritage, they should get married. They wrote to each other frequently and Monro came to visit Mary Jane in York.

But within a few days of the longed-for twenty-first birthday, Mary Jane received a letter from her future father-in-law, that caused her much distress. She wrote urgently to John.

27th January, 1827

I regret troubling you in the midst of your gaiety with my distress but I think it is of too great importance to require making an apology to you. You are aware from Mr Monro's recent correspondence with you, as well as with Mama and myself, of his undiminished attachment to me and his determination when ever he comes of age of fulfilling his long and repeated engagement, neither did a week pass, since he was here, without two or three letters to that effect, but he was anxious that it might be concealed until that period.

His last letter was Saturday the 13th wherein he mentions that while he was out to dinner the day before his Brother had acquainted his Father of his [Monro's] intentions towards me. The Father, who was not aware that our correspondence had continued, was very angry indeed at Monro concealing it but said that he had now no objections as Monro can provide for me fully from the estate. He hoped his next letter to me would pronounce everything comfortably settled for altho' his Father is very hot at first after reflecting some little time he always forgets and forgives. Monro requests me not to discompose myself, as it is only at him that his Father is angry for concealing it ...

But, my dear John, what was my astonishment upon Saturday last at receiving the annexed letter from his Father written four days after his son wrote to me. I can make no comment upon it but that he could not express greater indignation had his son been engaged to a person far beneath him. And for the fault of concealing it from him he will insist upon his son committing the most shocking of all perjuries at the very moment he was to have fulfilled his promises.

I thought it no business of mine to answer such a letter as I am convinced the old man, and I daresay the whole Family, object to the marriage in consequence of the settlements I might get which would not be to their advantage.

I directly sat down and wrote to Monro the anexed copy of a letter and enclosed his father's letter. I cannot understand how his Father has the power to put a stop to all future proceedings ... I need scarce add you will see the propriety of not mentioning this to a living creature.

Copy of Mr Monro Senior's Letter to Mary Jane
                                                   17th January, 1827
In consequence of Capt. [in fact Commander] MacDougall's reply to a letter I had the honor to address to him on a subject in which I am deeply interested, and of the utmost importance to my son, I take the liberty of addressing you.

I have with pain observed for some time a visable change in him, on enquiring the cause I discovered to my grief and astonishment that he had deceived me by continuing a correspondence which I had forbidden, and which he had promised to relinquish. He confessed that he has never been happy, but has been oppressed with the deepest remorse at the undutiful part he was acting towards his Father. While I heartily lament being the cause of giving you offence I deem it my bounden duty to lay my commands upon him to put a stop to any further proceedings in this affair. His youth and inexperience are sufficient fully to justify my present conduct. Trusting you will perceive the propriety of my interference on this occasion I have the honor to be, Madam, Your most obedient Humble servant, J Monro

Copy of Mary Jane's letter to Mr C.H.Monro, her fiancé
I have not words to express my surprise and astonishment at receiving inclosed most Extraordinary letter from Your Father; to which if he expects an answer it is quite impossible for me from its tenor to do so as I ought to to your Father. I regret to observe that he appears to have forgot what is due to me, or cannot properly be aware of the situation in which we stand. I therefore send his unfeeling, and I must say selfish, letter to you — who I think the

proper person to possess it. If I have done wrong in this I know I
have a kind advocate in your heart to plead my excuse. Painful as it
is to me and however incapable I feel I will try if possible and
follow your kind advice to discompose myself as little as I possibly
can, as on the 23rd your minority will end and you take all upon
yourself. I had hoped to have heard from you today and I will be
quite unhappy and distressed until I do. I must now conclude this
unpleasant letter which believe me has quite exhausted my
strength and spirits.

Monro's twenty-first birthday came and went but there was still no
letter from him to Mary Jane. Five days later she wrote again to John:

> 28th January, 1827
> I have not yet heard from Mr Monro since the receipt of his
> Father's letter altho three posts have passed that I ought to have
> heard since he came of age, the period he looked forward to with
> such anxiety and such decided certainty of being his own master
> and could and would, uncontrolled, fulfil his long engagement to
> me. I cannot possibly conceive what has prevented him from
> writing unless our letters may be interrupted by his Father, who
> from his extraordinary letter to me I think capable of doing
> anything. Still I would fain hope and flatter myself that Mr Monro
> can not possibly be capable of such long continued and deep
> deceit after all his letters, coming here so rapidly after our arrival
> and his repeated letters to you and Mama upon this subject. I will
> now conclude this painful and distressing subject which occupies
> my whole thoughts.

The state that Mary was now in was described to John the same day by
her mother:

> I sit down again to write in regard to our dearest Mary Jane, no
> letter from Monro today, and it is impossible for me to describe to
> you what she suffers, so completely has he gained her heart and
> affections; and it is not surprising as it has been his sole study for
> two years past and he succeeded. It appears to me quite
> impossible that any mandate of his Father's could so completely
> estrange his heart and affection from one for whom only he lived,
> those were his own words and writ even to me, and that so lately
> such very frequent long and loving letters acquainting and
> consulting with her upon every occurance, from those of
> consequence to the most trivial. He said his family had remarked
> his low spirits which were entirely owing to his absence from her,
> his anxiety for her, care of her health and every thing he thought
> would add to her comfort or happiness seemed to be his only
> study. At the same time he appeared anxious that his engagement

to Mary should not be known to his Father, altho he said the rest of his family knew of it.

Louisa Maxwell went on to suggest that, if John did not get a satisfactory answer from Monro, he should go and see the father and son and 'point out their high culpability to them'. Before this she had never seen Mary Jane in better health, spirits and looks but now, how changed was her appearance: 'Indeed, I could not believe so short a period could make such a change on any person.' The letter ends: 'I think altho his Father had imprisoned him he might contrive to write to her.'

So January passed with Mary Jane miserable and her relations in agitated sympathy and indignation. But by the middle of February young Monro had arrived in person at York. Now all seemed bright again, but only for a day or two.

Louisa Maxwell wrote to John:

18th February, 1827

Mr Monro had a note last night acquainting him that his Father was dangerously ill and insisted on his returning immediately and he sets out for Lymmington this evening. I suspect it is all a manouvere to get him down and make him sign some deed regarding his property as the father has both Lawyers completely upon his side of the question, I must fear they will prevail upon him. He has promised to return in a few days ... I suppose they don't want him to marry until they have first <u>plucked</u> him well.

Monro kept his word and was back in York within a few days. Whether 'plucked' or not the letters don't reveal, but his father seems to have given his consent to the marriage. Louisa Maxwell told John the good news: 'Mr Monro is here every day as usual and talks of his marriage as quite fixed and settled and has even acquainted several of his male friends of it. He says his Father has nothing at all to do or say in the matter as he has left it entirely to himself. Still I think in politeness he ought to have answered my letter which he never has.'

During the next month Monro's brother, who had told his father about Monro's engagement, became ill and died. He left all his money to his mother.

Louisa Maxwell told John that: 'Mary Jane has had a very kind letter from Monro's Father and most affectionate remembrances from the rest of his family which is all as it ought to be so I pray God she may now find everything agreeable and happy, his mother has succeeded to a good fortune by her son's death so that there is plenty of riches among them.'

But Louisa Maxwell's pious hopes for Mary Jane were for the moment unfulfilled. Mary Jane wrote to John:

16th April 1827

I would not have written to you so soon again had it not been in consequence of a letter I have just received from Mr Monro in which, after a good deal of prefacing, he says that altho' he had while in London told me and my family that he was to settle five hundred a year upon me at his death, he now finds in justice to his heirs, whoever they may be, he cannot do so and therefore has given instructions that instead of five hundred I should have three hundred per annum, and that he wishes to know from me that I am neither displeased or disappointed.

You may well suppose, my dear John, it was rather puzzling to me how to act as I am convinced, from what Monro has repeatedly acquainted me with, that his fortune is even better than he had anticipated when in London, and I rather suspect this is entirely a manouvre of his Father's who I suppose withholds his consent until the reduction of the jointure is made, and that Monro will not (and naturally) marry without it. No doubt you have cause to be displeased, which I have no objection they should know, altho' there is no good, but to the contrary, in my showing my displeasure as it might lead to further putting off and perhaps ultimately more disagreeable consequences.

I therefore in answer said: 'As you are so anxious, my dear Monro, to have my approbation for your curtailing the settlements which you so kindly made upon me be assured where I have so decidedly placed my sole happiness, heart and affections I likewise with confidence intrust to your care for my future comfort should I unfortunately be the longest survivor.'

Mary Jane's tactful letter to Monro seems to have averted a crisis and from now on arrangements for the wedding were made in earnest.

The bride wrote frantically to John: 'I have not had a farthing since I left London and of course cannot get even the necessities I will require for the occasion so, my dear John, I beg you may send me what will give me a proper rigging for to appear amongst Mr Monro's friends, with whom I am now a great favourite.'

Meanwhile Monro asked John to fix a day for the wedding, after the middle of May. He also asked for an impression of the MacDougall arms as he wished to put them on his carriage blended with his own. 'I saw the carriage the other day,' he wrote, 'I can assure you it is the most elegant but genteely plain one I ever saw — all ready for a start.'

Finally the wedding day was fixed for 1st June. Monro then thought up a plan involving the bride's sister Ann, which today sounds most peculiar. He told John:

I start again for York next Friday fortnight just to spend the few remaining Batcholor days I shall have with you, and then on first of June I think we must set to work and get that job over. I then propose starting for Lymmington in 'my travelling carriage' accompanied by Ann who is vastly delighted with the idea of going, I thought it would be more comfortable for Mary not feeling so lonely and altogether parted from her own family ... with the pleasant prospect of seeing you on the approaching signal event, an event which will set all York in a commotion and all tongues going.

The wedding duly took place and the young couple, accompanied by Ann, travelled to Lymington in the new carriage drawn by four horses. They broke the journey in London where, quite unexpectedly, they met several friends and relations from Scotland.

Soon after this they moved from Lymington to Monro's estate in Devon. He had inherited a large house there called Ingsdon House. The marriage seems, after all the vicissitudes which beset the engagement, to have been a very happy one.

A Marriage of Convenience

Compared with Mary Jane's warm and affectionate love affair her sister Ann's courtship seems cold and calculating.

About a month after Ann, like a guardian gooseberry, had gone south with her sister and brother-in-law on their honeymoon journey, John, as head of the family, received the following letter:

Sir, I went twice last year to Dunolly with the intention to lay the contents of this letter before you and your Mother and both times I found myself so much at a loss for want of expression upon such a subject that I have now taken upon me to use the liberty with you by my taking this mode of now laying before you that which I ought to have done when I last had the pleasure to be with you at Dunolly.

Both my brother and sister for these several years past earnestly entreated of me to take a Wife, last year both my brother and sister knew the intention of my Visits to Dunolly which really was to lay myself entirely at the disposal of your sister Miss Ann, my brother and sister are extreamly well pleased at the connection I wish to form and I hope it will meet with your approbation, your Mother's and Miss Ann's and I will look upon myself as a fortunate man if this my proposal to your Sister meets her approbation. If I am so fortunate as that my proposal meets with your concurrence I beg you will have the goodness to let me know whether you are first to acquaint your sister of this my proposal or am I to do it first, if the latter please have the goodness to direct me where I am to address my letter. May I expect the favour of an answer from you to these contents in course and I ever remain with the utmost Esteem, Sir, Your much obliged, Humble Servant Peter Campbell.

John gave the prospective bridegroom permission to write to Ann's mother, Louisa Maxwell, and at the same time wrote to her himself. Louisa Maxwell replied:

10th July, 1827

Your letter of the 28th ulto. with Peter Campbell Balivolan's proposal I received in course and immediately communicated the contents of it to Ann, with my own observations which were that if she thought she could overlook his age and appearance in every respect she might, if she approved, make herself comfortable in respect to his connections and fortune, but not to be biassed by any thing I should say but think seriously of her future prospects when I am gone, which by the course of nature cannot now be very long of happening. Poor thing she says she has had a good sample while even living with me here what it is to be in poverty and what will her state be when I go. Brothers and Sisters may be very kind but there is nothing like a home of ones own. No doubt John she says true and girls without money or much good looks must stomach many things for independence. So from her letters she does not object to his offer.

I have lived so long in the World that I have often seen these marriages of mutual convenience turn out as well and happy as your Love marriages. But you must inquire into what settlements the Brother proposes making upon them during his life and what jointure upon Ann at his death ...

Peter Bally [Balivolan] may really think himself a fortunate man if he gets Ann, she will brush him up and his whole family and with great economy will make a figure they never did in their old fashioned way, altho' I remember when there was scarce a family in the Country that lived more comfortably and respectably than the Balivolan Family did.

Immediately upon receipt of Peter Balivolan's letter I wrote him a civil acknowledgement of it and said I would communicate the contents of it to my daughter and acquaint him after receiving her answer. But now I think it would be as well, as the Old Colonel cannot come to you, that you should go to him and know what he intends to settle upon them during his life and what jointure at his Brother's death he will settle upon her ...

I told Ann to take time to consider before she answered me which she has done, and all her sisters approve of her determination as they can never keep house or even board themselves after my death, and those from whom they might expect a home appear as needful. You will go or write to Balivolan as they will of course be daily looking for my answer there from Ann.

Meanwhile Peter had told John:

> I received your kind letter of the 25th and I return you my best and warmest thanks for your having done me the favour to permit me to write to your mother upon the subject contained in the letter that I writ you prior to this one ... I have taken it upon me to send you here inclosed a letter for your Mother. After you have perused it I beg you will have the goodness to seal and direct it to your Mother. My reason for sending you the inclosed is that you may actually see all my proceedings regarding any proposal to your sister.

About three weeks later he wrote jubilantly to John:

> 20th July, 1827
>
> Yesterday afternoon I had the pleasure of receiving a letter from your Mother, dated the 11th inst. giving me the joyful news that your sister Miss Ann has done me the greatest favour that can possibly be paid to any person by her having the goodness to accept of my proposal ... If you desire it I will send to you by post your Mother's last letter to me. Your Mother has done me the favour to permit me to write to Miss Ann, inclosing Miss Ann's letter into one for your Mother, and I propose sending both in the course of a Post or two, unless you wish to see them before they are sent off, if so please acquaint me in course.

Peter's letter stirred up a fine flurry in the family. John was outraged: Ann had been far too precipitate, for the financial prospects were not yet clear, and he wrote to tell her so. His anger, however, was nothing to hers:

> 27th July, 1827
>
> Your surprise would not equal mine, I may say my mortification, when I this morning read the contents of your letter saying that I had accepted Mr Campbell's proposal to me without knowing or considering what settlements were to be made.
>
> How can I possibly be accused of doing so is perfectly unintelligible to me. In the first place he, Mr Campbell, has never written to me and of course I have not to him and any correspondence which has taken place between Mama and I on the subject could not, and did not, empower her to write to him in any such manner ... I told Mama that if Mr C. wrote to her to refer him to me.

If Louisa Maxwell was guilty of putting her daughter in this embarrassing position she wasn't going to admit it:

28th July, 1827

Your letter of 22nd surprised me not a little [she told John] as I had always understood that unless there had been a concurrance upon Ann's part there would have been no occasion for your communicating in any shape upon the subject of money with the Balivolan family, the sanctioning of which was all that I meant by my letter to Mr Peter Campbell, and her desire to be further acquainted with him and his family. I have no copy of my letter to him, that I know was the meaning I intended to convey and surely if his means does not please or personal appearance, upon further acquaintance I don't suppose Ann is in the least bound by what I could say, the former she could know as little of as of the later.

Both she and all her sisters seemed to approve of the marriage as well as you did in your letter to me, wherein you say 'that if Ann could divest herself of the feeling of getting a Young Buck everything else is equal to what she could have looked for'. Now Ann in both her letters to me, which I received before I wrote to Mr Peter Campbell, appears to have devested herself of that Feeling and in that case I make no doubt she might make herself happy otherwise God forbid she should ever enter the state of Matrimony.

The next letter to John was a somewhat worried one from the bridegroom-to-be. He was surprised that Ann's mother said she could not give her consent to the proposed jointure. Worse still, he had not yet received an answer to his first letter to Miss Ann. He had heard, however, that Ann was shortly to go to Dunollie and that he was to meet her there.

The meeting apparently went off well. A month or so later Peter's elder brother Charles, the Colonel, wrote to John:

20th September, 1827

I was favoured with yours of the 17th curt, by my Brother on his return from Dunolly, who I am happy to find is likely to form an Alliance with a family so highly respectable as yours.

The best proof I can give of my good will to the Match is my hearty concurrence to Grant, for the benefit of the young married pair, the whole of my Property in the Parish of Ardchattan together with the House, Furniture and Stock upon the Farm held in my own hands. I am also willing to let them enjoy the Meal, Kian, and Servitudes of my Lismore Tennants as now paid to myself, and I hope that one Hundred pounds Ster. by way of Board will not be thought too little so long as they can make my residence with them agreeable, but in the case I am obliged to reside elsewhere, which I will be very sorry for, the Meal and the Kian will then be required for my own use. I have this day written to my man of business to let you or your brother have a perusal of the Deed of Entail.

After this followed much correspondence about the entail and settlements. Louisa Maxwell was shown to have a business head as good as any man's. At one point poor Peter wrote in a state of great embarrassment: he had told John that the amount of oatmeal paid by the tenants for the use of the family was 35 bolls when in fact it was only 26.

> I really do not know how to make a proper apology to you for my commiting myself so grossly to you about the meal but I believe that my ignorance at present proceeded from this, that ever since my Father's death it appeared to myself that it would in me, as second brother, be highly improper to have it said of me that I was looking too much, and more than became me, into my brother's affairs. [Having got this off his chest Peter then broke into fanciful prose.] 'I wish that this old cold-hearted entail that hangs over this small Estate was in the heart middle of Mount Etna, spreading its pestilential vapours on all the natives of Italy.'

September came and went and then on 20th October Colonel Campbell wrote to John: 'I have written to your Brother Allan all that occurs to me on the subject of the Alliance betwixt your Family and this and as every obstackle, as far as I can see or remove, has been removed I imagine that the Marriage Ceremony may take place about the end of the incoming week — the day must be left to the Lady and yourself.'

But six days later the prospective bridegroom wrote to John in a state of agitation:

> 26th October, 1827
> My brother writ you and your Brother Mr Allan by the post of Sunday last and I am thrown into a stew-pan over not having heard from either of you since . . . I would like to know whether we are to remain the first night at Dunolly, or do we immediately set out for this, young Airds accompanys me to Dunolly.
> P.S. I beg you name an early day as Airds is obliged to leave the country in a week hence.

The bride, however, was not prepared to be rushed and the wedding date was fixed for three weeks ahead, on 16th November.

As soon as the date was decided, Colonel Campbell wrote to John:

> 1st November, 1827
> As I do not imagine it is the wish of the newly married pair to run away from their friends and scamper all round the country I hope you will find it convenient to accompany them hither without any

circumvendibus and see your sister installed here as Mistress of this Family. This will also give you an opportunity to assist them in laying down proper regulations for their domestic economy during their present circumscribed situation ... Before I send this epistle let me again intreat you to accompany your Sister, whom I very soon expect to call my Sister also, to this place bringing with you as many of the Family as this House can accommodate.

Louisa Maxwell wrote to John at the same time: 'I think the settlements for Ann are very respectable indeed and what none of us can object to, and as far as ever I heard of the man his appearance is the worst of him, which Ann must have always been aware of ... if she has not changed her opinion I think the sooner the better.'

The marriage took place at 11 a.m. on 16th November in the Dunollie drawing-room. It nearly didn't happen, as the family had forgotten about the banns, but they were reminded just in time by the Rev. McIntyre, minister of Kilmore, who was to take the ceremony.

Louisa Maxwell wrote to John from York on the day of the wedding: 'God grant it may prove a happy one to her so far as we could have reason to expect from the dissimiliarity in age ... I think, dear John, tho' I don't in general approve of crowds upon such occasions you have acted very properly upon the present one to invite your friends and neighbours to witness the marriage.'

A month later the family had decided that the marriage was going to be a success. Louisa Maxwell wrote to John: 'I am most truly gratified to understand both from you and Ann that she is so much pleased with her lot, and that she has cause to be so as she has got over the greatest bar — the man's age and appearance.'

Ann and Peter enjoyed only a few years of married life. Peter died three years after the wedding, and Ann was left to bring up their only child — young Donald.

Building at Dunollie; John's spells on land and at sea

It was not only the family who looked to John for advice. In July 1831 he received the following letter from Duncan Campbell of Lochnell:

I have a letter from Sir James Riddell this morning dated the 11th inst. in which is the following paragraph: 'We have a Report here that a vessel with cholera on board has put into Loch Don.' [Loch Don is a sea loch on the Island of Mull, opposite the island of Kerrera.]

This is of too serious a nature for the Country, I therefore send it to you in hopes you will be able to asscertain the truth or otherwise of the report as by your ferry you have daily communication with the near Neighbourhood of Loch Don, I trust it may prove a false report but if unhappily true we all look to you as most conversant in these matters to put the ship and if neccessary the whole opposite coast under strict Quarantine and to take every necessary step to prevent it spreading. [The ferry referred to went from Kerrera to Auchnacraig on Mull.]

Asiatic Cholera, a disease hitherto unknown in Britain, was at this time sweeping nearer and nearer across Europe from the East, killing many as it came. It finally arrived at Sunderland in October of that year, carried by ship. Presumably the Loch Don scare was a false alarm, but early in 1832 fears that the neighbourhood would be affected were renewed. John and his family were staying at Cheltenham on a visit to his in-laws. He received the following from his factor in Oban:

10th February 1832

You will see from the Papers that Cholera has appeared at Kirkintulloch within 7 miles of Glasgow and that some cases have appeared in Glasgow which alarmed us very much here. The Magistrates have written to the officer of Customes at Glasgow and have received Orders to put the Quarantine Questions to all vessils from the Clyde and if the least Symptom of Disease appear to order them to the nearest Quarantine Station. I sent Fletcher the Constable to Inspect and Report the state of the Tenants on your property. I sent him in preference to the Ground Officer as he could direct them what they ought to do much better having more experience.

He says they are much cleaner than he expected to find them but still there is much to be done, he thinks it will require 60 Barrels of shell lime to go over them all. I intend getting the lime as soon the weather permits and have it distributed amongst them. He has made out a list of the whole and a state as to their cleanliness and the number of persons in each family. He has ordered them to put all their Dunghills at a distance from their houses, to clean themselves and their bed cloathes and put clean straw in the beds which they have all promised to comply with ...

We are using every precaution that can be suggested to prevent or avert the virulence of the disorder should it unfortunately get among us. But our funds are getting low and little prospect of getting more ... I hope you all enjoy good health, you are fortunate to be so far distant from the Coast the risk of contagion will be the less.

At this time, and for some years before, John had been throwing himself with enthusiasm into improving his property. He had begun with new farm buildings in the stable yard and planned an addition to the

Sketch of Dunollie showing the house built by Alexander in 1745
on the left and the Georgian addition on the right

L-shaped family house built by his grandfather. The 'addition', as it was always referred to in the letters, turned out to be larger than the house itself, being a three-storeyed Georgian block filling in the L. There was much argument in the letters about its plan, an argument in which most of the family joined. John's mother wrote that she understood that the addition 'was entirely for the necessary accommodation upon an economical plan and not for appearance'.

John's brother Allan, however, thought looks mattered: 'The small embrassures on the porch are I think petty, particularly as there is nothing else in the new or old house like a castle or place of defence, I think a neat cornice would look much better and have less pretension about it.'

John was able to supervise the building of the coach house and the new byres, the stables and the dairy. But before the addition to the main house got under way he was given the command of a ship and sent to the coast of Spain. Nothing daunted, he solved the problem of the building in a bizarre way: he sent his wife and children (five of them by now) to Sophy's parents at Cheltenham and let the house and the home farm to an elderly Mr Douglas for about £200 a year (plus additions such as £12.12.0. for the hire of the piano!). Mr Douglas, it seems, was quite content to live among noise and inconvenience while the building was going on. He even kept an eye on the workmen, advanced money to pay them, and altogether behaved in a most long-suffering manner. As Peter, John's brother, remarked in one letter: 'there is no accounting for peoples' taste and we do sometimes meet with extraordinary ones.'

Peter disapproved thoroughly of the Douglas arrangement and wrote to John:

> 7th February, 1835
> Notwithstanding what I have said of Mr Douglas, and were Dunolly mine, I would see him or any other man <u>Damned</u> before they should build in my absence. Superintend your own building and do not leave it to any person, still less to a person you never saw. Listen instead to a person who feels deep interest in you and everything about the old place, and do not be led by those who cannot have this feeling and merely think of their own convenience without ever even dreaming of yours.

Allan, John's other brother and man of business, kept coming up from Edinburgh to look after John's interests. The correspondence of this period is entertaining, because Allan, Mr Douglas and the builder kept disagreeing, while John issued orders from somewhere off the coast of Spain which those on the spot felt to be quite impracticable.

While the house was being built John was in command of *H.M. Sloop Nimrod*. This was one of the naval ships sent by Britain to support the cause of the young Queens of Portugal and Spain in the revolutionary wars against two pretenders to their thrones — Dom Miguel in Portugal and Don Carlos in Spain. In 1834, when Dom Miguel was forced to relinquish the throne of Portugal, which he had usurped, the British Navy conveyed him and his suite to Italy. John took him to Lisbon in the *Nimrod* and was given a ring by him. From Lisbon to Genoa Dom Miguel travelled in *H.M.S. Stag* accompanied by the *Nimrod* with most of his suite.

The Captain of the *Stag* had written to John on 5th June, 1834, as follows: 'You are hereby required and directed, in pursuance of orders from Rear Admiral Parker, C.B. to receive on board the 'Nimrod' under your Command for general accommodation, the 23 Attendants of the Infante Dom Migual mentioned in the enclosed list, and to entertain them according to their respective ranks, and putting to sea with the 'Stag' proceed in company with her to Genoa, or Leghorn as I may deem necessary.'

In the following September John heard from the Admiralty that they had authorised the payment of £322 to him and his officers, due to them for the entertainment of Dom Miguel's suite, to be distributed as follows:

£184 to Commander McDougall for the entertainment of the suite at his first and second table.

£103.10.0. to Mr Samuel Northcote, Master of the Nimrod on behalf of the Gunroom Mess for the persons entertained at their first and second table.

£34.0.0. to Mr Michel Kelly, Clerk for the Midshipmens' Mess, on behalf of the young Gentlemen composing the Mess, for the Persons who were entertained at their table.

John's letters from home included one from Louisa Maxwell about his children (her grandchildren), who were staying at Cheltenham while the builders were busy at Dunollie:

11th November, 1834

One of my principal inducements to comeing here was the pleasure I anticipated in being surrounded by so many of my grandchildren and truly John you may be very proud of your little group for finer creatures I never saw. You must know that our landlord is a dancing master and your two boys and Sophy and Mary Jane's two eldest have entered with him and meet twice a week in Mr Hart's dining room. You may judge how proud I am to see them all with their happy faces sit upon a form and taking their lessons.

Your boys are all truly what I call stout well built little fellows with broad shoulders ... and all the little darlings are so fond of each other, indeed they are my great delight and I often think what you would give to have a peep in upon them all so happy and thank God in such good health ... I never saw Mrs MacDougall looking better, do you know I often judged your visit home last winter might have made an addition to your little flock but it is as well as it is perhaps.

The 'little' flock at the time consisted of five children, the eldest aged seven and the youngest one.

Sophy and the children had travelled from Oban to Cheltenham in the Dunollie coach. She had written that she did not want to do it again with such a family, 'knowing as I do the inconvenience of travelling with so much live lumber'. She added, 'I do not think that we should now feel inclined to move further than Edinburgh.' As to expense, she calculated that the journey cost about £70 each way.

In 1836 John was promoted to Captain — and in the same year he came home on half-pay. One of his former ship mates in the *Nimrod* wrote to him: 'If you should be appointed again to the Command of a vessel, I will always feel happy to join you, even tho' I should give up a better appointment, for all of the Captains I ever sailed with I never found one so impartial or gentlemanly in their admonitions, nor did I

The luggage of the family coach

ever find one that would go one inch out of their way to serve me, with the exception of Capt. Gordon, your own countryman.'

The new house was now finished — though much to everyone's distress it had cost £1040, instead of the expected £840. Mr Douglas was now reluctant to move out and was asking for a seven-year lease. Allan wrote advising John to give him one and not go back to Dunollie because: 'surrounded by friends, acquaintances and countrymen you could hardly avoid being more or less led to live in a manner not suited to your income ... The Melfords and other tribes would never be out of the house.'

This somewhat curious piece of advice was ignored. The long-suffering Mr Douglas departed and John, gathering up his family from Cheltenham, returned home to style and comfort in the new house. Meanwhile Allan, as John's financial adviser, saw fit to echo the gloomy forebodings of their father Patrick:

> October 1835
> As a warning to Highland Chiefs the sale of half Glengussie estate is just going round the papers ... In fact there are more highland properties now lost by the proprietors apeing the style of men in the South of three times their income than used to be lost by rebellion against the Throne or their superiors or the war-fare they waged amongst each other ... So much for what our poor father used to call 'your style & your comfort', a few Lowland Lairds and English Squires may to the end practice a life of both, but I cannot name a Highland Laird that has in my experience indulged in both that has been able to stand it.

In a letter to Allan Louisa Maxwell added her misgivings about the way Sophy was managing Dunollie:

> A numerous family in the country of children and servants requires an active person to superintend every department and not to sit up in their drawing room like a china ornament and entrust everything entirely to the management of servants, who don't care at what risk or expense the thing is done if it is done in appearance to please the Master or mistress.
>
> But why need I preach, my ways are only old fashioned ways which don't suit new fashioned people — but in all the places I have been in I see the World thrives best with those who look judiciously after their own affairs and circumstances in life.
>
> We are all too prone at aiming at a place in society which providence has excluded us and in immitating the follies of those who are called our superiors. But I must not commence moralising.

Judging from the letters, it seems that John was far from idle and threw himself with verve into the affairs of his estate and of the community. Not only the crops, the beasts, tree-planting and peat-cutting were his interest, but also the schools, the poor, the roads and the churches of the locality. Some of the letters concern dull routine matters, but some, such as the letter John received from the Minister of Kilbride, are amusing. (Kilbride is about three miles from Oban.)

> 15th June, 1840
>
> You asked my opinion in regard to the expediency of withdrawing the public house from Kilbride, I have no hesitation in saying that though opposed to having public houses in general in a country under present circumstances I do not see how the one at Kilbride could be dispensed with. There being no vestry, children brought to the church for Baptism are obliged to be kept in the public house during the time of service, and for the same reason, that is the want of a vestry, in rainy weather I am often obliged to go in there to put off my wet things. I must again repeat that I disapprove highly of the very great number of public houses in Oban and in this country in general and would rejoice to see many of the licenses with drawn.

In 1840 there was great agitation in the family when John's sister Ann announced that she intended to marry again. It was now ten years since her marriage of convenience with Peter Campbell had ended in his death, and she was now forty-one. Her brother-in-law Charles Monro, who had met the proposed bridegroom, a Mr Locke, gave John his views on the man:

> February 1840
>
> I have failed in my endeavours towards restraining your unfortunate sister from ruin and disgrace. I went to see her and it is sad to say that I left her as I found her ... The man she is about to adopt is as deficient in his external appearance as he is low in his mental qualifications, without the slightest pretensions to a gentleman either by birth or Education, in short as ... says he is a wretch you would kick out of your way. Income £35 a year.
>
> [Monro thought Ann's brother Allan, who was her child's guardian, ought to intervene.] He must know the depth of ruin she is entailing on herself and her innocent son who I am sure, even young though he is, feels the ignomony his misguided and faulty mother is attaching to her family and to herself.

Five months later Allan told John: 'I have had a letter from Ann announcing her intended marriage against which I have remonstrated for reasons which will have occurred to all who hear of it, but I have no doubt with very little effect. Ann will marry in haste and repent at leisure or I am much mistaken.'

The wedding took place soon after this and Louisa Maxwell wrote philosophically to Allan: 'God knows it is not likely my sojourn on earth can be long and I wish to be on good terms with all the world, particularly my own family ... I certainly never did hear anything against Mr Lockes's moral conduct yet that does not show he was at all Ann's equal or a proper person for her to marry. But now that is the case I believe our best plan is to make the best of it.'

Despite all the agitation this view seems to have been adopted by the rest of the family, and Ann's new husband was accepted.

Louisa Maxwell died the following year in Bath, and was buried in Bath Abbey. (Ann died in 1856, when the only child of her second marriage, Louisa, was about fifteen years old.)

Towards the end of 1840, John had a short spell at sea again, in *H.M.S.Pique*. He took part in the Battle of Acre before returning to Dunollie on half pay.

The bombardment and capture of Acre formed the climax of Palmerston's long-standing policy of preserving the Ottoman Empire. The Egyptian armies of Muhammed Ali and his son Ibrahim had decisively defeated every Turkish army sent against them by the Sultan, and the Ottoman Empire was on the verge of complete collapse (which would have allowed Russia to drive south to the Mediterranean and the Persian Gulf). The capture of Acre was the critical moment in Palmerston's successful plan to force the Egyptians to evacuate Syria, which Ibrahim had been governing (quite benevolently) since 1832.

John gave his brother Allan an account of the part he played in the Battle.

> H.M.Ship Pique
> St Juan de Acra
> 5th November, 1840

Your letter of the 22nd Sept. I got a few days ago ... You wish to know what the resolute Pashir is doing, I know not what is doing at Alexandra — But on this coast we are playing hell with his town and Troops. The night before last we attacked with the fleet Acra [Acre] the strongest fort he has got. The Garrison consists of 5,000 men and 300 Guns. In 2½ hours the Garrison struck [gave in] with a loss of 1200 killed and wounded and 2500 prisoners. Our loss was but in all 16 killed and 30 wounded in the whole fleet. Thank God I went to duty and had a finger in the fight. What the Pasha will think I know not for he thought it impossible for us to take it without a six month attack. The great loss on their side was caused by the blowing up of a magazine and no doubt they struck the sooner for it. But the firing from our ships was awful, nothing could stand it, the town is riddled and there are but 12 guns left that they could fire.

Royal Visit to Taymouth Castle

In 1842 John was invited to be present during the visit of Queen Victoria and the Prince Consort to Lord Breadalbane at Taymouth Castle. Afterwards, he wrote a long account of the visit. He described the Queen's arrival at the Castle on 7th September. The drive was lined with cheering Highlanders and Lord Breadalbane and his wife met theQueen at her carriage. They conducted her to the Drawing room where were assembled 'all the Peers and Peeresses':

> A platform was erected in front of the Drawing room windows on the ramparts, and Her Majesty and the Prince came out and on stepping upon it a Royal Standard was then held above her head. She appeared fatigued but her countenance instantly brightened on witnessing the splendid scenery from that spot and the warm and enthusiastic cheers from thousands and salute from the batteries.She remained there a few moments gracefully receiving the homage of her loyal Highlanders and then retired.

John had been asked to steer the Queen's Barge should her Majesty feel like a trip upon Loch Tay.

> On Saturday morning His Lordship announced that it was the Queen's intention to embark. Unfortunately the boat intended for Her Majesty only rowed 8 oars and there were at least fifty applicants for the honour of rowing in the Queen's Barge. A crew had been selected beforehand and the disappointed ones comforted themselves with the thought that from the state of the weather the Queen probably wouldn't trust herself on the loch to get wet perhaps and catch her death of cold.When they found that she was actually to embark their jealousy of the fortunate eight became great.
> All was in readiness about 11 and in the boats there never existed a body of men more anxious to do their best than the lucky eight men, more than cautioned by the others to row well and not to splash.
> Shortly afterwards Her Majesty arrived and, as the carriages drew up about 3 feet from the carpeting laid on the ground, Lord Kennaird gave the Coxwain [Captain MacDougall] a tartan shawl for Her Majesty to step on ... We pushed through the arch of the Bridge over which the Royal Standard was unfurled. Her Majesty was rapturously cheered in passing the Bridge and cheered and saluted by the gun boats anchored off the Island.The sight at this

moment was truly animating and seemed to those on the boats gratifying beyond description. Cold indeed must the heart have been that could have looked upon this scene without emotion.

John went on to say that those in the Royal Barge wished they had had a great writer with them to describe the scene and also 'our feelings at being the sole guardsmen of this youthful and interesting Queen, in a special bark on one of the largest Highland Lochs'.

Her Majesty and the Prince seemed delighted. The Plaid of the Coxwain [John] happened to lay over the back board which she observed and asked what tartan it was — and being informed that it was the MacDougall's his Lordship introduced the owner at the same time mentioning his profession and that the Brooch on his brest was once worn by Bruce. This led to a conversation on tartans, clans and Chiefs, a subject her Majesty appeared as familiar with as if she had been educated to occupy the musnud [seat] of a Highland Clan instead of the throne of the greatest existing Empire ... When she returned the brooch she asked the name of the centre stone and said she supposed the Pearls were fresh water ones. When Lord Bredalbane produced some that had been found on the Lochs and streams of his estate she admired them and His Lordship begged her Majesty's acceptance of them.

Family tradition has it that John felt the Queen expected him to beg her to accept the Brooch of Lorn, but in spite of all his fervent loyalty, this far he refused to go. The Queen then changed the conversation and asked if the water in the loch was good. Whereupon his Lordship, who, besides having the pearls in his pocket, seems also to have embarked with a quaich upon him, let her have a drink of the loch water.

There was a piper on board and John wrote that the Queen 'was much pleased with the Pipe Music and gave her preference to MacIntosh's Lament and the Reel of Tulloch'. The Duchess of Norfolk, who perhaps was feeling cold, requested 'There's nae Luck aboot the Hous'.

The Queen was also delighted with some Gaelic songs in which the whole crew united in chorus. On losing sight of Taymouth she said, 'Adieu Taymouth.' At one point it got a little chilly, and His Lordship recommended her putting on a cloak, but she declined.

John seems to have been much impressed by Her Majesty's stamina (she was twenty-three at the time). 'Although her Majesty was upwards of three hours on the water,' he commented, 'she did not seem to be in the least fatigued.' Something else impressed him too and he ended the description of the voyage with the following comment: 'On hauling the Boat into the landing place His Lordship was anxious to have her placed as near as possible when Her Majesty then said "she" (the boat) was far enough ahead.' John added: 'It is such expression and such acts as her Majesty is known to have exercised which makes her particularly the Queen of the seamen of our sea girt isles.'

Later on in that year John was invited to stay with the Duke and Duchess of Argyll at Inveraray Castle. He wrote to his brother Allan:

> 16th October, 1842
>
> After mature consideration, not withstanding the expence, I considered it right to go and have no reason to regret my resolution as the attention of the Duke and Duchess was most marked and gratifying. They insisted on my taking up my residence at the Castle, the County member being the only County man there but Aristocratic strangers to the amount of 30 filled the Ducal residence. The Meeting was a very full one and all were pleased I hope.

John went on to say that he needed to borrow some money until his rents were paid and explained: 'what with my boys, Queens and Dukes etc my expenditure has been great for the last three months.'

His eldest boy, Alexander, had recently been sent to boarding school at Woolwich which was a big expense and Pat, the second boy, had had to be fitted out when he joined the Navy. There is a sequence of letters from Pat, then fourteen, on the subject of a sword. This shows how his first tentative request grew in strength until eventually he got what he wanted.

> 13th October, 1842
>
> Do you think there is any use for me to get a sword as I would like to have one very much.

> 24th October
>
> I think I will need to get a sword for they all wear it on Sunday and on Court Martial days, you are obliged to wear them. I think it is better to get a sword rather than a dirk for in two years you are not allowed to wear a dirk and if I take care of the sword, which I certainly will do, it will come cheaper in the end. Grandmama says she will give me one but she is afraid it will be too large and is a very handsome one and it belonged to poor Grandpapa and I should not like to injure it in any way.

> 1st November
>
> I was sent yesterday to land some troops and I must get a sword for I am obliged to borrow one on these occasions and you are to wear one on Sunday properly and all the rest wear one so you would if you please get one and I will take great care of it.

> 15th November
>
> All the Volunteers here have Swords so I have got one and am very much obliged to you for it, it cost £4.8.0.

John Goes East

In 1845, when John was nearly fifty-five, his spell on land and his life as a country gentleman came suddenly to an end, and he went to sea again. This was a great surprise and caused a flurry in the family. His sister Colin wrote to their brother Allan: 'I sincerely hope he may have health to stand all the fatigue he will now have to encounter upon such a voyage and John is such an active minded person he forgets that he is no longer a young man.'

Sophy, his wife, also wrote to Allan:

> March 1845
>
> You may indeed suppose how thoroughly unlooked for was the announcement from the Admiralty. MacDougall had no more expectation of it than I had, and in fact he remarked only a few days before that there was little chance of his ever being afloat again — so there it is, we know not what a day may bring forth. As far as himself is concerned I do not consider that he will be a gainer in any point of view by this appointment, Certainly not in the exchequer but it may prove of great advantage to the Little gentlemen ... He will now have it in his power to make friends who may hereafter be very serviceable to them. Fortunately his constitution is still sound and when there is a call for it his activity is still greater than that of many men considerably his junior. Still at his time of life it is no joke commencing, or rather resuming habits so totally different to those he has been accustomed to during the last eight years. I flatter myself with the hope that his destination may not be a very distant one as these very large steamers are seldom sent to remote quarters.

The hope was a vain one: John was sent to very remote quarters indeed.

He wanted to take a piper with him, and Allan sought the advice of Lord Breadalbane's piper, McKenzie, and also his lordship's butler. He wrote to John:

> John McKay is son of the famous McKay and brother of Her Majesty's piper, and brother also to Donald who played to the Celts along with McKenzie during King George's visit to Auld Reekie in 1822.
>
> MacKenzie says John is an excellent pibroch and reel player, he was lately Lord Ward's piper, who occassionally lives at Glengarry. McKay asks and McKenzie says a Gentleman's best plan is to give the piper a sum of money as pay and for clothes and that he will dress himself well in plain clothes to act as your body servant and in the McDougall Tartan for pipe playing, if you will give him £50 and his mess per annum. I see there are no pipers at all

the thing out of places [unemployed], so I suspect if you want to give your sailors a reel to the Bagpipes you must give John McKay his own terms. McKenzie says McKay is a <u>Pretty</u> man and a first rate reel dancer as well as playing.

John replied:

30th March

I have received yours of the 26th in reference to the Piper John McKay. I will give him £50 annually, that is to make his pay up to that sum, he being rated my Servant, on the following conditions: he is always to be well dressed in the Highland dress when required to play Pibroch and Reels, or when desired. Engage him and send him with a good dress of the McD. tartan. He will mess with my Steward. I know nothing yet of my destination.

McKay was duly engaged. On being told to report to John's ship, the *Vulture* — a steam frigate — he asked for two day's grace as he was acting as Usher to the Lord High Commissioner of the General Assembly, which job he had had for the last three years. This was granted.

John sailed on 19th June. At the end of August Sophy wrote: 'Not a word have I yet heard of you since you sailed. At this I am greatly disappointed but a sailor's wife must learn to bear many trials and place her trust in that Merciful Being whose care extends over all regions and who has promised never to forsake those who trust in Him.'

In fact he had written to her on 23rd July — from Rio de Janeiro: 'You will have been informed of my sailing from Plymouth with sealed orders to be opened when clear of Europe. To my surprise I was ordered here with despatches for our Ambassador of the greatest consequence . . . I propose leaving this for St Helena next week enroute for Hong Kong.'

Sophy was left behind with nine children and the estate to manage. The family consisted of three girls and six boys. Sophy was fifteen, Louisa eight and Elizabeth (Kitty) only three. Alexander was eighteen, Pat seventeen, Charles fourteen, John twelve, Henry ten and Somerled six. Alexander was a cadet at Woolwich while Pat had already been at sea for three years. But the younger boys, Charles, John, Henry and Somerled, still had to be put into some profession. During the next few years their parents' correspondence was much concerned with future plans for them.

Sophy's Visitors

When John went to sea he had instructed Sophy (said to be an excellent manager) to supervise his affairs. He did not altogether trust Allan and Mr Baxter, the partners in the firm which looked after the Dunollie business, to manage things properly. This arrangement presumed what the men did not believe — namely that a woman could understand business matters — and it caused endless trouble and correspondence. But Sophy insisted on her rights. She wrote to her husband:

> 16th January, 1846
> I have at length got the statement promised me by Mr Baxter. Allan says he would have shown it me ere long since but was fearful you might resent him doing so. I told him there was no fear of that for that in your absence you had confided the superintendance of your affairs to me and that as the balance of the rents paid to my credit were so much smaller than you had led me to expect it would be, it was but natural for me to enquire what use had been made of the residue.

To make things more difficult for her, John's other brother, Peter, who was now a Colonel on half pay, moved into Dunollie to take charge — at least that was his idea. It certainly wasn't Sophy's! She wrote to John:

> You will no doubt be surprised at finding that the Colonel is off and in a huff too, and from the speciman I had of him yesterday I care not how long it be before he re-visits Dunollie ... I shall now make no further comment on his conduct than this — that I was never attacked in such a manner by anyone since I was born and you are the only person who has any right to speak to me as he did. Before we had the slightest difference of opinion I saw perfectly that he was dissatisfied at something ... It was evident to me that he was <u>disappointed at not having been left in full charge of</u> <u>everything</u> and he told me the last day that unless he had full powers to do just as he pleased he would have nothing to do with matters here.
>
> I told him as you had thought fit to entrust me with the management of this place, I certainly would not give up the authority thus delegated to me, that his advice and co-operation I should have been thankful for, but that I would not submit to be dictated to or called to account by anyone but you, neither would I consent to be a mere cypher in a house of which I was uncontrolled mistress in your absence.
>
> He was in a towering rage and summed up all by going to the Caledonian for his Breakfast. [Sophy added forgivingly]: <u>I shall</u> <u>never ask him</u> here but if he comes he will be welcome, only he must not think to rule us as if we were a parcel of recruits and so completely under his thumb.

The Colonel had hardly stormed off before another relative arrived who was to prove just as tiresome, though in a very different way. The

Colonel's visit had been short and explosive; Allan's was long and tedious.

Sophy told John, 'Allan has announced his intention of coming here next week with his "sole domestic", Ellen I suppose. What will the Col. say to his travelling with a maid servant.'

Allan had a reputation in the family of being something of a hypochondriac, but at the start of his visit Sophy was all sympathy. 'He shall have every care and attention whilst here and if he gets better I shall not grudge any trouble he may give.'

The Oban doctor could find nothing wrong that exercise and strict attention to diet couldn't rectify. Allan reacted to this by being out of doors by five in the morning and eating almost nothing. 'He depresses himself by over care,' complained his worried hostess.

Allan refused to join the family at meals. Sophy wrote despairingly, 'from what he says and from the number of packages he has brought he intends being here for months.'

After a time things began to look up and she reported the good news: 'he is quite well and eats now whatever is going and with us.' This improvement, however, didn't last long and soon she was writing: 'I despair of his ever being better. For the moment the least thing ails him he takes to his room and goes on in his usual way. The doctor has fine times of it, six visits last week!'

By the winter Allan had shown no sign of moving, and had dispensed with his maid. 'This relieves me of an extra mouth,' Sophy remarked.

To do him justice, Allan did try, when he was not retiring to bed, to be a helpful guest, and set out to rid the place of vermin. 'Uncle Allan,' wrote one of the boys, 'has been very busy killing rats since he came and has nearly destroyed them all.' While Sophy wrote, 'Allan is out shooting crows and I believe he fancies himself young once more, he certainly is the greatest curiousity I ever met.' Unfortunately on one occasion his shooting ended in tragedy. 'Fancy Allan killing poor old Touch [the dog] instead of a hare, he was sadly annoyed at the mishap.'

At the start of the second winter Allan announced that he was leaving. Sophy's relief can be imagined, having suffered from his hypochondriac ups and downs for nearly eighteen months. Then came the unexpected denouement.

One of the boys wrote to his father: 'Uncle Allan was to have left us this winter and gone to Edinburgh and was all packed up and ready to go this day three weeks ago, which was a beautiful day, but for some reason or other which no one knows but himself he did not go. His boxes remained fastened up and roped for some time and now everything is unpacked again and he is going to remain here during the winter.'

Allan wasn't the only visitor who stayed too long: there was also Bell, John's eldest sister. She hadn't had an easy life in her youth. It will be remembered that, having eloped, she married against her parents' wishes and then lost her husband two years later. She had had a struggle to bring up her two children but with them now off her hands she was, as Sophy put it, 'in high health and preservation'. Her mother had written of her some years before: 'I very much regret to say that poor Bell, like others of my daughters don't always choose to command their tempers or be select in their expressions.'

Sophy thought that as Bell was staying so long at Dunollie she really ought to contribute something towards the housekeeping. She told John that she feared that Bell 'would grudge paying anything handsome and even if she did I should not like her to be able to insinuate, as she might take it into her head one day to do, that during your absence she had partly supported your family.'

'I suspect,' she complained, 'she has no notion of moving.' She went on to sum up the situation in one expressive sentence: 'She has papered her room and bought a new carpet for it at Cumsties, which looks very ominous.'

In the end Sophy was so worried by her visitors — she now had twenty mouths to fill — that she wrote to her husband suggesting that she should let Dunollie and move into a smaller house. It would be more economical, and she added: 'I should have no visitors which would be a great affair.' Nothing seems to have come of this suggestion and on John's return to the country three years later she wrote to him of 'most annoying family coldnesses ... which I believe I may say our good nature brought upon us by permitting our house to be an assylum for all who chose to come to it. But that is at an end & I have no doubt that we shall find that short visits like short accounts make long friends.'

While Dunollie filled up with visitors, John was enjoying himself on the voyage to the East. His letters from Rio, St Helena and the Cape of Good Hope are full of enthusiasm for his new life, his delight in seeing new places and in being at sea again. 'The hills,' he wrote from Rio, 'are quite covered with all our most rarest shrubs growing as large as our birch trees.' At the Cape of Good Hope he was surprised while wandering on the shore to run into a pack of hounds: 'Jackels are hunted here as they do foxes in England.'

Distance from home, however, did not make John forget that his sons needed influence to help them in their careers. In those days, parents, whether they liked it or not, found it necessary to be on good terms with influential people.

With this in mind John sent home presents — but not to the family: 'I sent some seeds and a box of artificial flowers to the Marchioness of Breadalbane' he told Sophy 'and boxes of seeds to the Duchesses of Argyll and Sutherland. It is of great consequence to be on good terms with these people, a little attention may insure it ... P.S. I would send you seeds and artificial flowers but they are very dear.'

Then later from the Cape he wrote again to his wife:

> 30th September, 1845
> I wrote to you on my arrival here ... likewise to the Duchess of Sutherland and Marchinness of Breadalbane with boxes of seeds and to the latter the addition of a small box of <u>birds</u>. I think I hear you say <u>I think I might</u> have something, the fact is these things are very dear. Seeds will only do under glass and the other curiosities you will have plenty of on my homeward trip. Lady B. deserves all the little attentions I can pay her and the D. of Sutherland requested me to send her seed.

Meanwhile John's children wrote to him of home affairs. Johnnie was the child who enjoyed writing letters most, but because postage was so dear he had to be restrained. In November his elder sister, young Sophy, told her father: 'I have been intending to write to you for some months but Johnny always gets the start of all of us so early in the month that he leaves nothing for anyone else of us to say ... He is much disapointed at not being allowed to write this month.'

She went on to give rather charming cameo-pictures of all the children still at home:

> I wish you could see Pum [Somerled, aged six] he got on trousers for the first time about a fortnight ago and was as proud as possible of them and of his 'kinggairy' [Glengarry] bonnet which he wears when he goes out, he is learning to write and reads remarkably well. He is reading the history of Scotland. Baby [Kitty] is improving every day and is a very dainty pretty little body and a tremendous chatterbox. Johnny is as old-fashioned as ever as I daresay you will see by his letters. Charlie is growing very fast, he is as tall as Mama when he holds himself up, he is very much improved of late and not so shy as he used to be. Louisa is also growing fast. She is getting on really well with her music and other studies. Henry is as active and busy as ever and talks for all the family.

Later Johnnie wrote of how the Duke of Argyll had tripped at the opening of Parliament when walking backwards in front of Queen Victoria. The Duke was carrying the Queen's crown. 'The crown was damaged, and most of the jewels fell out. All those present were sadly annoyed.'

Some of John and Sophy's children

After a visit to the South, Henry described what impressed him most about Shakespeare's birthplace: 'We saw Shakesperes tomb and the house he was born in. I think the funniest thing in the room where he was born is the number of names on the wall, I could hardly find a spot to write mine on.'

Charles wrote of the proposed railway: 'The inhabitants of Oban are quite on the Qui Vive about the railroad and Cumstie [owner of the main shop] declares that Oban will become a Second Glasgow and that it will have all the trade of Ireland.'

The railway did not, in fact, come to Oban until thirty-five years later, but the prospect of it caused Sophy senior much worry. The first public meeting in Oban about the scheme took place just as John was leaving the country. (For a report of it see page 263). Since then Sophy had been bombarded with communications from the promoters needing immediate reply. Meanwhile her letters to John asking for his opinion, and his replies, were taking long months to sail across the world to and from Hong Kong.

Some of the proposed plans showed the railway running over John's property, one even just past the house. Obviously no one in the family wanted this but the problem was which of the other plans, if any, would be John's choice. 'Not that I mind my own trouble and anxiety,' Sophy wrote once, 'but I am so fearful of doing anything you may not approve.'

She herself was sceptical of the success of a railway to Oban in any case, and told John: 'They say the railway is likely to go on — and we hear a man is stationed near the Lodge to ascertain the numbers of passengers that pass daily. I think the results will not be very satisfactory to the share holders — how they expect it to pay I can't imagine.'

In September 1845 she wrote: 'The Marquis's scheme about the Railway has at length appeared in this day's paper and as might have been anticipated is not just the line that will suit this part of the country except for Tourists. It goes from here to Tyndrum, Glen Dochart and Callender — where it joins the Caledonian railway. I should think the Drovers will scarcely approve of sending their Cattle to the Markets by such a circuitous route.'

The following year she was still preoccupied by the subject: 'You will observe by the papers that the World has actually gone mad about railways, conceive a company starting one through the Isle of Man. This is if possible more absurd than our Railway.'

Sophy had yet another worry while John was away: a disastrous disease which attacked the potato crop all over the Highlands. She wrote in distress of the plight of their tenants, and how a mill was being set up in Oban to make potato flour.

Towards the end of 1846 she wrote to John: 'In consequence of an extremely wet autumn the rot got into the potatoes, and some of your tenents have lost 40 out of 50 barrels. Out of 45 carts dug here 5 were destroyed, and had I not made the men open the pits eight days after they were dug, and aired and dried the whole, putting some up with dry sand and some with lime, our loss would also have been serious.'

John arrived in Hong Kong in November 1845, five months after he had left England, as the *Vulture* had been detained at the Cape for repairs. In Hong Kong he joined up with his son Pat, who was transferred sometime later from his own ship to the *Vulture*. Pat was thus able to share in some of his father's exploits, which is fortunate, as his letters, though difficult to read, give more detail than his father's. One of these exploits, for which John was made a Companion of the Bath, was a punitive expedition up the river to Canton in April 1847 which Pat described in detail (see page 265). Shortly before the incident, in an earlier letter, he had written to his mother: 'He [John] is in splendid spirits at having something to do and I think if a row does occur he will show what the old Vulture will be able to do ... I never saw him at Dunolly look half so well as he is now.'

The reason for the expedition is given in a paper found among John's letters which states that it was 'to exact instant satisfaction (which had previously been repeatedly demanded in vain) for certain acts of sanguinary violence which had been inflicted upon some merchant sailors in the neighbourhood of Canton ... Another outrage was committed, in which a party of English gentlemen, including an officer of high rank, narrowly escaped with their lives.'

The Chinese authorities had treated the British demands for their redress with silent contempt as they knew that there was only a small force at Hong Kong. The paper continues: 'Under these circumstances it became a matter of vital importance to teach the Chinese authorities that the British Government could redress its wrongs much more speedily than imagined.'

It was a daring operation which involved first putting the forts on the Canton River out of action, before the ships could proceed upstream to Canton itself, and then compelling the Chinese authorities to put an end to their behaviour. At one point the troops had set out in range of a hundred guns, while further up the river they had had to embark in small boats amid a heavy rain of cross fire from the Chinese.

Pat wrote of his father:

The splendid way he led the boats in and his great forethought was the means of saving many lives, as if a shot had struck any of the boats, they being so full of men, they woud have killed a great many.

So our Pigeon as the Chinese call it, my great thing, is over having spiked 176 guns of very heavy calibre . . . without the loss of a man . . . Papa has been very lucky in being senior officer when it happened, if nothing else but for the benefit of the service, for I think that very few would have done so much with the small force he had . . . On the 14th the officers of the 10th gave the Captain and officers of this ship a dinner. I went and they drunk Papa's health with 3 times 3.

Even the Admiralty showed enthusiasm and the Secretary to the Lords Commissioners of the Admiralty had this to say to John's Admiral:

7th July, 1847

Having laid before My Lords Commisioners a Report from Captain McDougall of her Majesty's Ship Vulture respecting the combined Naval and Military Expedition up the Canton River and detailing the operations of which he had command, I am commanded to acquaint you that their Lordships entirely concur with your opinion that this enterprise reflects the highest credit upon the conduct of all concerned in it. The ease and rapidity with which it was executed correspond with a boldness of the design and show how little numerical disparity is to be reckoned upon as an element to success when met with by the combinations of superior skill . . .

My Lords compared with pleasure the smallness of the Force engaged upon this occasion with the largeness of the results, and they desire me to request that you will convey to Captain McDougall, the Officers, Seamen, and Marines under his orders the expression of their entire satisfaction at the gallantry with which a Service has been accomplished that reflects fresh lustre upon the British Navy. My Lords are fully sensible that what has been done could only have been accomplished by the highest discipline and the most perfect subordination amongst all concerned.

Pat wrote later to his mother describing a Chinese feast. His handwriting was very bad, as Sophy had recently told another member of the family: 'Long yarn from dear Pat containing a full account of the affairs with the Pirates. Poor fellow he has written me 14 pages of letter paper but his writing is not improving and I have consequently had some difficulty in decyphering it, most of it being crossed and written on very thin paper.'

But Pat's description of the Chinese feast, once deciphered, is vivid:

We proceeded up the Canton river to Anson's Bay for the purpose of the Governer holding an interview with Imperial Commissioner Keying . . . After the conference Keying invited us all to a feast . . . I shall now try and give you a sort of insight into Chinese entertainment.

They first begun their dinner with fruit, which was served in small sorts of cups of different shapes, but I dare say you have seen them without explaining any more about them. They then gave small cups of everything you can think of, changing the cup directly they see you have tasted, bird's nests, shark's fins, sea slugs and all the most extraordinary things you can think of were served to you. I think I had about 50 cups of different things handed to me one after the other.

The interpreter told me after all this that it was not half over. I looked behind me and saw fellows bringing in 6 tables of all sorts of meats. They then commenced carving them by cutting them in small thin slices. They then gave you a slice of each on your plate so I had about 20 sorts of things on my plate at one time. After this came the sweetmeats and rice.

The wines they had were Claret and very bad champagne, but the Chinese drink mostly very weak tea. They eat tremendously, I was very glad when it was over for I suppose we were upwards of an hour and a half at the meal.

The *Vulture* arrived home in 1848. To his disappointment, Pat was left behind in the East. He was disgusted with his new ship, *H.M.S. Ringdove*, and with her Captain, and the following are some extracts from his letters to his father:

7th April, 1848

At the Amambas Islands [between Borneo and Malacca] we watered, we had very hard work of it. I was in one of the Boats for two days watering, up to my middle in water and a burning sun over my head, but as I had a good straw hat I felt no bad effects from it.

They expose the men very much to the sun here and never think of spreading awnings, the first Lieut. says the sun does him no harm and he does not see the use of awnings. The Doctor has represented it but I am sorry to say the Capt. never interfered with any thing and is never on deck. All he does is Draw, Paint and Polish and he has got a Turning Machine in his cabin which is always at work. He has also got several experimental things which employs all his time and he leaves all the duty of the ship to the first Lieut. I do not think I have ever seen him on deck 4 hours since I have been in this ship.

I must say she is not very much like a man of war, men discontented, ship dirty and no system. Gunnery not attended to but polishing, carpentry and such like. I get on very well with the officers.

[The next day he added] I forgot to say that at the Amambas Islands the Captain and every officer in the ship landed in full dress to visit a Malay Chief. He received us in a horrible house, nearly naked, and we found out later he was a very inferior fellow.

Just fancy everyone in full dress and the Captain to be so particular that he made the officers wear blue trousers for the gold lace, with the thermometer at 90. I was told he had never worn Commander full dress before so I suppose he wanted to show off.

In another letter, he wrote of the ship's discipline:

16th June, 1848

Fancy officers of the watches being fast asleep and smoking in their watches at sea.

One day I could not make out what had become of my officer of the watch my attention being called to a heavy squall approaching ship. I found him fast sleep aloft and could not rouse him. I quickly, as I had too much regard for my own safety, got the sail off her, the howling of the wind and rain at last woke him but he was too drunk to do anything.

You will see the 1st Lieut. here carrying on duty with a cigar in his mouth, the men are also in a half state of mutiny.

And from Trincomalee, Ceylon, some more about the Captain and the ship's officers:

11th September, 1848

I have very little news to tell you since for the last 5 weeks we have been supposed to be going to sea every day and actually have hove sheet around Royal yards and every thing ready for a start. That is just the undecided way we have been going on. Captain does not seem to know his mind five minutes, our orders I know were to refit with all possible despatch and proceed to Bombay to be docked.

The Captain writes a letter every week to Admiral giving some excuse for detaining him, the first excuse was the disturbed state of the Island, than another was that the monsoon was too strong to attempt to beat against, then that one of his men was a witness at a trial and now that Fury is bringing some of the late Admiral's things for him so there is no saying when we will be off.

The Captain lives on shore and we see him about an hour twice a week. Our 1st Lieut. has been out shooting the fortnight we were here in the middle of refitting, he has now got rheumatism and has been living at the Admiral's house 3 weeks and says he will remain there as long as ship is here, he goes out in Palequins for a drive so there is not very much the matter with him. The second Lieut. has

Painting of John's ship, H.M.S. La Hogue

got delirium tremens through his drunkeness, the Third Lieut. is just promoted from mate and knows nothing and our Master is very little better than Mr William in the Banking line so you may imagine from what I have told you of them all what a nice state of discipline we are in.

I tell you fairly I never, since I have been in the service, was in or saw a ship in the state this one is in. I am glad to tell you that I keep perfectly clear of them all and attend to my duty but I shall be very glad when I get in a ship where there is some discipline and not in the state this one is in. I keep clear of all rows and never get into any and so I manage to slip along.

John arrived home in June 1848, and wrote to Sophy: 'Vulture was paid off about 12 o'clock today and I am again a <u>Private Gentleman</u>. My purse has gained little but I hope my reputation has, all agree that the Canton affair was Dashing well executed.'

Sophy had by now had more than enough of care and anxiety, and had written to John on his return:

May 1848
I do hope your health has not suffered, we are none of us getting younger but Jane [a cousin] says you are not the least altered. I cannot say that such is the case with me. I suspect I have got <u>old</u>

and <u>ugly</u> but perhaps I shall renew my youth now you are come home. I have had more care and anxiety during the last three years than in the previous 39 years I had lived in this troublesome world, nothing tells so quickly on the countenance than care.

Her mother wrote to John on the same theme: 'You will find your young ones much grown and improved, I cannot say any thing favourable respecting dearest Sophia's looks, she is very thin and looks careworn, which is not to be wondered at after three years and more of anxiety not only on your account but from the weight of responsibility that has naturally devolved upon her and other sources of anxiety.'

But there was to be little respite for Sophy: it wasn't long before John was again at sea, this time as Captain of *H.M.S. La Hogue*. In this ship he accompanied Queen Victoria on her visit to Ireland. He also joined the Experimental Squadron under Commodore Martin, based off Lisbon and in the Mediterranean, for the purpose of trying out the *Hogue*'s steaming and sailing capabilities.

In May 1850 John thought that Britain might soon be at war with Russia and France. He wrote to Sophy from Lisbon:

> By the Times of the 17th curt. it appears that the French Ambassador had made a sudden trip to Paris and that the Russian Ambassador was not at the Fete given by our Foreign Minister on the Queen's Birthday. There may be nothing in all this, yet it looks suspicious. Should a war take place with these Powers it would look very pretty La Hogue towing the 60 Gun Russian Frigate, laying here with the Emperor's Son in law on board, into Plymouth sound.

In a letter to Captain Eden at the Admiralty, written during the following month, John described his good-will exercise towards the Russians and the French — good-will mixed with warlike thoughts!

> I have had His Imperial Highness the Duke of Leuchtemberg on board here accompanied by his Staff, the French and Russian Ambassadors, the Portuguese Admiral etc etc. His Imperial Highness having expressed a wish to see the 'Screw' work, I started towards Belem rounding the Bows of the French Frigate Le Minerve, then cutting in between the two Russians giving them both a very close <u>shave</u>. His Imperial Highness hailed them asking how all his children were. They replied that their lives were at his service. You may believe that my teeth were watering for them. How beautifully I could have managed the three Ships. The 2 Russians are in good order, the Frenchman only so so.
>
> I relanded the Party at 5 p.m, all highly gratified and pleased, so will I be if you do not make me pay for the Coals. I conceive I was

perfectly justified in acting as I have done towards the Russian
Prince and the French Ambassador considering all that has lately
occurred. I lunched them all on board to the number of 40, and I
should be delighted to learn that your appetite was one third as
good as theirs.

Table Plan
Luncheon On board H.M.S. La Hogue

June 8th 1850

Rhubarb Tart	Roast Turkey	
	Oranges	
Rhubarb Tart	Flowers	Plum Tart
Dressed Dish	Ices	Dressed Dish
Pears	Strawberries	Green figs
Pigeon Pie	Cake	Roast Chicken
Tongue	Salad	Ham
Jelly	Cakes	Blanc Mange
Dressed Dish	Strawberries	Dressed Dish
Plums	Ices	Apricots
Iced Custard	Flowers	Iced Cream
Pears	Cake	Green figs
Veal Pies	Plums	Roast Duck
Cherries	Ices	Apricots
Dressed Dish	Flowers	Dressed Dish
Apricot Tart	Oranges	Cherry Tart
	Roast Beef	

The following year it was Sophy's turn to entertain Royalty, or rather ex-
Royalty. She wrote to John, still at sea: 'It is strange in this quiet part of
the world one can hardly go out of doors without stumbling on Princes,
Royal Dukes and Duchesses etc. Generally the ex-Queen [Marie-Amelie
of France] is to be seen with all her grandchildren playing round her at
Port More [the shore below the Castle] and cook has met her twice
down at the ashpit.'

The 'ashpit' was the Dunollie rubbish dump!

Marie Amelie, with other members of the ex Royal family of France,
with their entourage, arrived in Oban by sea in the *Dolphin*. One of
Sophy's daughters wrote:

We went down to see their arrival, the whole population of Oban
and neighbourhood having turned out to welcome them. We
hoisted the flag on the Castle and the whole of Oban and the
steamers were decorated. A Royal Salute was fired from the
battery ... and there was a great deal of cheering and waving. The
ex-Queen seemed a good deal agitated and walked up to the
Caledonian Hotel where she had previously engaged a large

public room upstairs, a small sitting-room, and five and twenty bedrooms. The Duchess of Orleans and her sons and suite had taken seventeen rooms in the Royal Hotel.

During the next day or two they all turned up to see the Castle and were then asked in to partake of wine and cake in the Dunollie drawing-room. Beside the Queen herself were Princes, Princesses, Dukes, Duchesses, Counts and Generals, a Priest, Her Majesty's Physician, one or two gentlemen who had charge of the little Princes and two old ladies who appeared to be Governesses to the Princesses ... They all chattered away a great deal both in English and French. They had two servants with them, one was very smart in green cloth embroidered with gold.

On another day some of them came to lunch. Before the Queen went south she came up to say goodbye. 'The Queen took my hand in both of hers on leaving,' wrote Sophy, 'and said "You will not forget me will you? I shall never forget you." The Duc of Nemours, who was with her, said how much the children had enjoyed playing in the grounds. 'He is,' Sophy remarked, 'a very gentlemanly aimiable looking person — not like a frenchman as he is fair and has no moustache.'

The day the Royal party left Oban all the family got up early and intercepted the carriages as they passed the lodge at 7 a.m. Sophy presented the Queen with a basket of fruit and a bouquet of flowers from the Dunollie garden. 'The Queen,' she wrote, 'seemed quite overcome: "Oh this is really kind and so early too," mutual compliments and exchange of good wishes. Behind the royal party was a carriage filled with the Queen's suite who all raised their hats as high as they could and bowed tremendously.'

Marie-Amelie wrote a grateful letter to Sophy and sent her a present of a vase 'pour mettre les belles fleurs de votre jardin.' Sophy replied in suitably flowery tones:

September 1851
Believe me Madame I esteemed any little attention I had it in my power to offer your Majesty and your illustrious family was more than repaid by the opportunity your condescension afforded me of receiving at my house a Lady whose exalted virtues shed a lustre alike over the splendours of a throne and the retirement of domestic life.

The elegant Souvenir your Majesty has been pleased to send me will be treasured in my family, a precious memorial of one whose character we have long admired, but whom the last few weeks have taught us to love.

Accept, Madam, the expression of my highest esteem, together with my heartfelt aspirations that it may please the Allwise disposer of events to shed his best blessings on yourself, and every member of your family, and allow me the honour of subscribing myself, with the most profound respect, Your Majesty's Very Humble Servant, E. S. MacDougall.

And Sophy wrote to one of her family: 'The Queen is really a delightful old lady [She was sixty-nine]. I quite rejoice at having it in my power to contribute to the pleasure and comfort of this illustrous but unfortunate family during their sojourn in the highlands.'

Three years before the visit of the ex-Queen to Oban, Sophy had written to John as follows:

9th March, 1848

Strange events have happened since I last wrote to you. The Sagacious Louis Phillippe, [Marie-Amelie's husband] who it was supposed could so completely control the turbulent French people is now a fugitive at Claremont (Leopold's place near London) and a great part of his family with him! In the midst of the fortifications which he himself has raised and surrounded by nearly one hundred thousand troops he was glad to escape with his life from a Parisian Mob!

I am sure this news will amaze you beyond any thing as I know you, like many other people, entertained a high opinion of his prudence and forethought — nevertheless he seems to have been taken completely by surprise and to have resigned his Crown without a struggle, his exit from the stage has really been most ignoble — all the ex-Royal family actually landed in Britain without a change of clothes even. France is declared a Republic and the Provisional Government professes themselves most desirous of maintaining peace with all the world. It remains to be perused how long this will last.

Young Sophy's Romance

It was during the year of the ex-Queen's visit (1851) that the romance between young Sophy, John's eldest daughter, and Sir Angus Campbell of Dunstaffnage began. Sophy senior wrote many letters to John at sea, describing the progress of their daughter's love affair. She was not enthusiastic about the romance, not because she disliked the young man but because she did not think his intentions were serious. She felt that the less her daughter saw of him the better. However, fate intervened and successfully sabotaged her efforts to keep the two apart.

On 1st May, 1851 Sophy senior wrote to John: 'Sir Angus Campbell was here this morning. He is not what I expected being not so tall as I thought he would be and stout, very dark of course after his long spell in China. He seems a nice unassuming youth . . . and has apparently a good deal of his late father's knowingness.'

Portrait of young Sophy, c.1850

A week later Angus came to stay at Dunollie. 'Sir Angus has been here a couple of days and I think him a fine young man ... He seems very much attached to his family which has raised him many pegs in my opinion. He is not very fond of his profession though.' [He was in the Navy.]

A month later: 'The young Bart. left us on Monday. I had a long letter from his mother thanking me for my attention to him. She says he enjoyed his visit here so much and wrote in great praise of all the family particularly of my <u>Eldest daughter</u> who he says is very ladylike and accomplished. I shall not encourage the young gentleman to be here much more as unless something is likely to come of it the less he is here the better.'

In her next letter Sophy senior continued to fuss: 'The Bart has contrived to find his way here most days ... he is gone over today to Salmore and I hope will remain there as in such a gossiping neighbourhood as this I should feel as well pleased in his absence. Sophy has gone to Gallanach for 3 days ... I am not sorry to get her <u>out of the way</u>. Fancy Mousey [Kitty, aged nine] saying "Sir Angus and Sophy are very fond of each other."'

After this there is a gap in the letters. In November young Sophy was sent to London — ostensibly to visit the Great Exhibition, but perhaps also to get her away from Angus. She returned in time for Christmas, accompanied by her brother Johnnie, who was at that time working as a clerk in the War Office. Their journey was tedious: having got as far as Edinburgh it took them three days to reach Oban. Johnny recorded:

Thursday 4th December, 1851

Started from the Railway Station at Edinburgh at 10.45 a.m. for Glasgow where we arrived in about an hour and a half. Proceeded at once on board the "Duntroon Castle" steamer for Oban ... advertised to start at 1 p.m. but instead thereof did not leave until nearly 3 o'clock, and we had hardly proceeded 5 miles down the River when we had to come to a standstill in a thick fog, and had to remain moored at Renfrew for nearly 5 hours ... Went ashore and visited the village which is a very dirty inferior looking place.

Shortly after 8 o'clock again got under weigh the fog having partially cleared away and arrived at Greenock about 10 p.m. where we were detained upwards of an hour taking in cargo. At last started about 11.30 p.m. and shortly after we retired for the night.

Friday 5th

About 5 o'clock this morning we were aroused by the Steamer suddenly striking on a rock. We instantly went on deck and found that she had struck a rock near the Island of Sanda. Some time elapsed before she could be worked off and as she leaked considerably it was deemed advisable to return to Greenock so at 2 p.m. we had the satisfaction of finding ourselves back at Greenock instead of at home as we had expected. Engaged rooms at the Tontine Hotel where we dined at 5 o'clock and amused ourselves as best we could during the evening.

Saturday 6th

We left Greenock at 10.30 a.m. by steamer for Loch Goil Head where we arrived about 1 p.m. After a short delay proceeded by a very slow Coach along a very bad and hilly road to Inverary which we did not reach until 4 o'clock. Immediately ordered a Converyance and pair of horses to proceed to Dalmally.

The Carriage was prepared with wonderful dispatch and we accomplished the first stage (16 miles) in about 3 hours. Detained for upwards of half an hour at Dalmally Inn. Started for Taynuilt about 8 p.m. and arrived there at 10 o'clock. After a slight delay procurred another conveyance and to our great joy reached Dunollie shortly before 12 o'clock ... Retired to Bed shortly after considerably fatigued.

Soon after their return, Sophy senior wrote to John:

13th December

Poor Sophy looks very thin and pale but I trust she will come round. She merely requires strengthening — perfect quiet and pure air will soon set her to rights I hope ... The Bart has been here two or three times since Sophy's return and seems just as he was but I do not intend giving him any encouragement whatsoever and if needful a hint must be given — it is as you say a delicate affair and Sophy is very sensitive. I cannot quite make him out — he undoubtedly admires her much and has given me to understand as much but nothing further has transpired. To me he has never said anything to lead me to guess at his intentions.

In the first week of the New Year Sophy senior again reported to John:

Sophy is getting much better. She takes a bath every morning with just the chill off and is well rubbed afterwards. She requires bracing and strengthening and as any excitement is decidedly bad for her the quiet of home is better for her than a town life. She is very anxious to pay her Edinburgh visits but I think it would be suicide to let her run the risk of more gaiety until her health is thoroughly established.

The next letter to John described the terrible weather that the new year had brought, and Sophy is not mentioned:

13th January

We have had dreadful weather and last Thursday was such a day

that few even of the oldest people ever saw the like. In the morning
it was snowing heavily — about midday it turned to rain and until
dark it fell in perfect torrents. The Distillery resevoir burst and
innundated Oban. The Mill loch did the same ... The Bridge over
the Feochan is gone and the Bridge at Salmore, which Gallanach
says you always prophesied would not stand, is down — the
foundations it seems gave way. These Bridges will be a nice
expense to the county.

Then a few days later: 'Still the same wretched weather. I never saw
anything like it — we have only had two dry days this month and the rain
comes down in such torrents that every place is literally deluged. You
have no idea what a state the country is in. The Bridge near Stonefield is
down ... and a large sewer has burst near Dunach leaving a wide chasm
in the road so that it is almost impossible for people to get about.'

At the end of January Sophy was still worrying about her daughter.
'Sir Angus goes to Edinburgh early next month which I am glad of. By
the way I am much puzzled what to do about Sophy. The Bowies and
Hopes [cousins] both expect her and of course she is very anxious to go.
I think she is much better here both on account of her health and in other
respects for if the Bart means nothing it is not desirable that he should be
dancing after her any more, and of course in Edinburgh they would
often meet.'

Although young Sophy's mother was trying to discourage the affair
with Angus she took a rather dog-in-the-manger attitude towards any
one else who seemed to be trying to catch him. The Maclaine girls from
Lochbuie on Mull were her especial worry and when Angus went to
Edinburgh she wrote: 'I suspect some ladies will follow him there but
they may save themselves the trouble or I am much mistaken.'

And the next day she told her husband with delight:

The Lochbueys have gone to Lochbuey. All they have gained from
the winter's campaign being the Baronet's dog which he did not
know what to do with!

He is gone to Edinburgh and intends trying for a ship soon ...
Sophy is far from strong and I have decided upon her remaining
quietly at home in spite of all the arguments that have been used to
induce me to let her go to Edinburgh ... A certain gentleman said
all he could on the subject but had there been no other objection to
her going at present I should have wished him out of the way first.

It was a month later that fate put an end to Sophy's separation from
Angus. A letter arrived from a young cousin in Edinburgh, Hopie
Bowie, asking Sophy to be a bridesmaid at her wedding, which was to
take place shortly.

Sophy senior wrote to John:

> 26th February, 1852
> Sophy has told you of the forthcoming marriage in the Bowie
> family. Of course the parties met here for the first time and Sophy
> declares it was clearly a case of "<u>Love</u> at first sight .." Sophy is
> quite delighted at the idea of being at the wedding which takes
> place in a few weeks it seems ... The Edinburgh gaieties will be
> over by that time which is what I so much dreaded for Sophy, and
> the Bart I hope will be off.'

On 13th March Sophy set off for Edinburgh. In spite of Mama's hopes
Sir Angus was waiting for her at the station when she arrived, having
already met six previous trains in vain. 'I only trust,' [her mother wrote
to John] 'she will not over-exert herself. I have lectured her much on the
folly of dancing till she is knocked up. I hope one day she will be
comfortably settled but she is better as she is until a <u>really</u> eligible match
offers. The young Bart stays in Edinburgh over the wedding. I suspect
he has no idea of matrimony as yet ... he is very <u>thoughtless</u> and
<u>extravagant</u>.'

Young Sophy wrote to her father on 30th March:

> The marriage last Wednesday went off remarkably well ... The
> six Bridesmaids were all dressed alike. At 11 we sat down to a
> beautiful supper. Sir Angus took me down to supper and he
> returned thanks for the Bridesmaids when their health was
> proposed. After supper dancing was resumed till nearly four a.m. I
> did not dance polkas or waltz but I danced the Quadrille and five
> reels. Then we had a country dance which Sir Angus and I led off.

On 5th April the young couple were still in Edinburgh and Sophy senior
wrote to John: 'I have received yours from the club and am indeed
rejoiced to find you have been granted a month's leave ... I intended
begging you to come by Edinburgh as Sophy will of course wish to be at
home whilst you are and I am <u>very</u> desirous to have her back. The Bart is
still there and evidently most attentive, which of course pleases her but
an end should be put to the present state of things.'

At this point there is a gap in the letters, John having come home on
leave, but by 20th May the marriage seems to have been fixed up. Sophy
senior wrote to John: 'By this time you will have received Sir Angus and
Sophy's letters and will see by them that he is <u>very anxious</u> to have his
affairs brought to a speedy conclusion.' She then goes on to say that
though she has hardly told a soul about the engagement so many people
seem to know even their own son Johnnie, who is working in London,
has been told of it there by three different people and has written

begging to know if it is true. She ends with 'here it must be pretty well guessed at any rate, as he is here from 11 every day and would think himself very hardly used if he were not.'

From her next letter it sounds as if the bridegroom-to-be, having kept them all guessing for so long, was now impatient for the wedding: 'He is most assiduous in his attendence in fact he seems miserable when he is obliged to go away for a few hours. Sophy says he is in the horrors at the idea of waiting beyond August to be made happy.'

Angus's mother wrote wishing the bride every happiness. Sophy remarked: 'I suspect she is not very much charmed at the prospect of becoming a Dowager just yet. I can quite enter into her feelings, nevertheless the step he is about to take may possibly prove the saving of himself and his prosperity as I think if he went to sea and left all in the hands of the Lawyers he would find things in a pretty mess on his return.'

Everything now seemed to be going very well when suddenly a cold wind from the east blew through the letters. Sophy's brother Pat, who was still at sea, wrote to his father:

> I had a letter from Louisa [Sophy's sister] and to my astonishment I find Sophy is to be married to Sir Angus. He is a very wild young fellow and got in bad scrapes when he was a mate. I doubt if he has got much beside his Baronetcy, but you will see to all this. On the whole I am rather sorry to hear of the match ... I shall not be sorry if it does not come off as a pennyless Baronet is not a great acquisition for a Highland Laird's Daughter ... I do not think much of Sir Angus Campbell from what I have heard of him he will never get on in his profession which I hope he will leave if he ever gains possession of Sophy's hand.

However, Pat's opinion seems to have been of no importance to the family. From then on preparations for the wedding went on apace. The only setback was Angus' illness which delayed the two Sophys' visit to Edinburgh to buy the trousseau. Sophy senior told John:

> 16th June
> The poor Baronet is just now very sorry for himself, he has been taking blue pills under the Doctor's directions and I suspect he has got cold. His throat and face are very much swollen and so painful he can take nothing but spoon meat. He has taken a course of calomel often in China but never experienced any inconvenience but this medicine requires great caution in this climate.
> 19th June
> Poor Sir Angus is still very poorly — he is completely salivated and has been unable to take anything but liquids since Sunday last, his liver being very out of sorts.

23rd June

Sir Angus is better but he cannot yet take anything but soup and slops. The doctor was rather shocked yesterday at the state of his mouth and said he had a patient who had taken blue pills for a much longer time without being the slightest degree affected by it. He has now prohibited the pills which he ought to have done before and cautioned him against cold for there is a great difference between taking calomel in this country and India.

(Blue pills and calomel, which were popular in Victorian times, were derived from mercury, a cumulative poison which can be stored in the body and built up over the years, eventually causing death. Angus' symptoms sound very like such a poisoning.)

When he had recovered, young Sophy and her mother set out for Edinburgh. Sophy senior wrote to John from there in July:

We have got very nice lodgings £1-15-0 a week. I thought they would be cheaper now. We have <u>commenced</u> operations. You may depend upon my getting what is required as economically as possible. What Sophy has I should like to be good of <u>their kind</u> and <u>useful</u> but I think it great folly to have a great many dresses. The Edinburgh shops are really <u>most tempting</u>. I have ordered the <u>cake</u> as it ought to be made at <u>least six weeks</u> before it is required other wise it will not cut ... Do you still think of giving Sophy a dressing case? They may be got here most elegantly fitted with silver for £16 ... I am told these kind of things are much cheaper in Edin. than in London.

<u>The</u> dress [of Limerick lace] with a satin slip and a lovely bridal wreath arrived today from Dublin. Aunt Bell has really <u>done the thing well</u> ... She is, I really belive very generous at heart though she <u>sometimes rather regrets</u> of it <u>afterwards</u>.

The wedding was now fixed for the beginning of August but the family had reckoned without the Admiralty who refused to grant John leave, and of course the marriage could not take place until the bride's father came home.

Sophy was displeased and wrote to her father: 'It is exceedingly annoying that they should keep you so long in suspense, particularly now that everything else is ready for the marriage. My maids' Trousseaus etc arrived last week and even the Cake has arrived as everything was ordered to be ready by the beginning of August. Angus is quite in despair about it.'

Sophy senior wrote to John towards the end of August: 'Can you be here by the end of next week, if so the 7th or 8th might be fixed for the marriage, as if you let me know who is to be asked to it, and what you wish done, all can be forwardness by the time you arrive.'

244

HIGHLAND POSTBAG

The marriage eventually took place on 22nd September and there still remain the plans for the day, written by John on a scrap of paper.

On Wednesday Morning September 22nd Flag to be hoisted at the Castle. Piper playing "the Campbells are Coming" and "Mac-Dougall's March". Breakfast at ten, after which dress for the Marriage which will take place at one o'clock — after which Cake and Wine handed round. Half past two carriage and four to drive up to the door for the Bride and Bridegroom. At three o'clock the Tenantry, with the Dunstaffnage ones, to sit down to dinner in the laundry and Milk house, and dancing in front of the house to take place afterwards if they choose till half past five.

At six the visitors in the house to dine off the following: Two soups and two fishes.

1 roast leg of Mutton, 1 Ham. 1 Turkey. 1 stewed Beef. 1 curried Fowl. 1 Dish dressed Cutlets. 1 stewed Duck. 1 Chicken vol au vent. 2 Lobster pates. 2 Rissoles. 2 Games.

Vegetables, potatoes, Beans, French beans, Cauliflower, Cabbage, carrots, Turnips.

2 Jellies, 2 Trifles. 2 Blanc-manges. 2 fruit tarts. 2 puddings. 2 tartlets. 2 Arrowroots. 2 dishes Grapes. 2 Peaches. 2 Nectarines. 2 pine apples. 2 apples. 2 Pears. 2 Nuts. 1 large Cake.

wines — Port. Sherry. Claret. Champagne.

Sophy's brother Johnnie wrote in his diary:

This is the day appointed for the marriage of Sophy with Sir Angus Campbell Bart.

Disappointed by the morning being wet, but fortunately towards noon the clouds cleared away, and the sun shone forth brightly ... Occupied in the forenoon decorating the avenue with triumphal arches of flags etc.

At 1 o'clock Sophy, who had been invisable all the morning, was led from her room by the Chief. The Bride was attired in a beautiful dress of Limerick lace with a magnificent scarf and veil to match. On her head she wore a wreath of orange blossom.

The Bride was followed by four Bridesmaids, Louisa, Kitty, [sisters] Alice Melfort and Louisa Locke [cousins] all dressed in white with pink scarfs and sashes ... The Marriage Ceremony was performed in a very impressive manner by Mr Campbell, Kilmore. Sophy at first appeared rather nervous, but soon recovered her self possession.

The ceremony took place in the drawing-room and was witnessed by the family and about twenty friends and relations. Outside in front of the house, attended by two pipers, were a hundred people, 'the assembled tenantry, and their families of the two estates who cheered vociferously'.

After the ceremony was over the young couple 'partook of lunch and about 2 o'clock drove off to Dalmally where they passed the night in a carriage and pair amidst loud cheering.'

As soon as the bride and bridegroom had departed the tenants adjourned to dinner 'and frequently drank the health of the happy pair', after which, for those who were able, there was dancing in front of the house. In the evening the house party partook of a huge meal with song and dance to follow.

The Family Careers

By the time of Sophy's wedding John had decided on the careers of all his six sons and the older ones were well established in their professions. Alexander was in the Army and lately back from Nova Scotia; Pat was in the Navy, at sea in the Mediterranean; Charles was in the Army in India; Johnnie was working as a clerk in the War Office; Henry had just started to train as a doctor at the Edinburgh Medical School, and Somerled was at Merchiston School in Edinburgh waiting till he could enter the Navy the following year, at the age of fourteen.

The family's letters by now provided plenty of interest — and some anxiety — for their parents. While young Sophy and her mother were shopping in Edinburgh for the trousseau, Pat's ship was nearly wrecked. He wrote to John from Malaga:

28th June, 1852

We had a very narrow escape coming in. The fog was very thick and we thought we were 10 miles off the place steaming along 5 knots when the Capt. observed the water rather discoloured but the master said it was impossible we could be in soundings, but Capt. ordered a cast of deep sea lead and to his surprise got 9 fathoms. We immediately let go the anchor. When the fog cleared up we were within ½ mile of the shore. Going steam on we had turned ½ a point too high, five minutes more and we should have been wrecked if we had struck. It would have gone hard with the Cap. and Master, in the first place moving in the fog and not having leadsman in the [word torn], so you cannot be too cautious on such occasions.

A few weeks later Pat described a very different scene off Malaga:

10th August, 1852

We arrived at Malaga on the 29th and gave a grand Ball the same day having upward of 300 people on board. The whole affair considering the short time we had to prepare, went off capitally

and pleased the Spaniards beyond anything. We had all the
authorities on board and a very good display of fashion and
beauty. What we intended was to have about 70 people off and
you may imagine our surprise when the Consul told us that
everyone had begged for an invitation and one party would be
offended if they were not asked as well as others and he had in
consequence certainly invited at the very least 300.

We kept it up from half past nine till daylight, the ship was very
nicely cleaned and everything went off capitally. The Spanish
papers are full of it and I fully expect to see it in the British papers.
The merchants of Malaga have written the Admiral to beg this ship
may be sent there again, they want to give us a return ball, but I
doubt if the Admiral will do this. Next forenoon we were going out
with 45 Bullocks so the whole affair seems like a dream.

Soon after this Pat came home on leave. He wrote to his father: 'We
were paid off on Saturday, nothing could have been better than the
behaviour of the men. I discovered that I was a great favourite amongst
them and many came up to me saying they would join any ship that I
went to. I was surprised at all this as I certainly was the strictest with
them on board and never looked over an offence.' (He was twenty-two
at the time.)

In November, Charles wrote from India that he had had some leave
and visited the nearest range of the Himalayas.

I enjoyed the trip very much as when we left Lahore the weather
was very hot and a great deal of sickness going about, but after
ascending to an elevation of about 6000 ft from sea level the
climate became beautiful and the mornings and evenings quite
cold, the air was so much clearer and rarer ...

Indian corn is the principal grain cultivated which was ripe at
the time we were there, the bears being fond of it came down from
the higher hills to feed on it and the acorns in the oak woods, where
they remain during the day and at night commit great ravages in
the corn so that the unfortunate people are obliged to keep watch
all night on a raised platform in their fields with a fire burning to
drive the animals away.

Altogether I enjoyed the short trip very much although we had
to rough it a little sleeping on the ground and three of us living in a
very small tent, everything had to be carried up the hills on the
heads of coolies so that it is necessary to march light, it being quite
hard enough work climbing the hills without a load.

Nearer home, and a month after the wedding, Johnnie caused his
parents anxiety by getting into what the family referred to as another
scrape at the War Office. His first one had been during the previous

year, but what he had actually done is not divulged in the letters. His brother Alexander had written then to his father from Canada: 'Johnny's scrape seems to be a very serious one. I did not see anything of it till in some of the papers that arrived by this mail, however he has been well cleared of any imputation.'

Charles wrote from India: 'I was sorry to hear that Johnnie had got into some scrape ... It was lucky that you were in London at the time so as to assist him out of it but I suppose it was nothing very serious.' A friend of John's wrote: 'It was a lie trumped up by a young scamp to extract money from an inexperienced lad launched into the great ocean of London.'

Of the second scrape his mother wrote, 'Let us hope for the best and commit poor Johnnie to a merciful Providence who can, if he sees fit, bring good out of evil.'

After an inquiry Johnnie was again acquitted. But his father decided that he should leave the War Office. Sophy wrote to John: 'If Johnnie leaves without any stigma attached we may indeed be thankful ... I trust the severe lesson he has had will make him more cautious not to run the risk of making mistakes for the future — the ommision of a few words in that ill-fated letter have indeed cost us all dear.'

After this Johnnie went out to the West Indies. But the move does not seem to have stopped him from getting into trouble. He hadn't been long in Jamaica, when his father received a letter telling him that his son was accused of 'a frightful Crime'. Again, there is no indication of what the crime was but there was a court case and Johnnie was proved innocent. His future career was rather unexpected, as will be seen later.

In 1851 Somerled had entered the Navy as a cadet. He was most indignant when he failed to pass his examination for promotion to midshipman. He wrote to John:

You will be sorry to hear that I have not yet passed. I cannot make out what the Captain is about as He still goes on asking me questions about the planets and questions in Astronomy that have nothing to do with my examination. He has never asked me anything about knotting or splicing or boat sailing. The Commander tells me he has done everything in his power to get Him to sign my certificate but he would never give him any answer. The Naval Instructor has told Him that I passed him.

I asked the Captain the other day if He could tell me how long I was turned back for and He told me to wait and find out. I do not think he has treated me at all fairly and He forgets that I am all this time losing time as I ought to have had my certificate 3 months ago.

John evidently wrote to the Captain to find out what this was all about, and received the following reply:

> A glance at the notes on the other side will show you the cause of the delay in your son's passing from Cadet to Mid. Poor boy! it was not his fault that he had no means of instruction in other ships; and that even here he had been climbing up the ladder without an idea of the very first steps. It is amusing to think of working a day's work without having any idea ... of working chronometer and getting the latitude by sun and moon, and yet imagining that the earth revolved round the moon and other errors.
>
> I could not conscientiously pass him in this state; and by withholding his certificate till he had satisfied me I made him work in earnest to make up for former leeway. This he has done about a week ago and I consequently gave him his certf. a week before I received your letter today.

In 1854 the Crimean War broke out against Russia. By this time John had been appointed Superintendent of the Packet Service at Southampton. To quote his own words, he 'had a very arduous duty to perform in Superintending the embarkation of Troops, Horses, Stores etc.' His son Alexander was one who embarked and a cousin wrote to Sophy:

> I feel much for all those whose friends and relations are involved in this dreadful War and wish that Alick's departure for the Crimea could have been deferred until the Spring, but you have the comfort of knowing that the Artillery have fared throughout better than the rest of the Army from having been able to carry their tents and a portion of baggage in their Gun-Carriages.
>
> I trust Alexander will have the more serious evils remedied before his arrival, though it is sad to think of the sufferings our poor men have had to endure from the mismanagement of their commanders.

It is not clear from the letters whether or not Alexander took part in the fighting in the Crimea. One of his jobs was recruiting mules for the Army and in June 1855 he received the following letter from the Director General, Land Transport Corps, Crimea, written to him at Turin.

> I beg to express to you how fully I appreciate the valuable services you have rendered to the Army in the Crimea by the continual supply you have maintained for twelve months of transport mules, Men and Equipments.
>
> It required indeed an officer of no ordinary capacity and vigour to obtain within that period, from a Country already freely drawn upon for its own wants, 5000 Mules which were second only to the

First-class Mule of Spain, with 1200 Drivers superior in every respect to other Foreigners engaged in the service and Equipments of every description, all excellent of their kind.

But all this you did unaided and to my entire satisfaction and I beg you to accept personally my best thanks for the thorough support you have afforded me throughout a very trying period.

Meanwhile, Pat and Somerled were both serving in the Baltic Campaign, though on different ships. Attacks were being made on the Russian Forts by combined British and French forces. The British Admiral, Sir Charles Napier, has been criticised by historians for being far too timid and, at sixty-eight, too old for the command. Pat's comments, in his letters to John, agree with this.

> 20th June, 1854
>
> We heard of the French fleet being off Nargan so we proceeded to join them and all anchored in Line again. We have been fraternising a good deal with the French and there was more nonsense receiving him [the Admiral] on board than when His Majesty came aboard. They kept us 3 hours at dinner during their presentations and nonsense. They say the French Admiral is an old woman, so I do not know how we shall get on between the two. One thing certain is that if the Admiral shows as much indecision and nervousness as he has done as yet I think we shall do nothing, and if we do we shall make a mess of it. That I believe is the opinion of many in the Fleet. Everyone agrees that our Navy's business was very bad and that we either ought to have left them alone or destroyed their forts.

In August, he wrote from *H.M.S.Bulldog*, off Bomersund:

> The Admiral has his flag on this ship ... I will point out to you the very great disatisfaction there is in the Fleet from the Captains downwards at the indecision which has marked all our movements. It is really disgusting and to the last the Admiral could not make up his mind whether the Ships should go out or not, and when he shifted his Flag to a small steamer we saw it was all up for our having any part in it. The French Admiral in his Flag Ship led the way and our Admiral in a wretched steamer brought up the rear.
>
> I hope our Commander in Chief will act more vigorously than he has yet done. His old followers say he is broken up. But I hope a little active service will buck him up again. I must say what I have seen of him he is not the man to Command our Fleet. He is very undecided and I may say nervous but I hope he will prove himself a true Napier when we come to real work. [Admiral Sir Charles Napier had in his younger days been admired as a competent, decisive and courageous officer.] We get on very well with him on

board, but I supect the Captains of some of the ships do not love
him, he pitches into them right and left.

Besides being critical of the Admiral, Pat was appalled by the
inefficiency of some of their equipment. Mortars were very important
weapons but they were continually letting them down.

> The Mortar boats stood capitally but there is something radically
> wrong with the mortars which the contractor of them ought to be
> very seriously taken to task about. The Artillery officers say the
> metal is bad, and the vents instead of sloping forward, as in a gun,
> slope aft and consequently put such a stress on the chamber that
> after heavy firing it gets soft, honeycombed and bursts exactly in
> half right down the centre. The escapes the men have had is
> wonderful, one mortar burst, one piece went overboard and the
> other flew into the yards; another piece flew forward on the
> forecastle and another turned completely round and the muzzle
> part went where the chamber was before. Out of 16, 3 burst, 7
> were next door to it, and the remainder were beginning to give.

The detailed description Pat gave to his father of the bombardment of
Sveaborg will be found on page 270.

On a lighter note he wrote: 'Somerled has got his things, the shirts
were very acceptable to him as he had only three clean ones left. He has
only, with them, got 32 — little enough I think but he gets them washed
on board.'

Deaths in the Family and John's Declining Years

The year 1857 brought the first death to the family circle. Before the
decade was out there were to be two more. Young Sophy had been in
indifferent health on and off for some years but what she was suffering
from is not apparent. The only clue is in a letter written not long before
her death, about a cow:

> We have had a sad misfortune in the death of the low Country
> Cow Papa gave me. It has been gradually getting thinner and
> thinner for three months without any apparent cause though
> eating well, latterly we have been giving it corn meal and milk and
> hot mashes but it still got thinner. It was really frightful to look at
> and at last died — they say it was a kind of consumption. I believe
> it must have been something of my complaint.

Although in bad health young Sophy had, that year, been writing
cheerful letters to her mother (who was staying in the south at the time)
about her life at Salmore — or, as it was later called, Dunstaffnage
House.

Yesterday we had another dinner party ... We had great fun altogether — first of all the preparations. George and Angus [her brother-in-law and husband] were very busy making milk Punch and Salad, Islay [sister-in-law] whipping cream and I concocted a curry and some pork cutlets and tomato sauce which I considered a great triumph of art.

George is very fond of cooking on a wet day. It is a useful accomplishment as the Cook, though a good willing creature, is by no means proficient in the art.

In the evening the Gentlemen played whist and Islay and I favoured them with our duets, then Pat performed two songs and George played and Sang. His spirits are beyond any thing I ever saw he kept the whole party in fits of laughter all the evening ... The party broke up a little after Eleven.

Another letter about dining out spoke of the problem of what to wear. Young Sophy was at that time in mourning for her mother-in-law.

29th January, 1857

On Friday we all dined at the Friths. We ordered a closed carriage to be here at five, but we waited and waited and no carriage came. So at five and twenty minutes to six we had to get Paddy harnessed and Angus, The Colonel, Islay and I set off in the Dog cart with Pat following on the poor little pony. It was snowing and a real cold night but we were so wrapt and covered up that we were nearly suffocated. We were not many minutes late after all. I was provoked at it as it was the first time we had dined there.

I was rather puzzled what to wear, my only evening dress being covered with crepe to hide its defects, so I thought I might go into half mourning and wear my lavender silk dress, which I trimmed in a nice cheap way ... I took off all the border and had the jet bertha Mrs Towers gave me at Cheltenham put on as a cape with some black lace of my old silk body and then made under sleeves of the lace hood of my silk cloak. With my black shawl it looked very tricky and cost nothing. I was quite proud of my contrivance.

I left off all my black crepe last Sunday. I got a very neat black and grey straw bonnet at McKays for three shillings and Ramsay trimmed it with the ribbon I had last year on my Cavendish House Bonnet, it will do I expect till I go out of mourning.

Sophy was hardly out of mourning when, after a very short illness, she herself died at the age of twenty seven. She had been married for only five years. She was buried in the old chapel in the wood at Dunstaffnage. Angus died six years later. The family thought his death was due to mercury poisoning and blamed the doctor for giving him lime mercury pills without warning him what they were.

Sophy's mother wrote of Sophy to Charles in India: 'our family circle
had so long remained unbroken that it seemed as if it <u>could not be</u> that
one of our loved ones was no longer with us.'

To Johnnie in the West Indies she wrote in July: 'She is gone, how will
her place ever be filled. She was a being rarely met with in this selfish
world. She was beloved by high and low. The thought will arise why
one so calculated to make others happy and fulfil the duties of her
station has been snatched away, but let us hush every murmur.'

A Victorian letter of condolence from a cousin, Lady Hope, still
exists; the following is an extract:

> The Lord saw that she 'was ripe for Glory' and took her to Himself.
> She is 'not lost but gone before' and has left a bright example
> worthy of imitation by old and young. It is difficult at such
> moments to say 'Thy will be done' when the 'delight of your eyes'
> has been snatched from you and all your fond hopes for her
> blighted, and laid in an early grave, yet take comfort mourning
> Parents, she was only lent to you by her Heavenly Father for a time
> and he has recalled her to Himself.

A month before young Sophy died John had been made a Rear Admiral,
thus achieving what he once wrote was his great ambition. Johnnie wrote
to him from the West Indies: 'There are now Several Admirals, both on
the Active and Retired list, verging on 90. I see no reason why you may
not with care be preserved by Providence to attain the very highest
Rank in your noble Profession.'

(John became a Vice Admiral in 1863.)

By the time John had left his job at Southampton, and was home again
on half pay, the Indian Mutiny had broken out. Alexander had sailed for
India and wrote to his father during the voyage from the Cape de Verde
Islands:

> 27th August, 1857
> We arrived here this morning and remain a day or two to coal after
> which we make the run direct to Madras. We have come here
> under half steam, a fair fresh breeze the whole way, and I have
> been <u>sea-sick</u> the whole time. <u>I funk awfully</u> the rest of the voyage,
> it weakens me so, however I have two or three days rest here. It is
> blowing so freshly off shore that no one has been able to leave the
> ship as we all meant to have done tho' it is a bleak hot sandy place
> with about half a dozen houses on.
> We are most comfortable on board and fed splendidly,
> champagne, Port, and claret daily, fresh rolls, milk, half a dozen
> different dishes at breakfast. Bread and cheese at lunch, as good a
> dinner as you would see on board a P. & O. ship daily, tea in the

evening and the E.I. [East India] Company pay all our expences except £5 so we get all this living, with as much Wine, spirits, beer, soda water as we want for £5. I don't enjoy much of them tho' not having once dined in the salon since we left the Start, but the stewards make me any thing I ask for and I live off tapioca, <u>dry mustard</u>y ham sandwiches and soda water and brandy.

I have a capital stern cabin, and as in the trades the wind is always aft I am very cool, tho' in the salon the thermometer has been 86. They supply us with sheets, towels, lots of fresh water and we could not be more comfortable in any passenger steamer. All the officers but one are nice fellows, the ladies are muffs ...

Don't let Henry go to India if you can help it, three out there is quite enough and one son ought to stay at home. But whatever he does don't let him be such a fool as to enter the Navy or Queen's Army.

(Henry was by now a qualified doctor. The following year, taking no notice of Alexander's advice, he joined the Indian Medical Service!)

Whether or not Alexander was involved in the Indian Mutiny is not evident from the letters; he seems to have stayed in India a very short time. His brother Charles, who was in the Indian Army, saw much active service: he was three times wounded and on one occasion his horse was killed under him. He was at the siege and capture of Lucknow, and was said to have had many amazing escapes from death. At the end of the war his mother wrote, 'in fact, my dear boy, a kind Providence seems to have watched over you on many occasions.'

No letters from Charles written at the time of the Mutiny exist. One from his mother to him survives, which gives her ideas on the subject:

16th October, 1857

Troops must now be arriving in numbers so we may hope the salutary dread that has hitherto been felt for British soldiers will effectually extinguish all further rebellion.

I only hope a few of the ringleaders may be captured and made to expiate their crimes, as far as they can do, by an ignominious death. Surely there will be no <u>half measures</u>, neither will there be any more mistaken delicacy as to sparing the feelings of <u>high caste Sepoys</u> etc. I should think those who have proved themselves the most ruffianly, treacherous beings on the face of the earth will be dealt with as any other miscreants would be who have broken the laws of God and man.

The papers will tell you what a magnificent sum has been subscribed for the relief of the Indian sufferers and also that the Fast day was most solemnly kept. God grant the prayers then offerred may be heard and answered. He will surely avenge his own cause and then I trust a brighter day will dawn on India.

This country seems now to see the false policy of keeping the millions under one sway in the darkness of heathenism. It is clearly our duty as Christians to endeavour to enlighten the poor <u>ignorant</u> Hindoos — ignorant at least of that knowledge which alone can make them <u>really wise</u>.

We have had a fine specimen of what the <u>religion</u> is that we have been so careful not to interfere with — let us do our duty and above all live up to our <u>professions</u> and God will assuredly bless us and our endeavours.

By 1857 the family had heard from Johnnie in Trinidad that he wanted to take Holy Orders and become a student at Codrington College, Barbados. His father offered to allow him £30 a year for this purpose. Johnnie thanked him but pointed out that this was not enough. John was displeased, but by 1859 he was again willing to help. Johnnie wrote:

24th December

I have yours expressing your willingness to defray the expenses that will be incurred to complete my studies for Holy Orders at Codrington College; I beg you will accept my most sincere and grateful thanks for so promptly acceding to my request, and for the kind disposition you have shown to forward my views; your letter has relieved me of a heavy pressure of anxiety lest I should be prevented — owing to the want of necessary funds — from carrying out the object upon which my heart was so steadfastly fixed, that of becoming a duly ordained Minister of the Gospel.

Johnnie sent his father a copy of the Testimonial he had had from the leading people of Grenada, where he had worked as a lay reader. It read: 'we have much pleasure in certifying to the regularity and zeal displayed by him in the discharge of his duties as a Reader and Catechist, and to the general correctness, sobriety and morality of his mode of life, and to his becoming deportment and conversation.'

The last heard of Johnnie during the period covered by these letters was in a letter from Alexander, in 1861: 'I cannot conceive what Johnnie expects to do with himself by coming home, he cannot possibly become a Divine in this country and there is nothing else he can turn his hand to.'

(Johnnie came home eventually, after his father died, and was ordained as a curate in the Church of England in 1869. He is said to have made a good clergyman.)

The year 1860 brought serious worries to John and Sophy. To begin with money seems to have been short. Sophy wrote to John, away in Edinburgh:

I have been making a calculation as to money and the said ·

calulation has made me feel quite ill, yet we have been as economical as possible.

We [herself and the two girls Louisa and Kitty] have done as yet with our last winter's dresses, but have had to get some warm under clothing and <u>head gear</u>, these last named articles run away with a good deal — though I myself have only got a cheap black bonnet. However, as I have before remarked, one must be <u>Clothed</u> even at home.

Considering their financial position at the time it is not surprising that the announcement of Alexander's ill-starred romance with a penniless Irish girl, Anna Barclay, was not well received by his parents. Although John seems to have been a kind father he was (like his forebears) obsessed with the idea that the eldest son must marry money in order to support the tottering financial state of the property — and so save it for posterity.

Until now, Alexander — though very much chased by the ladies — had looked upon his female admirers with a somewhat superior tolerance. He had written a year or two before from Gosport saying that he had been going to many tea parties and Balls. But he added: 'I do all this to please the ladies not myself, poor little parties you must oblige them occasionally.'

But now, at thirty-three, Alexander had fallen in love — with a girl thirteen years younger than himself. From Ireland, he wrote to his mother, breaking the news of his engagement:

Sunday 13th January

As I shall be coming over to you early in Feb. I shall postpone full explanation of what I am now going to tell you until then. I yesterday afternoon proposed to the lady I have mentioned to you in former letters (Miss Barclay) and was accepted ... God only knows how it will all end in a pecuniary point of view, of course you will both think I have acted foolishly as there is no money, in every other point I have suited my own inclinations and time alone can only show whether they were right ones or not ...

Of family relations, connections, I know nothing all I know is I have a simple, good affectionate girl, and we will leave all discussion on the event until we meet. I hardly know if my father is in Edinburgh or Dunollie so I wish you to send him this letter and let him remember, as you may too, that I intend to do nothing either rashly or against either of your wishes.

There are of course many difficulties and obstuckles in my path, money being the chief one ... Nothing whatever in the way of womankind will ever lead me into matrimony against both or either of your wishes, but on the other hand it is to be considered that I have lived in the world some 12 or 15 years, I have known and been thrown with every description of woman, and <u>never</u> met one whom I could not make like me or <u>much more</u>. I am sick of worldly women and now want a quiet life ...

You are to say nothing of what I have been writing about to anyone, except my father, until everything is settled, in cases of this sort the less Publicity it gets the better. In her family it is confined to her mother, step-father and sister, tho' this is such a town for gossip it may get about at any time, and when it does I shall have a nice hornet's nest about my ears.

Sophy sent the letter on to John, saying: 'I felt sure you would be annoyed at it as we all know how important it is that he should get <u>money with a wife</u> however you must not let it worry you for as you will see he is perfectly aware of the difficulties that lie in his way, and is also determined to do nothing against our wishes. It would have been better had he consulted you before he compromised himself with the Lady but we must hope for the best.'

After hearing from her husband again Sophy wrote soothingly by return of post. A few years before this John had had some kind of apoplectic fit and she feared this annoyance might bring on another.

I grieve much that Alexander's matrimonial intentions have distressed you so much. You must try however not to allow this or anything else to prey upon you mind but trust that all will be well and wisely ordered by that merciful Providence which has hitherto kept us as a family from many evils, and enabled us to keep up our position whilst so many of our neighbours have been absolutely ruined. Remember of what great importance your health is to us all and do all you can to preserve it.

But John refused to be comforted and a few days later Sophy wrote again: 'I am more grieved than I can express at finding how much you still feel the news conveyed in Alexander's letter, <u>you must not</u> allow it to annoy you so much. Remember that you have never concealed from him how family matters stand consequently if he commits an imprudent act, and has to fight on through life with a small income, he has no one to blame but himself.'

In July, Alexander wrote to his parents with an ultimatum: if he could not marry the girl he wanted, he would never marry at all.

With regard to my marriage there are many difficulties in the way and I fear for the present and perhaps for ever marriage may be wholly out of the question, but no woman but Miss Barclay, while she remains as she is at present, will ever be my wife.

I have lived long enough in the world not only to see the misery of marrying without the means of proper support but also the wretchedness of marrying for money. I have had many opportunities of the latter but none to my taste.

This ultimatum had no effect on his parents' feelings. The engaged couple remained unmarried till after John's death.

(To finish the story, although it is beyond the dates covered by this book, Alexander and Anna were married at Limerick in 1867. When the couple arrived home at Dunollie a great reception met them at the lodge gates. The horses were taken out of the shafts so that the carriage could be pulled up the avenue to the house by tenants, employees and friends. Rejoicing swiftly turned to sorrow: there was some kind of accident and one of the men pulling the carriage was killed.

The tragedy was keenly felt by all the family who, beside mourning the loss of life, also looked on the incident as a bad omen for the marriage.

Seven weeks later Alexander died after a few days's illness. He and Anna had waited seven years to be married.)

In the summer of 1860, John and Sophy received a most disturbing letter from Pat, who had seemed all set for a very successful naval career:

> H. M. S. Mohawk, Gibraltar
> 18th May, 1860
>
> I am sure you will be as sorry to hear as I am to write that a very severe ulcerated throat brought my original illness back and has so reduced me that the Surgeons informed me that to save my life I must go home instantly in the Mail, and that I have remained out too long as it is, everyone from the Admiral downwards said the same, and I have been invalided and to go home at once.
>
> You may imagine the pain this has caused me, but what could I do. I am skin and bone having lost 2½ stone. I am recommended at once to go to my Native air as the only means of restoring my health. I am broken hearted at leaving the ship and I fear I shall never be the same person again.
>
> If I am well enough when I arrive I am recommended not to go to Hospital but at once to my own home, this must depend upon the state I am in when I arrive. If I can I shall go to London first and get medical advice, seeing Sir J. Leddell. I can write no more.

Pat's native air did not restore him and he died the following year at the age of thirty-one. He was in Edinburgh at the time under the care of the famous Dr Duncan. Although he was very ill his death was as unexpected to the doctor as it was to Sophy.

She felt that Pat had not been properly prepared for death and wrote in distress to Charles in India:

Oh! how bitterly I now regret not having made greater efforts to lead our dear one to think more of these things which belonged to his everlasting peace, but as you know he was a difficult subject to deal with and then the Doctor always urged the necessity of keeping up his spirits — still he <u>may</u> have <u>thought</u> more on this subject than we know. Let it be a warning to us <u>all</u>, my dear Charlie, for we know not how soon our summonds may come!

The year following Pat's death John was made a Knight Commander of the Bath. In becoming a knight he fulfilled a prophecy made by his mother in a letter written forty-seven years before! By this time he was seventy-two, but apparently still eager for active service.

His doctor son Henry wrote: 'I was very glad to find that your health was so good as to induce you to volunteer for Service in the event of an American War, at the same time I think you allowed your zeal to outrun prudence and am very glad indeed that matters turned out that your services were not required.'

Early in 1865 John went to London on business concerning the coming railway to Oban. He went also to see influential friends who might be able to further Charles and Somerled in their careers. A cousin who saw him there wrote that he looked wonderfully well 'considering that he had, contrary to the advice of everyone, come up from the North during very severe weather'.

John's homecoming after this trip is described in a letter: 'He arrived here in an open gig having slept at Kilmartin and started at 5 a.m., it was a horrible day snowing and so cold. He was quite wet and had a very bad cold.'

Apart from the cold John seemed to the family to be in his usual health. He fell asleep in his armchair in the drawing-room during the afternoon. When he awoke he was confused and stone deaf, and behaved in a peculiar way. He never became himself again, but took to his bed, refused all food and medicine, and in a fortnight's time was dead. The cause of the illness was said to have been a blood clot pressing on the brain.

There were about three hundred people at the funeral. The coffin was borne shoulder high from Dunollie to Oban, and right on through the town, on its way to the family burial ground at Kilbride. All the shops in Oban were shut and every flag flew at half-mast.

Somerled wrote of his father from abroad: 'The Navy has lost one of its best officers and one who would have laid down his life any day for his Country.'

Henry, in India, wrote to Charles, who was also there:

My Mother certainly has had her fair share of trials during the last few years but has borne up nobly under them all, and placing, as she does, her trust in God and enjoying thereby the consolations of religion I doubt not she will have strength given her to support her under this, I suspect, the heaviest trial she has yet had. I fancy few couples have ever spent so long and happy and loving a career, and that there can have been few, if any, instances of so devoted a wife and so excellent a Mother.

We have many blessings to be thankful for but for none more than such excellent parents. Whatever may have been the lot of any of us in after life we can none of us trace back our misfortunes, as many can, to our parents. If they have erred at all it was on the side of kindness, but I do not even think we can blame them for over indulgence which I think almost as harmful to the young as over severity, or even neglect.

If any of us marry I hope our sons and daughters may be able to look back with as much satisfaction to us as Fathers as we can on him who has passed away to a World where we all hope to meet again, and be as united a family as we have been on earth, for thanks goodness there has as yet been no estrangements between any of us.

Family Post

The Battle of Algiers

John to Louisa Maxwell, 27th August, 1816

(The British and Dutch victory at the Battle of Algiers resulted in the release of 3000 Christian slaves who had been captured from ships of all nationalities sailing in the Mediterranean, and who were being held in appalling conditions by the Turks.)

At 5 a.m. hoisted all the boats out and prepared them for action. Admiral made signal that cooking and meals to go on as usual although signal to prepare to Action be made. At noon English and Dutch Squadrons in company standing in for Algiers. Admiral annuling Flag of Truce ...

At 2.46 opened our fire, upon time the Enemy commenced a heavy fire. At 4 observed our shot had made considerable impression upon the fortifications, answered signal to send boats manned and armed to the Admiral and observed one of the enemy's Frigates in flames, at this time the Algerians were gaulling us very much with musketry. At 8 most of their frigates were on fire, our men much exhausted, at 8.30 our powder nearly expended orders were given to fire at those places only where the enemy were most active.

We now had leisure to view the scene around us which was the most awful and grand that can be conceived and baffles all description. The whole of their navy in flames illuminating the town and Bay to a considerable extent all round, with vivid flashes of lightning and tremendous peals of thunder.

About this time one of the flaming Frigates drifting out of the mole caused the greatest alarm for the safety of the Queen Charlotte (the ship of the Admiral, Lord Exmouth) when the wind fortunately carried it up the Bay clear of everything. The enemy still keeping up a fire from places we could not get our guns to bear . . .

At 9.40 observed ... the enemy's fleet, consisting of five Frigates, six corvettes, besides Brigs, Schooners, and upwards of fifty Gunboats, in flames, their batteries demolished, the greater part of the town in ruins and on fire and the ramparts heaped with killed and wounded.

At 10 began to haul out of action. Found 2 midshipmen and 14 men killed, Captain King severely wounded by a splinter in the leg, Two Lts., 3 Midshipmen, 56 men wounded severely. Lt MacDougall, 2 midshipmen and the Boatswain and 84 men wounded slightly.

At 11.20, being without range, firing ceased on both sides, all the Squadron ... sailing for Anchorage. At 2 a.m. anchored. Found we had now 16 men killed, our masts, rigging and sails cut to pieces. At daylight turned the hands up to repair damages and Buried the Dead.

(Elsewhere John tells of how, as a lieutenant, he ended up by having to take command of the ship — his wounds being slight in comparison to those of his superior officers.)

Sixteen years after the battle John bought a picture of it from an Admiral Chambers who wrote: 'The weather to which you were exposed all that night up on deck would defy the first artist that ever lived to do justice to.'

A Turtle for the County Meeting at Inveraray

John Campbell, Customs, Greenock to John MacDougall, October 1822

I wrote to you last evening mentioning that I had procured a very fine turtle for your meeting. I will see it put safely on board the Toward Castle tomorrow morning and I spoke to Johnston the Master who has promised to take care of it.

I am most happy that I have it in my power at the same time to send you a parcel of nice limes for punch to relish your Turtle, part of a present I received this day from a young friend of mine at Demerara. You may send the money for the Turtle by Johnston Master of the Toward Castle.

The Turtle was the only fine one to be had and was just about being embarked for Glasgow when I got hold of it.

A Nervous Traveller

Robert Roy from Edinburgh to John 24th July, 1823

If your kind offer, of taking under your protection at Fort William my Mother, does not interfere with your other engagements I find by a letter just now received that she will be there on Friday evening the 1st of August.

Altho' she may, when left alone, be causing herself annoyance and uneasiness from being so very seldom a traveller I have no fear that she could reach Oban safely, altho' anxious enough ... But to speak truly I never felt more obliged by any attention than your considerate offer and, if there has not since occured any thing to make it inconvenient, you will save me no slight uneasiness ... My Mother is easily alarmed and never put foot on board steamboat, so you will do both her and me an act of great kindness.

John becomes an Archer

David Paterson to John from 49 Castle Street, Edinburgh, February 1824

Sir, I have the honor to acquaint you that you were admitted a Member of the Royal Company of Archers, Kings Body Guard, on the 26th January last and that your Diploma is ready for delivery on payment of the Fees of admission.

The Fees are Five Guineas of Entry Money — and one Guinea of Annual Contribution for 7 years or Ten Guineas in full of both.

I also beg leave to mention that the members of the Body Guard lately entered into a Voluntary Subscription of one Guinea each, for the purpose of purchasing Plate for the use of the Company which I hope may meet with your approbation and support.

I have the honor to be, Sir, Your most obed. servt.

David Paterson, Treasurer.

Ladies in India

Baldwin Timmins (Sophy's cousin) from India, 1832

You say it is the fashion for people who have been in India to underate their own country. Pardon me for insinuating that this failing chiefly rests with the Ladies and the reason is obvious.

Civilian or officers' wives high in their respective Services in India are paid great attention to and made Goddesses of by the admirers of folly when perhaps, and generally it is the case, they possess not an atom of merit beyond the entertainments that their husbands' purses enable them to give.

When these folk return home they are surprised to find they are not of the same consequence, are horrified at servants and shopkeepers presuming to be independant of them and gladly fly back to their old and more congenial avocations, flirting, abusing servants and giving dinners. So much for India, but at the same time be it understood this is by no means applicable to all, but to those who have been entirely brought up and perhaps born in it, and those who have resided in it for perhaps twenty years and upward — having but little or nothing to recommend them at the outset.

A Grateful Nephew

Neil MacDougall writes to John, from India, 1833

Neil was the twenty-two year-old son of John's widowed sister Isabella.

I now sit down to perform a duty which I ought to have executed long ago, you are one of the first to whom I should have written on my arrival in this country to have thanked for all the kindness I have experienced from you. I am afraid you will attribute my silence to a want of gratitude and affection — and not without reason, but I can assure you this is not the case for no person could cherish a keener affection or a warmer sense of gratitude towards you than I do for your kindness in protecting an orphan and enabling me to enter as a gentleman this honorable profession to which I belong.

When I look back on my past life, and view, through the lapse of time, the many indiscretions of my youth, and the many plausible reasons which they afforded you for casting me off it is with a sense of liveliest gratitude that I admire the high motives of honor which actuated you, and you alone, of all my Uncles and relations to stretch forth to me, however undeserving, the more than protecting arm of a parent. I can assure you, my dear Uncle, that altho they do not appear in my actions these sentiments are indelibly engraved on my heart.

I have now been in the Country nearly six years.

First sight of a train

Louisa Maxwell from Bath, 1840

Charles came over the other day by rail road to see me in about 20 minutes from Bristol ... I went with him to the station house when he returned, it is a truly wonderful sight to see all those carriages going by self motion, one would suppose.

The high cost of coal

Sophy, to John, from Dunollie, 1845

A strike has raised coals to an enormous price, they were selling in Oban last week at 18/- a ton. Fortunately we got 20 ton not long since.

(At the end of 1844, coal in Oban was 11/- a ton.)

Potato disease

Sophy to John, 1845

The potato disease has scarcely proved so bad as was anticipated, but the continual wet is much against those in pits and of course many have not houses to store them in, particularly as they require to be thoroughly dried and placed in layers. Ours have not gone much since the first and the pigs and poultry have been fed on the diseased ones after cutting out the affected parts.

Cumstie and MacArthur are very busy erecting a mill for making potato flour at the Tannery, it is to go by steam and is to cost a very large sum of money.

Pat to his mother from Hong Kong, 1847

I am very sorry to hear of the Dreadful state of the Highlands in consequence of the failure of the potato crop. Every paper you take up is full of it.

Charles from India, 1851

I see from the papers that part of the Western Highlands and some of the Islands are again in a very bad state, I suppose they trusted too much to the potato.

The Proposed Railway

Letter to John, sent on to Hong Kong by Sophy, 10th June, 1845

Sir, We beg leave to send you Copy resolutions agreed at a public meeting held at Oban this day. The project laid before the meeting was for the formation of a Railway from Oban by Loch Etive and the head of Loch Etive to Inveraray there crossing Loch Fine and proceeding by Loch Eck to Kilmun. From thence by Steamboat to the terminus at Helensburgh of a projected Railway from Glasgow.

It was stated by the Gentlmen who brought forward the project that it had the support of the Edinburgh & Glasgow Railway Company who would take Shares to a Considerable amount & that the portion of it which extends from Kilmun to the Banks of

Loch Fine has already been determined upon with the Sanction of the landed proprietors of the Line.

The meeting were unanimous as to the very great advantage to be derived from Railway Communication with the South and the great importance of securing as soon as possible a benefit which must eventually be obtained.

They were not however unanimous as to the adoption of the line proposed. The general impression seemed to be if a practiable Line could be found without the intervention of ferries it was much to be preferred and that all events the Sentiments of the Landed Proprietors who may have a Deep Interest in the Line of the proposed Railway, as well as in the prosperity of the County, should in the first instance be ascertained.

Several lines were mentioned as worthy of examination in order to avoid the inconvenience of the two ferries.

One by Tyndrum and Loch Lomond through Glen Falloch, another by Glendochart and Lochearnhead.

We beg however to call your attention to the fact that a Railway Company is forming for the purpose of carrying the project laid before the meeting into effect, and there seems little doubt that the requisite Capital will be subscribed. If therefore no Company will be willing to undertake the execution of any other line we trust you will not refuse your Sanction to the line now proposed passing through your Property.

As the Supporters of the project laid before the meeting are naturally anxious to have an expression of the feelings of this part of the Country as to its merits & advantages we request the favour of an early answer as we shall be under the necessity of fixing a day for the adjourned meeting as soon as possible.

Copy of resolutions at Meeting

1. That this meeting aware of the advantages of Railway Communications are of opinion that it would be of vast importance to connect the extensive and populous Country of Argyll and other parts of the W.H. & Islands by Railway with Glasgow and the large towns and Markets in the South, and that such would be a great National as well as local benefit.

2. That a line of Railway connecting the whole Western Districts and Islands by a direct route from Oban to the South would accomodate the large export traffic that already exists in Cattle, sheep etc etc as well as the return traffic in manufactured goods and would also command an extensive passenger traffic from the great population of these districts.

Midshipman in Trouble

James Black, Midshipman, to John MacDougall, Captain of *H.M.S. Vulture*

28th February, 1847

Sir, As you announced to me yesterday that it was impossible on your part to overlook the disgraceful conduct I have been guilty of, and that I must either leave the ship or stand the consequences which certainly would be fatal to my prospects in the Service, if not a final dismissal therefrom.

I beg again most humbly and sincerely to express my contrition, and implore your forgiveness, pledging myself that a repetition of such conduct shall never again occur, and that my conduct in future shall be, to the best of my ability, regulated to gain your approbation so deservedly lost, if in your goodness you permit me to remain in the Ship under your command which I have no wish to leave.

I beg further to state that I do not make this humble request so much for my own sake as that of my parents, for whose feelings I hold the greatest respect and as much as any disgrace befalling me would consequently affect them and I be rendered doubly miserable; hoping that your forgiveness may avert this.

I beg to subscribe myself, Sir, Your most obedient Humble Servant, Jas. Black, Midshipman.

The Taking of the Bogue forts

Pat to Sophy, 1847

(This is a description of a combined Army and Naval operation under the command of John. The ships taking part were John's ship, *H.M.S. Vulture*, *H.M.S. Espiegh* and the Hon. East India Company's steam vessel *Pluto*. The hired steamer *Corsair* went with them. The army troops concerned were from the 10th and 42nd Regiments. The object was the taking of the Bogue Forts up the Canton River, and to push up and land the troops at the Factories at Canton.)

April 1st You may fancy Hong Kong is all bustle and confusion on account of this expedition. At 3 p.m. our paddle box boats, getting ready to receive troops aboard. At 5 all ready to receive troops but these soldiers take longer than sailors getting ready ... Papa dined with the General and made all his arrangements. You may fancy he has lots to do. I am helping him as much as I can.

At 11 the soldiers and officers commenced coming aboard with plenty of traps and eatables which soldiers are very particular about. At 12 sent boats to embark the troops. I went with one division. These soldiers are precious clumsy fellows in boats and I had a great deal of difficulty with them. I am sorry to say that a good half of the Regiment were drunk and you may know what a drunken Irishman is. The whole of the regiment are Irish. We have hired the Corsair steamer for the expedition, she takes troops likewise.

April 2nd At 2 a.m. the troops being embarked to the number of about 850, we having aboard nearly half, we made signal to weigh anchor and fired a gun. We were obliged to ease the engines occasionally on account of tows, having two lurchers with ordinance stores on tow. [A lurcher was a large, single-masted, oared Chinese craft used in the Canton river.]

At 7 a.m. cleared for action, shotted the guns, got the troops ready. I have only had half an hours sleep last night, Papa none, but I am in high spirits as is he.

At 10 run close in to the Starboard batteries, these include the Bogue forts. Lowered Vulture's and paddle box's boats and filled them with troops.

We were within ½ pistol shot and within range of 100 guns so I call it a very daring thing as we did not know then but that the forts were manned. I went in one cutter, a Lieut. in the other boats. The boats shoved off and landed and spiked the guns, the Chinamen running away.

At 10.30 Corsair and Pluto having come up I went with cutter and paddle box boats with Col Breeton of the Artillery to be taken in tow and proceed to the Port batteries. We spiked all the guns of the Port batteries and then Vulture came over to us. Having spiked all the guns and destroyed all the powder we weighed anchor and proceeded to Whampoa — where we found Corsair and Pluto. We then rested for the night.

April 3rd At 3 a.m. we were all up busy getting ready to proceed to Canton on the Corsair and Pluto. Vulture not being able to go on account of our draft of water being too great ... At 1 the Espiegh arrived with the 7 fast boats with stores for the troops. At 6 a.m. all the troops, but 100 to guard the Vulture in the absence of her boats, had embarked aboard the steamers. The force was this:- Pluto, 2 lurchers with ordance stores, Vulture, paddle box boat, gig and cutter, Espiegh, pinnace, gig with 300 of the 10th, Corsair with 2 ordance lurchers and rockets ...

At 8.30 the tide suited and we weighed and proceeded for the Barrier Forts about half way from Canton. About 10 we passed the Stakes and the steamers anchored off the fort to cover the boats' landing. The boats then shoved off ...

The first fort shut their gates on us, which were soon blown in. The others ... opened fire on us, when we were within 50 yards,

with grape canister and chain shot. We pulled for the angle in the
Forts and all their shot went past us, but the other fort's shot went
very close to us and we had a cross fire. They had 15 shots at our
division of boats. One fell close to the Gig which Papa was in being
the headmost boat, but the splendid way he led the boats in and his
great forethought was the means of saving many lives as if a shot
had struck any of the boats, being so full of men, they would have
killed a great number. Each boat was full of troops. I was in the
Cutter at this time, about 3 yards astern of Papa's Gig. After firing
those horrible cowards cut, the steamer's shot astonishing them.
We did not fire from the boats.

We spiked all the guns here and blew up all their powder. Their
guns are larger than the Vulture and smaller than a 30 pounder,
some of them are upwards of 130 cwt. Their batteries are
immensely strong and well built and they ought to defy any nation.
I saw all their forts.

At 12.0, all the guns being spiked we re-embarked and the
Corsair being aground we took advantage of it and gave the men
their dinner.

At 1.30, being afloat, we proceeded and pushed up for Canton,
spiking the batteries as we went up. We had some very close
shaves coming up, the river being so crowded. At 4, we anchored
opposite the factories.

Painting of John's ship, H.M.S. Vulture (foreground), depicting the
expedition up the Canton River in 1847

The factories were covered with merchants in a great stir because by this time the Chinese were acquainted with what had been done and were very likely to attack the factories. Every place was also covered with Chinese rather surprised to see us.

By sunset all the troops were landed and housed in the factories. They had very comfortable quarters. Directly all the troops were landed I made Papa aware of it and dined with him aboard Col. Breeton's lurcher. Papa is a great favourite of his and he says if it had not been for Papa the expedition would have failed entirely. These soldiers, the General included says Papa, are the most helpless useless fellows we ever came across. The privates a noisy, drunken, useless set of fellows. The Vulture men behaved admirably ...

Everything has been done without the loss of a man. It was Papa planned the whole thing. The General wanted to leave troops in the forts and not spike the guns, the Consequence would have been that if any thing had been wanted to be done up here the General would have found he had no men.

April 4th At 2 a.m. we disembarked all the artillery and ordinance stores. At 11.30 Keying (the Imperial Commissioner) visited the General to negotiate.

The mob seemed inclined to give annoyance but we flogged 2 or 3 of the ringleaders which had a great effect. One of the men had flung a stone, hit an officer who had his horse pulled down ...

April 5th ... Everyone this evening is getting ready to attack the city in the morning. The Merchants have formed a body of Volunteers to defend the factories while the troops attack the town. The city is to be attacked at 10 tomorrow if Keying will not come to terms. We are all ready.

April 6th At 8 a.m. Keying gave in to everything. The burning of Canton, which would have been certain if we had attacked the city, would have been a dreadful loss of life. We were going to open a very heavy fire from the steamers and boats and also the artillery and Rockets. We have regularly got Keying under our feet so he thought it best to give in to our reasonable proposals.

April 7th. Today, everything being done, we sent our boats, with the exception of the pinnace and Gig, to Vulture and sent 300 of the 42nd in the Corsair to Hong Kong ... In the afternoon we heard that if Keying would not give up the Chinamen to be flogged in our presence we would burn Fuskan, a town about 10 miles from Canton, but in the evening he gave in and so everything is settled.

April 8th At 5 a.m. Papa and some of the officers saw the

Chinamen flogged, it was for insulting and wounding British subjects.

All the troops but 100 embarked in the Pluto for the Vulture ... I was getting very tired of Canton indeed ... The Espiegh remains up for a time and the Pluto returns to Canton in case of a disturbance, but I do not think there is the slightest chance. At sunset all the troops were aboard and all the boats ready for a start.

April 9th At 5 a.m. we took the 2 lurchers in tow and weighed and proceeded. At 7.30 we cleared for action and shotted the guns. At 8.30 we passed the Bogue Forts. All their embrasures were open and they were full of men but I do not know whether they had cleared their guns of spikes, but we were all ready for them if they had been treacherous at all, keeping our guns bearing on them.

At 4 we anchored at Hong Kong. We immediately out boats and got rid of everyone. These soldiers are precious dirty fellows and it will take some time to clean the ship.

Lord Palmerston, Her Majesty's Secretary of State for Foreign Affairs, commented on the operation:

There never was a Military and Naval operation in which not only the common feelings of humanity but the still higher qualities of generous forbearance, noble disinterestedness and self-denial were more splendidly displayed by every man engaged, from the highest to the lowest; and, if the Chinese are not in their moral Constitution essentially different from the rest of the human race, the admirable conduct of the British soldiers and sailors on this occasion must produce as forcible an impression on their minds, as the proofs which have been afforded of the irresistible superiority of Englishmen in Naval and Military matters have no doubt created on their prudential fears.

Income Tax

Sophy to John, 1848

Truly we are living in strange times and who can say when the present rage for Reform and change will stop.

We were threatened with 2 per cent to the income tax but such were the very strong feelings against it that Lord John [Russell] has with drawn it. Probably the French minister's fate may have influenced him to some degree.

(Note: income tax was then 7d. in the pound.)

Court Martial

Pat to his father, from *H.M.S. Firebrand*, at sea, 9th June, 1852

We joined the Admiral on 2nd June at Port Mahon (Minorca)
having experienced very boisterous weather on our way down,
getting a strong gale out of the Gulf of Lyons.

We arrived just in time for a court martial on one of the Lts. of
Trafalgar for sleeping on his watch. Strange to say they made out
the charge for the wrong day and consequently it saved him his
commission, a great piece of luck for him.

The Bombardment of Sveaborg

(This action was part of the Baltic campaign during the Crimean War).

Pat to his father, from Sveaborg, 11th August, 1855

On Sveaborg [on a fortified island off what is now Helsinki] from
the top of the hill to the water's edge is one mass of guns — and all
the islands extending from Helsinfors and the island of Sandham
bristle with cannon.

[The battle was fought with six British sail of the line and a force
of small craft. This was joined by a whole French squadron.] Our
ships were anchored in two columns out of range abrest the works
of Sveaborg. The frigates were in a position in line about 400 yards
outside the mortar boats, the gun boats were 600 yards inside the
mortars and steaming round in a circle. The French were in
position with our own vessels.

The bombardment began on the morning of Aug. 9 at 10.30 a.m;
the town appeared on fire in two places and at 11 a heavy
explosion took place in the heart of one of the batteries, the fire of
the mortars was admirable, some of them in two and a half hours
having thrown 80 shells. The fire of the gun boats did little
execution, the range being too great.

At noon a series of heavy explosions took place in the heart of the
forts, the whole island appeared to be going up in the air, guns,
stones, large timber stores etc were scattered in every direction.
For upwards of three minutes this continued and all the ships
rigging, and topyards were manned with men, the cheering must
have been distinctly heard on shore. Our success at this time was
beyond all expectation and we all thought if as much damage had
continued to be done during the rest of the day the large ships
would have gone in and made a finish — but I am sorry to say even
at this early time the mortars began to complain ... The spare parts
being on board the Volcano which ship was at Nazen 30 miles off.

By 4 p.m. our fire had slackened considerably and the Russians
had nearly ceased. This was the only time our large ships might
have done their part well as the Citadel, and many of the buildings

close to their guns, were on fire, and it appeared from the ships that it was quite impossible that they could work their guns for the heat. Now would have been the time, as our gun boats had advanced considerably, but I suppose our Admiral did not like to run any risk taking these ships in.

Towards the close of the day the gunboats appeared to have got their range better and did good execution, at 9 the Rocket Boats of the fleet were sent in. During 4 hours of dark they threw in an immense number of Rockets but their long range did I am afraid little execution. The enemy treated them with Contempt, never firing a shot, they ought to have been considerably closer.

The sight from the ships in the night was beautiful and the whole town appeared to be in a blaze, and the constant discharge of the rockets and occasional shell had a very imposing appearance.

The bombardment went on for most of the night but there was trouble with the mortars. Three of them had burst on board, luckily hurting no one, five others were disabled — but by 5 a.m. the steam Factory boat, the Volcano, had arrived and rendered the Mortars servicable.

At about 2 p.m. the next day there was a tremendous blaze in the town which we supposed to be the boat sheds and Dockyard ... By 4 p.m. the Citadel had fallen in, taking with it the fort and its staff which made the Frenchmen greatly excited.

[Early the following day the bombardment was discontinued due to failing equipment.] All their barracks, publick buildings and all their naval premises had been destroyed, not to mention the damage that had been done to the place itself by the explosions which, it is natural to suppose had cost them many men, and strange to say not a single casualty has occurred from the enemy's fire on our side.

If the mortars had lasted another day I believe the whole place would have been destroyed, we then should have hauled in and bombarded Hilmapas. I cannot make out why the Government did not send out some spare mortars. I think this bombardment will prove that with 100 mortarboats we could destroy all their seaport towns including Arnstadt and the whole of their fleet. A blow of this sort close to their Capital I think would bring them to their knees, we ought to have 100 gun boats too, half the line of battleships would be quite sufficient.

[Pat's opinion was that they should have advanced the mortar boats much closer, their rocket boats were also too far off. The Admiral, he supposes, dreaded any casualty.]

One great mistake I think we committed, was not throwing up sandbag batteries in the Islands within range, we laughed at the Frenchmen doing it but their batteries ... played capitally on the town.

Good Appetite

Young Sophy to her mother, 1853

William [young Sophy's brother-in-law] is quite well apparently, walks three or four miles a day and eats like <u>three</u> ploughmen. We dine now at half past two and Papa was amazed the other night to see him devouring a <u>whole</u> shoulder of lamb with his tea.

The Wallace Monument

Allan to the Schoolmaster at Lismore, 1855

Dear Sir, The London Times Newspaper and some of the English people challange our right to erect a monument to Sir William Wallace. Scotchmen cannot allow this, we only regret that a monument to commemorate his great achievements as Liberator of his country was not raised centuries ago. Let it be our pride that we are about to do what our forefathers ought to have done. I hope you will assist me in getting subscribers. If we can raise one penny from every soul in the parish we will contribute a very useful sum to the fund.

Horsewhipping the Colonel

Sophy to Charles, 1863

(Louisa Locke was John's niece and daughter of Ann by her second husband. Donald was Louisa's half-brother.)

Louisa Locke has got herself and her friends into a nice mess. Donald had to <u>Horsewhip</u> the Colonel of a Regt. now at the Castle on her account — it took place in the Club and yr Father was present, you may suppose the excitment it has caused in Edinburgh and I fear may bring Donald into trouble ... There is no doubt she has been very <u>Imprudent</u> and the <u>Gallant</u> Col. must be a <u>consummate villian</u> — <u>he is</u> a married man with a family. I have <u>no doubt</u> the affair will get into the Papers, as it has been the <u>last 9 days</u> wonder.

Second Sight

Elizabeth (Kitty) to her brother Charles, May 1864

The poor Murray Allens are in such distress, their eldest girl Maggie had got over the measles and was carried off in a few days with diptheria. And now Johnnie, the only boy is dead. They only buried Maggie on Monday and he died on Thursday.

Now I must tell you an odd thing. At the time Maggie died, 2 am., I heard a melancholy sound like an Aeolian harp, and then I dreamt I saw her grave and an open one by it. I said next day I hoped no more of them were going, and now the grave I saw will be filled in a few days.

6

Themes in the Letters

It is now time to consider a few of the themes which run through the 150 years of the letters — themes which could for the most part apply equally well to other contemporary families — and to note the changes during those years.

In any history of the West Highlands during this period the great changes which took place are rightly stressed. Yet on reading the letters it is perhaps surprising to find how little change there was throughout these years in some important aspects. On the other hand there has been much change between the end of the period and the present day.

The threads that are gathered together in this last chapter can, to a certain extent, evolve into a pattern of the social life of the times. But the pattern must of necessity be incomplete for only that which went into this family postbag can come out of it and it is realised that some important themes are missing. Some trivial ones have been given space, but that is the way in a postbag — the important and the trivial lie close together.

One of the most important changes, which affected everybody in the Highlands, was the ending of the powers of the clan chiefs by the Act of 1747, abolishing the Jurisdiction of the chiefs. This is not mentioned directly in the letters but there are a few indications of how the lives of the chiefs changed and how the heads of this particular family saw their roles.

At the beginning of the period Iain Ciar was acting as a traditional chief, leading his clansmen into battle at Sheriffmuir, and writing to his wife that the few who had deserted and gone home would feel the whip when he eventually returned. After the battle he instructed her to send more men, adding that if they disobeyed, 'for my pairt I fully discharge my interest in them'. Thus he conveyed that the principle of mutual benefit that existed between chief and clansman would be wiped out. When he was a fugitive, and his possessions were forfeit, the clan system was reflected by the fact that his sons' education was undertaken by more fortunate clansmen.

Few letters survive the period after Iain Ciar was pardoned and came home, but one from 1730 shows that, although his lands were forfeit, he was still acting as a chief towards his clansmen; in this case organising a search for a clansman who appears to have been kidnapped. MacDougall of the Exchequer wrote from Edinburgh: 'I am surprized how your neighbours are guilty of man stealing, I assure you it is not an easy crime. Your son has been very diligent in making search for Mr McDougall but has not hitherto been able to find out where he is, but methods shall be fallen on to make Menzie's son accountable for him at the first of his appearances here.'

Letters of the time of Alexander, Iain Ciar's son, give some clues that the attitude of the chief in changing social conditions was still one of responsibility towards his clansman.

In 1746, the year before the Act, Alexander was trying to resettle some MacDougalls whom the government had evicted from their land in the aftermath of the '45 Rising. His friend the Chief of the Lamonts, to whom he sent them, wrote that they were 'very sensible of your Friendship to them and all of their name'.

Fifteen years after the Act a MacDougall in Mull demanded Alexander's opinion when he was arrested over a dispute about recruiting. He said his Chief had told him and his brother to let him know if anything should happen to them. Maclean of Torloisk, who had caused the arrest, wrote to Alexander: 'To obviate any foolish notions these ignorant People may have of the support of a Chief, right or wrong, would be glad you give your opinion of the matter to satisfy the People.'

The principle that the chief was a father to his clan seems to have lived on in Alexander's attitude towards his tenants. When his son Patrick became heir on the death of his elder brother, Alexander hoped that he would have the greatest concern for the place, the family and the 'dependents'. This sense of responsibility is seen again in a letter describing how Alexander had overwintered his tenants' cattle during a bad year. Referring to his tenants he wrote: 'I'll give them all the Indulgence in my power.'

Patrick wrote: 'every man I am satisfied must attend to his estate as he does to his family — Therefore two principles I would lay down, moderate rents and keeping the land in good heart.'

In 1847, a hundred years after the Act abolishing the chiefs' powers, John was fighting with enthusiasm for a Queen belonging to the Hanoverian line, a line against which his great grandfather Iain Ciar had fought with such dedication. Although this John was a naval captain of the nineteenth century he did not forget that he was also a clan chief, for he took with him into battle a piper wearing MacDougall tartan.

Infant Mortality and Medical Matters

One of the most important and consistent aspects of life during the time of the letters was the large number of children born to most families. At Dunollie a total of forty-five children were born to the four chiefs, and it is easy to forget that but for the number of miscarriages, of which there is evidence in the letters, there would have been still more.

These large families caused problems, especially in a part of the country where much of the land was unproductive, and the rest mostly shallow and acid — and where the wind, rain and lack of sun made harvesting a gamble. What money was earned could support only a few and many of the family had to find work elsewhere.

But if families were large, the infant mortality rate was high — right until the end of the period. Although the Victorian children of the Dunollie family all survived other families were not so lucky and children's deaths are often referred to in the letters.

During the eighteenth century this high rate of childhood mortality is reflected by a pessimism which seeps through the correspondence.

Iain Ciar wrote to his wife: 'let me know how the children are or if they are in life.' In another letter he told her she must not grudge the loss of her children 'if it be god's pleasor to inflict you with it being comon and natural to all flesh'. Again he wrote of his children, who had recently been reported to be in good health: 'God Grant you may not have the cross of their Death.'

Later in the century, when Patrick's firstborn died of smallpox he was told: 'God giveth and God taketh away, there is nothing in this world to be depended upon so we should all be resigned.' When flourishing twins were born next, Patrick's brother wrote: 'Their life is very precarious, the loss of them is less to be regretted when they are young and the mother is safe.'

A curious custom was the giving of a dead child's name to another born to the family later on. There seems to have been no superstitious feeling attached to this practice which was common in many families of the time. Iain Ciar's first John was replaced by another; in the next generation Alexander replaced his Allan with another, only to lose him. However, when his first Alexander died the second one survived. Among the girls the unlucky name seems to have been Jean — both Jeans died. Alexander's son Patrick was more persistent: his first Mary died and so did the second but the parents, undaunted, gave the name to a third child, and this Mary survived into old age. It does seem that much importance was attached to carrying on ancestral names.

A very common cause of death in the eighteenth century was

smallpox, which could lead to life-long disfigurement, if not death. Macaulay describes it vividly: 'Smallpox was always present, filling the churchyard with corpses, tormenting with fears all whom it had not yet stricken, leaving on those whose life it spared the hideous traces of its power.'

People even dreamt about it. A friend of Iain Ciar's wrote in 1730: 'I am afraid that my father will be snatched away by the small pox for I had a foolysh dream which I hope is but a dream.'

The first mention of inoculation against smallpox found among the correspondence is in a letter of 1752 from Crieff: 'innoculating for the small pox is so frequent and successful here that we were perswuaded to make little Dunky under go the opperatione.'

The idea of inoculation had been brought to this country earlier in the century by a society lady, Lady Mary Wortley Montagu, the wife of the British Ambassador to Turkey. So impressed was she by all she saw of the practice of inoculation there that she made it her mission to persuade doctors in this country of its efficiency. The inoculation was made using a mild strain of smallpox itself. If all went well the patient developed a very mild attack of the disease (which incidentally he could pass on to someone else), and then he was immune.

In 1754 the Royal College of Physicians of Edinburgh pronounced inoculation 'to be highly salutary to the human race'. It was not, however, without risk, for in some cases, owing to the difficulty of assessing the virulence of the strain, the patient had a full-scale attack which could be fatal.

In 1787 Alexander wrote from Dunollie that several of the family had been inoculated and that he had arranged for the inoculation of his tenants. 'There was 80 souls last weak in Kerrera Innoculated for the small pox.' he wrote in one letter.

Once into the nineteenth century the scourge of smallpox began to recede as vaccination, discovered by Dr Jenner, was gradually accepted by the medical profession. Dr Jenner, who was a country doctor in Gloucestershire, had often heard the saying that anyone who had had cowpox was immune from smallpox. This gave him the idea of using cowpox vaccine to protect his patients from smallpox. By the time of his death in 1823 many of the public thought of him as a national hero. This is reflected among the letters in a verse copied out by John's wife Sophy — who had all her children vaccinated a few months after birth and lost none of them.

Dr Jenner

Beneath this stone immortal Jenner lies,

His Soul is mounted to its native skies,
Born for the world his comprehensive mind,
Soon found its way to benefit mankind.
Awed by his word the dire contagion fled.
In ancient time a custom t'was to grace,
Who saved a member of the human race,
With an oak crown: to him what laurels then.
Reader bedew this marble with a tear,
For Jenner who preserved thy life lies here.

(Jenner's memorial marble is now high on the wall of Berkley Church and anyone wanting to bedew it with a tear would have to be something of an acrobat!)

Apart from the discovery of vaccination, and later in the nineteenth century of anaesthetics and antiseptics, neither of which are mentioned in the letters, medicine seems much the same at the end of the 150 years as it did at the beginning. Bleeding, the application of leeches and blistering were the main treatments to which the letter-writers were subjected for every kind of ailment.

Blood-letting is referred to throughout the period. It is first mentioned in 1719 when Iain Ciar wrote from France that he had been bled twice for a 'damnable Rumatick pain'. He added, 'I hop this will prevent fevors and any distempers.' Lucy, Alexander's daughter, was bled and blistered at the same time for a 'fever of cold'. Her brother Dr Sandie snatched their brother Duncan from death with a penknife:

> This morning was likely to present a scene in this family the most wretched it ever saw. Duncan and I were sitting before breakfast together in the dining-room making very merry at some of Duncan's Jokes when all at once he gave a loud scream and dropt to all appearance dead upon the floor, his Eyes fixed, his Pulse gone and every other Symtome of instant disolution. He continued in this state for about 10 minutes. Having no Lancet in my pocket I took blood from his Arm with my Penknife and every thing else you may believe I could think of until at last he came to himself and is now out of danger.

It was the same Duncan who, about ten years later, was distressed that none of his household sent for a doctor to bleed his son when the child had been badly kicked by a horse.

Being pregnant was no protection against being bled. During the first half of the nineteenth century Mary Jane became ill during her pregnancy. Her mother wrote: 'She was profusely bled, leeched, blistered and had quantities of medicine given her.' The baby was not surprisingly stillborn and three months premature, though the mother survived.

Later in the century Peter, the Admiral's brother, was freely bled for an apoplectic fit; his sister-in-law wrote: 'I think he ought in future to be bled every eight or ten weeks as it is evident notwithstanding his low diet that he makes blood very rapidly.'

Blood was drawn both by the lancet and by leeches, often mentioned in the letters. Twelve leeches could rid their victim of a pint of blood. They fed until they were gorged and then fell off and had to be collected from bed or floor. A description of leeches at work is given in one of the Victorian letters: 'I am now writing to you from a sick house, dear Cameron is laid up with fever and just had all his hair taken off, I am writing to you while his temples are covered with leeches ... On another couch my poor Missy is lying burning like a coal, I have had leeches on her little head and cut off her hair.'

In a chemist's bill of 1855 leeches cost 6d. a dozen and the account is credited with some which have been returned.

Blistering was often combined with bleeding, and one member of the family was long before his time in questioning its efficiency. He wrote in 1780: 'Your mother applayed a Blister to her back some days ago for the Rumatism I think she is greatly the worse of it.'

If the doctors' treatments described in the letters are obsolete today, their frequent advice to take more exercise has a modern ring. Fresh air was also recommended, and people taken ill while away from home were often advised to go back to their native air. The family attributed several cures to 'Dunollie Air'.

There is another more trivial but entertaining theme which runs alongside descriptions of the doctors' treatment: the medical advice the letter-writers gave to each other. For whooping cough in a child, which could be very dangerous at the time, one of the family wrote in the late eighteenth century: 'Change of Air is the best cure for that bad Complaint. I wish you had mentioned whether he Vomits. If he does you may depend upon it there is no danger to be apprehended.'

In Victorian times the advice given was to feed the child on gruel and treacle and dose him with castor oil.

In 1795 the brotherly advice to Patrick for an ordinary cough was: 'You must give up your favourite Grog for some time as I reckon Port wine is very bad for a cough, a little Rum and Water with sugar and fresh Fruit is the best licquor for a Cough.' Rheumatism could be cured, according to one correspondent in 1820, by wearing 'a brown paper jack coat next the skin' and the writer added that he knew several people cured by this method. The last medical piece of advice found in the letters is that sea sickness can be treated by eating 'ham sandwiches very dry, mustard and pepper, with soda water gingered as hot as you can take it and a little brandy.'

Gout was a common complaint and, at the turn of the century, one brother wrote to another:

> I received your letter informing me that your pains had descended from your haunch and laid hold of your Great Toe ... I cannot hesitate to pronounce it a Gout, which I never look upon as dangerous while it remains in the Extremities, at the same time I earnestly recommend you to treat your illness as a Gout and endeavour by every possible means to Arrest it in your foot. You must eat sparingly and drop a Tender and Parting tear to poor Grog.

In the early nineteenth century a son of the family wrote of the affliction: 'Our dear mother and father thank Providence enjoy perfect health except that he had the Gout which I think nothing of comparitively speaking, some people say in such a constitution as his it drives away all other complaints.'

This is not the only time that the theory that one ailment can keep away another appears in the letters. In 1770 one of the family wrote from a ship bound for India, that he was suffering from prickly heat, a rash which he reckoned was a good symptom, as it was said to prevent fever and most other complaints. A letter from John from Hong Kong in 1847 repeats the same kind of theory: 'I have been all covered with vile bites a common and purilent complaint here, they say it keeps off the fever.'

Advice on diet is occasionally given. Allan wrote to his sister Ann in the 1830s with some advice on the feeding of her child, who was then about eight: 'I hope Donald eats no trash, everything but porridge and milk, potatoes and broth and a little animal food and plain biscuits ought to be carefully avoided whatever his wish may be. If he is hungry some of the things above would do him good.'

About the same time the Duchess of Sutherland advised Louisa Maxwell: 'I am very sorry to hear of your illness. There are so many remedies for that sort of complaint and I imagine the simpler the better, one I was told of lately as very useful is to eat brown bread and butter at Breakfast, a course of which they say cannot fail to move the bowels. I heard it from one of my visitors, the loss of whom since we all much regret.'

Money Problems

As well as matters of health, money and the economic climate were often mentioned in the letters. Patrick, the most frugal of the four heads of the family, described money as 'the father of all disputes', and added 'I wish that Mettale had never Existed.'

Economy was a constant theme in the letters. Alexander wrote that though parsimony and frugality were necessary they should never be accompanied by meanness. Patrick practised his economy by refusing to copy his neighbours in apeing the more expensive life-style of those in the South. His son John, who had no such inhibitions, was still conscious of the need to economise, and wrote from Hong Kong to his wife: 'I feel very much the way you are pinched for money but what can I do. We must just economise.' He himself, unlike other officers, was walking, instead of riding in a sedan chair!

Throughout the period money seems always to have been short. It is clear that each new head of the family inherited debts, a situation found in many Highland families of the time. They did inherit land from which rents could be expected but in bad years these were often ill-paid — and rent-reduction was a common occurrence. Rent-paying was affected not only by a rough season but also by outside influences such as war or political moves like the introduction of free trade.

Charles, who was to succeed his father, the Admiral, wrote in 1851: 'Since the introduction of the Free Trade and the consequent depreciation in value of all sorts of grain and live stock the tenants must have great difficulty in paying the same rents as formerly.' He advises a just reduction of rents and adds: 'I suppose rents must be lowered all over the land and in fact everybody must come down a peg.'

Beside income from rents the MacDougall family depended, like so many others in the Highlands, on the sale of black cattle, which were driven to the marts at Dumbarton, Crieff or Falkirk. This source of income fluctuated for everyone as the price of cattle rose and fell at the markets, or as the season proved harsh or mild. After Patrick had reported a good season his son Sandy wrote enquiring whether the cows looked as if they would buy him a captaincy.

In the nineteenth century potatoes were an important crop. Louisa Maxwell, having taken her daughters to Edinburgh on a social spree wrote home to her husband: 'what a sale of potatoes etc must be when I get home to pay for all this nonsense.' The potato disease which ruined crops in the mid-nineteenth century was a tragedy for the Highlanders.

As is well known agriculture made great advances during the 150 years covered by the letters. Through the correspondence runs concern for improving the breed of cattle, for overwintering them efficiently, for growing new crops such as potatoes and improving the old ones such as oats, and for fertilising the land.

With large families one big drain on the finances was the children's education. This was looked upon as of the greatest importance throughout the period: primary schooling took place at local schools during the eighteenth century; in the nineteenth tutors and governesses were employed to teach the children at home. And in all the generations sons and sometimes the daughters were sent away for their further education to Crieff, Perth, Inverness or Edinburgh. It was also to Edinburgh that the sons were sent to be trained for medicine and the law. The fact that all the heads of family had, at one time or another, to borrow money to pay for education did not at all deter them.

It was not only schooling that was such an expense for fathers of the time: the pay at the start of many careers, such as the Navy, the Army, Medicine and the Law was so low that the sons needed the support of the parents for quite a number of years. Also there was, in each generation, one who, through inability, laziness or extravagance, expected to be supported for a longer period of time.

For instance, Patrick seems to have failed to make money in his profession of W.S. He had to be partly supported by his father to save him, according to himself, from 'rotting in a debtor's Dungeon.' His son Allan repeated history by being no success as a W.S., and for many years looked to his brother John for financial support. Eventually John, having come to the conclusion that it was laziness that made his brother indigent, refused further help. Soon after he received a letter from his man of business begging him to rescue Allan from the prospects of the 'horrors of a debtors' prison'. In the next generation it was Johnnie in the West Indies who kept begging for money from a somewhat reluctant father.

Marriage

With finances usually, as Alexander put it, in a tottering state, all through the period the heir to the family was expected to marry money in order to keep the ancestral estate together. In 1781 one of Patrick's brothers advised him to get married 'providing the fair one is mistress of at least £1500 or £2000, otherwise by no means.' Another brother aimed higher for Patrick and suggested a minimum of £3000 or £4000 as necessary with a wife. In the next generation John was told: 'I wish you could fall in with some rich one, it won't do without the needful.' His mother wrote, 'I wish you would lay seige to one of the Miss Beaufort's good forty thousand, I think it would be the best ship you could get.' John's wife Sophy wrote in 1860 of their eldest son Alexander: 'we all know how important it is that he should get money with a wife.'

In spite of all such advice most of the heirs took no notice and married girls of their own choice who could contribute little to the family coffers. Tradition says that Alexander's wife brought enough money with her to build the new house but there was none left over. Patrick's wife brought little, John's wife could bring no dowry (though her father did help later with the building of the addition to Dunollie), and John's heir married a lass with no money at all.

As to the many daughters, it was considered important that they should marry, not only for their own sake but to prevent them being a financial drain on their fathers. In order to find suitable husbands it was thought worthwhile to send them into a wider social circle even if it meant borrowing money to do so. This was lucky for the girls, since their delight in these rare jaunts away from home comes vividly through their letters, whether from Edinburgh, Inveraray, or Cheltenham.

Travel abroad and at home

The theme of sons who went abroad hoping to make their fortunes is one that runs through the history of many Highland families. Often they took with them sons of large families of tenant or crofter. One such was the miller's son who went with John on board *H.M.S. Leander*.

John wrote home in great distress in 1817: 'I am extremely sorry to say I have lost poor McCallum and fear much he is Drowned. The day after we arrived at Quebec he went on shore with me and I desired him to be down at the Warf by 10 o'clock ... he has never been heard of since then and it was reported next morning that two men had been drowned one of them belonging to the Leander, he was a most attached good man.'

However, there was a sequel to this sad story: three years later a man from America brought the news that John McCallum was still alive and had been seen in the province of New York. He had decided to embark upon a new life in a new country and, together with the other man said to be drowned, had deserted. Patrick wrote to John with this news and added: 'This Intelligence I gave to Old McCallum the Miller who seemed Joyful at his son being in Life but was greatly hurt at the thought of him Deserting from you.'

Between them the sons of the Dunollie family travelled almost all over the world — to America, Canada, Australia, China, India, Africa, Russia, the Mediterranean and the Baltic, and innumerable islands such as Madeira, Teneriffe, the Azores, the West Indies, the Cape de Verde

Islands, Corfu, and the Amambas. They saw and wrote home about such varied sights as icebergs and Chinese feasts, coral islands and the leaning tower of Pisa, St Peter's at Rome and the Himalayan mountains They brought home presents as varied: a barrel of sugar from St Kitts; a cage of bright birds from the Cape of Good Hope; the model of a Chinese junk from Hong Kong; and from India a deer the size of a dog — which unfortunately died just before reaching Britain and had to be stuffed.

Travelling in this country became much easier over the 150 years owing to improvement in the roads and, in the nineteenth century, the coming of the railway. But the railway did not reach Oban until 1880 and so travelling from there during the period covered by the letters was wholly dependent on the horse. Journeys to Glasgow and Edinburgh on horseback were often undertaken by the family and others in the district, during the eighteenth century. Even in the nineteenth century John made a rapid ride from Glasgow hoping to be in time for the birth of his first-born child in 1827.

Gradually, travelling by wheeled vehicle became the norm, whether by gig, carriage or coach. Most of the journeys in the Highlands were a combination of land and water travel: a favourite way of getting to Edinburgh was on horseback or by gig to Inveraray, taking a boat from there to Glasgow and then a coach or, after 1842, a train to Edinburgh. When John succeeded to the property he invested in a family coach, complete with coat of arms on the door. In this he made his honeymoon journey from the south of England to Dunollie. The coach was used for journeys to Edinburgh and even went as far as Cheltenham on visits to Sophy's parents.

Carriage accidents are sometimes recorded in the letters, as in the case of Sophy's aunt: 'The horses ran away with the carriage which so alarmed her that she sprung from the vehicle and unfortunately falling on her head she received a wound that rendered her insensible and she expired the following day.' A few years later, in 1844 a friend in Edinburgh wrote of a different kind of accident: 'The horses ran off and lept over a bridge into a ravine, the phaeton was upset and one of the horses was killed on the spot. Aunt Agnes' face is much cut with the glass ... David and I fell together we both got blows on the face, I bled a great deal, the coach man is bruised and the manservant was dazed by being thrown into the water.'

Travel by sea from Oban advanced very much during the period with the coming of steam. The first steam boat to ply between Oban and Glasgow was the *Comet*, in 1812. Patrick wrote in 1820: 'The Conveyance in this Country is much improved by the steam Boats ... so that you may Breakfast here the second day from Glasgow for a Mere triffle of Expence.'

Journeys to London by ship from Leith were often preferred to travelling on land. In 1801 John took five days on the passage and it was cheaper than going by post chaise which then cost £14. The sea voyage could, however, be dangerous at times. In the 1780s Dr Sandie's wife was drowned on her way to London when the ship she was in went down in a storm. In the next century John, who had just survived a hurricane in the West Indies in which many were drowned, nearly lost his life in a shipwreck between London and Leith. Even after the coming of better steam ships Allan wrote with anxiety to his brother in 1840: 'I hope you will not leave me longer of hearing from you that you are safe in London. One of the London steamers has been missing for several days.'

Another sea route to England was from Glasgow to Liverpool. In 1844 John's son Alexander thought of coming via Liverpool, on his way from Woolwich to Dunollie, but being such a bad sailor he decided to travel on land instead. He proposed coming by train from London to Newcastle, and then by coach from Newcastle to Edinburgh. The 1st class train fare was £4.3.0., the 2nd class £2.18.0. The fare for the coach from Newcastle to Edinburgh was £2.0.0. for an inside seat, and £1.1.0. for an outside seat.

Although it was December, Alexander wrote: 'I of course would go on the outside from Newcastle to Edinburgh as I do not much like travelling inside coaches.' The stuffiness and the sway of the coaches in those days could, it seems, have as bad an effect as a rough sea. As to the train, he wrote: 'It would depend on the fineness of the weather whether I would go in the 1st or 2nd carriages.' (Second-class carriages at that time were open to the wind and rain.) From Edinburgh Alexander planned to go by train to Glasgow and take a boat from Greenock to Inveraray and hence home by gig to Oban.

Bound up with travelling is the theme of hospitality, a virtue very much part of Highland life. Iain Ciar wrote from exile of a seaman he had met who had visited Mary, his wife, in her cottage on Kerrera. 'I was rejoyced of the account that the poor lad gave that tho' the house was small there was meat and drink waiting a stranger.' And this attitude continued down the years. Patrick, though unsociable in his later years, then wrote cheerfully of how some strangers and their children had been given food and beds at Dunollie 'for their convenience'.

Hospitality seems to have been on a wholehearted scale: guests could arrive with no warning and stay for months rather than weeks. Often the house was overflowing, a problem sometimes solved, especially in the eighteenth century, by sharing beds. One letter remarks that all the beds were full and 'the spit in constant motion'. Relatives seem to have thought that Dunollie was a home for them whenever need arose for one. This continued right until the end of the period although towards its close Sophy, John's English wife, found Highland hospitality more than she could stand. In one letter she begged her husband 'that the house should no longer be an assylum for all who chose to come to it', adding that short visits make long friends. It does not seem that her protests made much difference.

Ethics and Religion

References in the letters to every kind of situation indicate that ethics and attitudes altered very little from the beginning of the period to the end. Marriage, for instance, was consistently seen as being for life. There are examples, though not in the family, of wives putting up with cruel and violent husbands without a thought of divorce. Divorce is very occasionally mentioned and in each case the cause was the infidelity of the wife. Much sympathy was usually expressed for the aggrieved husband. In one of the Victorian letters, however, there is no sympathy for the husband whose wife had just gone off with another man to America: 'for the world attaches blame to him for neglect and unnecessary marked attention to others which gave rise to scandalous report ... It is said that Mrs C. [the deserting wife] gave each of her seven children a lock of her hair the evening before her departure.'

Correspondents were tolerant of the young men sowing their wild oats, and it does not seem anything to be worried about in a prospective bridegroom. Such remarks as 'he has been as most young men gay and foolish enough but of course is to turn over a new leaf when he marrys,' or, 'he has told me frequently that he has been very wild for some years past but he now intends to reform,' come into the letters as written of suitors considered perfectly suitable for the girls. Even in Victorian times the family did not seem at all upset when they heard that young Sophy's husband-to-be had the reputation of being a very wild young man who always got into bad scrapes.

The fathering of illegitimate children was also tolerantly looked upon through most of the period. So common was it that it seemed almost to be taken for granted and was no shame. In Victorian times, though the problem was still common, it was not taken so lightly.

Drunkenness was taken lightly but only if it was not carried too far. Duncan wrote of his fresh stock of Capital Whisky: 'It will intoxicate you into Drunkeness and not a headache in a Tun of it.' But on another occasion he wrote sternly to his brother: 'I am sorry to hear of the accident you met with, I suppose you were drunk for God's sake give up that trade it will ruin your excellent constitution.' The family lawyer wrote with no shame from Edinburgh: 'I must do my best to write to you today tho' I was dead drunk yesternight.'

In one letter a story is told about a relative of a local laird who was found dead drunk by the roadside in a shocking state, and was rescued by some passers-by. These he later charged with stealing his gold watch and snuff box, but at the trial it came out that the gentleman had been drinking in a low hostelry and that was where he had lost his valuables. 'In short,' wrote Louisa Maxwell, 'he cut a very bad figure.' An Inveraray acquaintance got little sympathy when having drunk too much wine he fell to his death from the dicky of his carriage: 'he made but a poor figure in life and a shocking exit out of it.'

The feelings of son for father appear from the letters to have been respect and often gratitude. In 1770 a son wrote: 'All the attention and regard I can pay you will nor can in any way recompence what you dear Father have done for me.' Another, it may be remembered, wrote: 'I shall always honour and esteem you as my father yet at the same time I should be particularly proud of considering you as my best friend and intimate companion.' In the Victorian age the sons were still grateful and one wrote: 'I am sure we ought all of us to be extremely thankful for all the trouble and expense you have been at to give us a good education and settle us in life.'

That a Father's word was law is evident throughout the period. Patrick wrote to his father in 1782: 'What you say of this profession I follow being my choice what was then my sentiments I durst not have contradicted what you suggested.' And in the next century Johnnie wrote: 'If I were allowed to chose my profession . . .' When a son went against his father's advice the father felt quite justified in cutting off all communications with him. The erring son, however put out he was, usually remained respectful. One wrote: 'I shall always show the respect I owe to a parent be his conduct to me never so Improper.'

Alexander, who seems otherwise to have been a kindly man, cut off his son John for several years after quarrelling with him about his career. He only made it up when his son sailed for India. A decade later Alexander had a serious quarrel over money with his son Patrick and was about to cut him off entirely when his two other sons persuaded him to see reason. Patrick himself was later to cut off all communication for a time with his son Peter, because of the young man's extravagance. In Victorian times it was Johnnie in the West Indies who was in trouble with his father and for two or three years received no letter from him.

Occasionally it seems that it wasn't altogether clear what the trouble was about. One son whose father had not answered letters for some time, wrote: 'The cause of this Extraordinary Neglect you Certainly have some reason for, I myself am perfectly Ignorant of any ... where now the Umbrage lies I am a stranger.'

These temporary quarrels do not seem to have diminished the sons' affection. John, the eldest son of Alexander, writing soon after the silence between them had been broken, says: 'I have never yet had cause to charge myself with a thought but of those of the most tender affection for you'. Peter wrote of his father from Australia: 'When I think of all his kindness to me I may say from my Birth and the little prospect I have of ever seeing him again it distresses me very much.'

Religious belief is a strong theme in the correspondence throughout the generations. Iain Ciar in particular looks on God (often written by him without a capital G), as a personal protector and friend in all his considerable troubles. After the Battle of Sheriffmuir he wrote: 'god is still in heaven on whom I have still my dependence.' When he broke the news to Mary that the '15 Rising had failed and he was now a hunted man, he added: 'Pray take nothing in bad pairtt for god who provided hitherto for us will not forsake us.'

When Alexander had just lost his wife and only four of his fifteen children were still living he wrote: 'I have reason to thank God for the great and Many blessings I enjoy by the company of the few remaining members of my family.' When Patrick, in the next generation, lost his eldest son he wrote: 'His death is a severe loss to us all but God's will be done.' In Victorian times Henry wrote of his mother that her trust in God and the consolations of religion would give her strength to withstand the blow of her husband's death.

The will of God often comes into the letters and was not to be questioned. But at times it does seem that the will of the individual was ascribed to God. When Mary Jane wanted to continue her enjoyable social life in Cheltenham she wrote to her father saying she was sorry about the expense she was causing him, 'but God's will be done'.

The whole household gathered together morning and evening for family prayers. This was the tradition of the family in the nineteenth century and probably before. The family attended the Church of Scotland at Kilmore or Kilbride. But in the Victorian age John showed a religious tolerance not so common then: he allowed his family to be brought up as Episcopalians by his wife, though he himself remained loyal to the Church of Scotland, often riding on horseback to Kilbride, sometimes accompanied by his family in the carriage.

The Letters Themselves

One thing which never changed during the 150 years was the number of excuses made for not having written before! The following selection will give an idea of how varied they were. In one case it was a severe attack of dysentery, in another the time taken in drilling at Holyrood for the visit of George IV to Edinburgh. A young bride's excuse was that she had had twenty people calling on her each day. A boy at boarding school wrote: 'Every night I have put off writing to you I have always been employed in something useful.' Then there is the extremely honest: 'the truth is I much hate writing.' One married daughter simply wrote to her father: 'Your last three letters before me condemn me so much that I cannot get a sufficient excuse fore myself fore not writing to you before now.' A young lady sent a message that she could not write because she was trimming a bonnet for Queen Charlotte's mourning.

A prospective bridegroom did not write to the bride's father about the state of his finances because: 'I have reason to believe that in the present juncture most letters especially those directed to the coast are inspected at the post office.' (Britain had recently become involved in the American War of Independence.) The same man's excuse some years later was the harvesting of seventy acres. However, on second thoughts he continued: 'Yet I will not even plead that as a Sufficient excuse. I know you'l say had I not one half hour neither evening or morning surely, and therefore the proper excuse with generous Spirits is I plead Guilty, not doubting of pardon from you.' During the time when letters had to be paid for on delivery, there was, when all else failed, the excuse already mentioned in Chapter 1 of not wanting to put the recipient to expense.

During the earlier letters the spelling seems to be at the whim of the writer, the same words being spelt in different ways in the same letter. The correspondents were not even consistent in the way they spelt their own names! The spelling of some words altered over the years: for example the letter *y* was used during the eighteenth century where it would have been an *i* at the end of the period. Allan wrote in 1739, 'I have toyl and fatigue enough,' and in 1776 Alexander wrote that his mother had 'dyed at Dunollie'. Such words as *met, get,* or *yet* were written *mett, gett,* or *yett* in the earlier letters. The spelling of *honour* and *colour* was then *honor* or *color* as it is today in America. Some words changed their meaning during the period, such as *to admire* which in Iain Ciar's time meant *to wonder*.

Abbreviations were much used in the eighteenth century, such as *qch* for *which*, *oyr* for *other*, *yr* for there and *fayr* for *father*, but these died out during the next century.

The construction of the sentences improved steadily throughout the time. Some of the sentences in the earlier letters hardly made sense, and punctuation made matters worse rather than better. Even into the 19th century much of the punctuation seemed to have no point at all.

The writing was, for most of the period, done with a quill pen. Its legibility varied as much with the individual as it does today. A few of the letters of Iain Ciar's time are easier to read than some of the Victorian scrawl. Children's letters were usually beautifully written.

Criss-crossing the lines of writing became a habit in the nineteenth century. This is not too difficult to read when it is on thick paper, but after 1840, when letters were paid for by weight and not by the distance they had travelled, a fashion for very thin flimsy paper came in. This made the criss-crossing almost illegible as the writing on the other side tended to come through.

Until the Victorian age capital letters were used very freely. This was usually for emphasis. Sometimes the key word of a sentence had a capital letter — for example: 'I beg you would Comfort her', or 'distinguish themselves in Acts of the most Cruel Murders'. However, in the earlier letters, some words which would normally be written with a capital letter had a small one. Iain Ciar was not the only God-fearing man who wrote *God* with a small *g* at times. In a letter written by MacDougall of Lunga in 1776, *god* is written with a small *g* in the same sentence as *Rum* is with a capital *R*!

Once into the Victorian age capital letters mostly gave way to underlining. 'I have been <u>sea-sick</u> the whole time. <u>I funk awfully</u> the rest of the voyage.' Or again: 'she has been very <u>Imprudent</u> and the <u>Gallant</u> Col. must be a <u>consummate villain</u>.'

As to the length of the letters, the nineteenth-century ones tend to be longer than those of the eighteenth. One of the shortest, written in the 1780s, conveys a wealth of fact and feeling. 'Dear Sir, Alas poor George Wright he droped down stone dead in the street as he was going home to Dinner on tuesday. Good God!' A sentence describing someone who had just moved house also conveys a great deal in a few words: 'She was up to the eyes in confusion and furniture.'

Several letters were never meant to survive and their postscripts seem to be pointing accusing fingers to the future. There is one from Duncan: 'I need not recommend to you to destroy this letter'. In the next century Louisa Maxwell instructed John: 'I beg nobody may see this letter.' Bell writes to her brother: 'If I thought you kept any of my scratches a moment after you read them I would write to you no more.'

There is the letter already quoted, written after the failure of the '15 Rising by a friend of Hanoverian allegiance. He warned Mary to hide her cattle and other valuables for he was coming with another government emissary to take an inventory of her possessions in connection with the forfeiture. Under the circumstances his 'P.S. Madam burn this when you read it,' sounds more than reasonable.

Appendix

The MacDougalls in Earlier Times

The Clan MacDougall, although now small in numbers, is one of the oldest in Scotland. In early history they were powerful in Argyll and the islands and maintained a considerable fleet of galleys for use both in war and for supplying their island fortresses.

The clan takes its name from Dugall, one of the sons of Somerled. After Somerled's death in battle in 1164, Dugall held most of Argyll — and the islands of Mull, Lismore, Kerrera, Scarba, Jura, Tiree and Coll. He took the title of King of the South Isles and Lord of Lorn. His son Duncan founded Ardchattan Priory on Loch Etive.

As the family held their island possessions from the King of Norway and their mainland ones from the King of Scotland the third chief, Ewan, found it hard to remain loyal to both, when the respective kings demanded his support in wars against each other! Finally, in 1263, he decided to support Alexander III of Scotland and handed back the islands to the King of Norway. When Norway ceded the Hebrides to Scotland three years later the islands were returned to Ewan.

The marriage of the fourth chief Alexander was disastrous for the clan: his wife was a Comyn, whose nephew, the Red Comyn, was murdered in a church at Dumfries by Robert the Bruce. This started a blood feud and the MacDougalls, who before had supported Wallace and the patriotic side, now became the enemies of Bruce. They defeated him at the battle of Dalrigh, near Tyndrum, but were themselves defeated in 1308 in the battle of the Pass of Brander near Loch Awe. As a result the MacDougalls lost their castles of Dunollie and Dunstaffnage and all their lands. Dunollie, most of the mainland possessions and the island of Kerrera were later returned, but Dunstaffnage remained in the hands of the Campbells.

The seventh chief, Ewan, married a granddaughter of Robert the Bruce. The marriage produced no son and a cousin became the eighth chief on the death of Ewan, circa 1375. The Lordship of Lorn, however, passed with the marriage of Ewan's daughter to the Stewarts, ancestors of the Stewarts of Appin, and then to the Campbells who later became Dukes of Argyll.

During the seventeenth century civil wars the MacDougalls supported the Royalists and fought alongside Montrose. At the siege of Dunavertie in Kintyre in 1647 many of the clan were massacred. More of the clan lost their lives when a MacDougall castle, Gylen, on Kerrera was burnt by General Leslie's troops. After the Restoration the MacDougall lands were returned.

The MacDougalls were strong Jacobites and the year 1715 saw Iain Ciar, the 22nd chief, fighting on their side.

*

Other important MacDougall families in the district were the MacDougalls of Raray, Gallanach, Lunga, Soroba and Ardencaple. Like the MacDougalls of Dunollie the descendants of the first three mentioned still live on their family lands.

As in all Highland clans many MacDougall families through the years have settled in Canada, America, Australia and New Zealand.

Select Index

293